WINGS OF WAR

For the military veterans of this great country of ours — your

dedication and enduring service to preserving our freedoms can

never be measured. We as a nation are forever indebted to all

of the sacrifices you have made.

Quarto is the authority on a wide range of topics.

Quarto educates, entertains and enriches the lives of
our readers—enthusiasts and lovers of hands-on living.

www.quartoknows.com

© 2015 Quarto Publishing Group USA Inc.
Text © 2015 James P. Busha

First published in 2013 by Motorbooks, an imprint of Quarto Publishing Group USA Inc.,
400 First Avenue North, Suite 400, Minneapolis, MN 55401 USA. Telephone: (612) 344-8100
Fax: (612) 344-8692

quartoknows.com
Visit our blogs at quartoknows.com

Motorbooks titles are also available at discounts in bulk quantity for industrial or sales-promotional use. For
details contact the Special Sales Manager at Quarto Publishing Group USA Inc., 400 First Avenue North,
Suite 400, Minneapolis, MN 55401 USA.

10 9 8 7 6 5 4 3 2

ISBN: 978-0-7603-4852-9

Library of Congress Cataloging-in-Publication Data

Busha, James P.
  Wings of war : great combat tales of Allied and Axis pilots from World War II / James P. Busha.
      pages cm
  Includes index.
  ISBN 978-0-7603-4852-9 (hbk.)
  1. World War, 1939-1945–Aerial operations. 2. Air pilots, Military–Biography. I. Title.
  D785.B88 2015
  940.54'4–dc23
                                        2015013800

Acquiring Editor: Erik Gilg
Project Manager: Madeleine Vasaly
Art Director: James Kegley
Cover Designer: Faceout Studios
Page Designer: Lee Ann McKevitt
Layout Designer: Helena Shimizu

Printed in China

WINGS of WAR

GREAT COMBAT TALES OF ALLIED AND
AXIS PILOTS DURING WORLD WAR II

JAMES P. BUSHA

ZENITH
PRESS

CONTENTS

FOREWORD

STEVE HINTON, PLANES OF FAME MUSEUM, CHINO, CA

Why do you read an aviation history book? Is it to learn about the amazing aircraft, the people who flew them, and the role they all played in history? Is it because you appreciate the information and lists of facts about the aircraft performance? Or maybe it's just to see cool photos of the great aircraft in our world's history, perhaps as reference material for squadron markings and paint schemes. Whatever the reason, this book will satisfy all your requirements.

Wings of War is a combination of firsthand stories from very different aviators who share their life-changing events from the very beginning of World War II up to the last atomic mission flown. All of their combat tales are laid out in chronological order, spread out across the entire globe, and they share their experiences in a wide variety of aircraft that all helped to shape the world as we know it today. These combat veterans all have a common bond as they all flew and fought in World War II, though in different military forces, in different aircraft, and in different battle zones. These men flew fighters, bombers, and reconnaissance aircraft for the US Army, Navy, and Marines, the German Luftwaffe, and the Royal Canadian and British Air Forces. Each of the stories brings a very descriptive review of some truly unique events and all are told firsthand by these pilots who were there. They place you center stage inside the various cockpits with the brave airmen who flew these harrowing missions and will help you understand what it must have been like during aerial combat.

Some of the personal and descriptive accounts of unique aerial combat events include aerial combat over the Pacific flying off of aircraft carriers, island-hopping campaigns against superior forces, night fighters over Europe, and chasing the enemy across borders wondering if they will make it back home alive. These veterans' compelling stories are written in a way that tells the human side of the story behind the combat. Although they are all heroes in their own right, most will proclaim they were just doing their job as they set out to fly and fight for what they believed in. No matter if you were Allied or Axis, both sides experienced heavy losses as these young men all played the deadly game of aerial warfare, with the loser facing deadly consequences.

Jim Busha has put this collection of accounts together in a way that has made an impression on me personally. I have worked in aviation for over forty-five years, flying historic aircraft at air shows and the air races, flying in television and motion pictures, and personally restoring and flying many of the World War II aircraft mentioned in these pages. As the president of Planes of Fame Air Museum for the past twenty-three years, I have had the good fortune to be surrounded with and to fly most of the aircraft that are described in detail in this book on a daily basis. Even though I was never a military pilot and I do not pretend to know what aerial combat was like, I now have a much deeper appreciation for what it was like after reading this book. As I turned the pages I found that these veterans have told their stories with detail I can relate to. Whether at the controls of a Spitfire, Lightning, Hellcat, Bf 109, Fw 190, Thunderbolt, or any of the other aircraft mentioned, I now have a better understanding of the total picture of the air war in World War II as seen firsthand by these brave men.

To learn more about Steven Hinton and the vast collection of historic aircraft located at the Planes of Fame Air Museum, please visit their website at planesoffame.org.

INTRODUCTION

GREAT COMBAT TALES THAT WERE ALMOST LOST

When I began interviewing World War II veterans almost twenty years ago, I merely did it because I was interested in hearing from an actual pilot of that era what it was like to fly in combat, under extreme conditions, with an airplane similar to the one I own and fly (a 1943 Aeronca L-3). Now I understood that my L-3 was used primarily as an artillery spotter, and in some instances as a stateside trainer, and I wanted to hear what the veterans thought about it. Little did I realize at the time that my first interview would turn into hundreds more as I began a quest to capture as many of their tales as I could before there were no more stories to be told. That was a fact that became crystal clear when my good friend and professional aircraft photographer John Dibbs told me about a friend of his who was writing a book on the Civil War and wished he had some Civil War vets to interview—of course, they had all passed away decades ago.

Although I liked to "scribble," I never considered myself a writer—still don't. But I knew I couldn't simply capture these stories, listen to their words myself, and just pack them away. I wanted the rest of the world to know and become educated on what these men had to endure when many of them were barely out of high school.

I began to write a few articles and send them off to aviation magazines, such as *Flight Journal* and *Fly Past*, and I was shocked when the editors asked if I had any more! I knew then that the descendants of those men who flew and fought in World War II were hungry to hear more about what it was like to fly these historic airplanes. I told many veterans I interviewed that I wished I had started twenty years sooner. Almost all responded the same way: they told me they wouldn't have talked about the war back then. The only reason they were doing it now was because they wanted their children and grandchildren to know what they did and, more importantly, why they did it.

There are many famous aces and other pilots of World War II who have been written about extensively; many are household names. Although I admit that most of these guys were my heroes growing up, I really wanted to target those veterans who, by all accounts, were just doing their jobs. Some, as you will read, were aces; one of them was a Medal of Honor recipient; and others flew for the Axis. But the one common denominator was that all of them had fascinating stories to tell that I, along with most other people, had never heard before. For close to twenty years, I tried to locate and reach out to these men. Most were very courteous and allowed me the honor of listening to them regale me with their tales of incidents that happened over sixty years ago; there were others, however, who were not ready to talk about the war, and I had the utmost respect for their privacy.

As a police officer for the last thirty years, I understand the importance of not interrupting someone when they're talking, even when they pause for an extended period of time to think about what they will say next. More times than I can remember, the pilots I interviewed would respond with crystal-clear details of flying, recalling events as if they had happened minutes ago.

This book is dedicated to all of the brave men and women—worldwide—who served, represented, and protected the countries for which they fought. Many veterans will tell you they were just doing their jobs, but most of the pilots I interviewed admitted that although they faced overwhelming odds and adversity and lost close friends, both in training and in combat, they found some joy in what they did. They would pause, reflecting back on their wartime experience and their flying days in particular; they would lift their heads slowly, smile, and say they were the best years of their lives.

As my interview tapes began to stack up and file cabinets began to overflow, others took notice, and I was asked to write more for other magazines, including those belonging to the Experimental Aircraft Association (EAA) right in my own backyard. I became editor of *EAA Warbirds of America* eight years ago and then added another editor role when I became EAA Vintage Aircraft Association editor three years ago. Although I still wear those editor hats, I added yet another one when I retired from law enforcement, recently becoming the EAA director of publications.

Unfortunately, about a year ago the interviews had slowed to a trickle, because veterans are leaving us at an alarming rate. As the seventieth anniversary of the end of World War II was fast approaching, I knew I wanted to recognize my heroes before they were all gone. In looking at the vast collection of interviews I had conducted over the years, I realized that for the most part I had more than enough to fill several books from the very beginning of the war right up until the final B-29 atomic mission of the war. What I find unique about this book is that it not only gives the reader an up-close, inside-the-cockpit feel of the war from both the Allied and Axis perspectives but also a comprehensive snapshot of World War II combat in the air that spans the entire globe. I hope you agree with me, and I hope you never forget what these brave men had to endure to ensure that our freedoms would be forever preserved.

—James P. Busha, 2015

1939

WAR CLOUDS
ON THE
HORIZON

LEARNING TO FLY THE LUFTWAFFE WAY

GUNTHER VOLTZ

Even though World War I had ended ten years earlier for Germany and we only had gliders to fly, we did have a "secret weapon" at our disposal that the Allies had overlooked. The stick-and-fabric, powerless sailplanes we flew seemed harmless to the Allied observers, but the World War I combat veteran pilots who were our mentors taught us the basics of flight as we became the foundation of the soon-mighty Luftwaffe.

I had learned to fly a Zögling primary glider on a large grassy hill near my hometown of Erfurt in 1929, when I was only fourteen years old, and the knowledge I gained from both my mentors and my time at the controls of this and other gliders only strengthened my desire to become a proficient glider pilot. I and my brother Gottfried, who was a few

Gunther Voltz poses in the front of the Storch that he operated over the Russian front.

Gunther, standing in the middle, along with fellow glider students and their instructor. Many German pilots in World War II cut their flying teeth on gliders, and this early stick-and-rudder instruction created very deadly Luftwaffe pilots.

Early German glider instruction was given by former World War I pilots. These instructors had been masters of the air in the Great War and provided invaluable insight to these fledgling glider pilots.

A Fieseler Storch on a German parade ground attracted attention wherever it landed. These airplanes are considered by some pilots to be the predecessor to the helicopter, as they could operate in and out of very confined areas.

years older than me, both dreamed of flying an airliner route in South America some-day—unfortunately, our dreams would never be realized as the war clouds in Germany began to rise. In 1935, the Luftwaffe was formed in Germany, and there had been a decree from the air ministry stating that pilots who were trained by the Luftwaffe and wanted to continue flying had to sign up for twelve years of service. At the time I thought that was a lifetime commitment, so I declined to join the German pilot corps. But in late 1939, the twelve-year rule was lifted, and I traveled to Berlin to get into the act.

At that time, I had over five hundred hours of glider-flying experience, and I was seriously considering joining the airborne paratrooper corps called the Luftlande Geschwader. The Germans were rapidly building up this airborne assault group, as they had already proven themselves by capturing and annihilating the Belgian defenders of Fort Eben-Emael. This stronghold had been reported to be the most impenetrable fort in the world—until the German glider forces proved them wrong. Just before I was about to announce my intentions to join the glider corps, I received a phone call from Gottfried, who had become a test pilot for Willy Messerschmitt. He warned me that if I kept push-ing my glider bit I would definitely end up flying with these guys, and he reminded me that glider flights were always a one-way trip! I followed my brother's advice and became a power pilot in the Luftwaffe instead.

FLEEING MY HOMELAND

LUDWICK MARTEL, RAF

My early fighter training was performed in my home country of Poland during the spring of 1936. While in secondary school, I learned how to fly gliders, which I felt helped me prepare for powered flight. By July of 1939, I was flying P.7 open-cockpit, high-wing, fixed-landing-gear fighters and was delighted at the chance to become a fighter pilot for my country. I only flew the P.7 for a short time, though, because I had to flee Poland from the blitzkrieging Nazis. I joined the Royal Air Force (RAF) while I was still in Poland and was attached to a unit. Our orders were to proceed to France, where we would collect the English fighters, and then we would make a stand and fight the Germans. I was transferred by bus across Poland to the French border and then had to figure out any way possible to get across without being stopped. It wasn't all that hard, especially considering how chaotic things were at the time with the Germans hot on our heels. I eventually made my way to Paris and arrived there in October of 1939. We reorganized the Polish Air Force while in France, and we were prepared to take our country back from the Germans. The problem was the French wanted us to join their air force. I refused, and they in turn refused to let us train and fly the English airplanes. While the Germans ravaged my homeland, I was stuck on the ground. Eventually I made my way across the English Channel to a country that would allow me to seek my revenge on the Germans.

Here, a Polish Spitfire pilot poses with a ground crewmember on the nose of his fighter. The red-and-white checkered box on the nose signifies this aircraft is flown by a Polish pilot. *Collection of John Dibbs*

A man without a country: Ludwick Martel rests between missions as he waits for the alarm to

Ring the bell and run like hell! RAF Spitfires prepare to launch from an English airfield to repel another Luftwaffe onslaught. *Collection of John Dibbs*

1940

OUR BACKS AGAINST THE WALL

To the neutral observer, especially those individuals living comfortably and relatively free in early 1940, thousands of miles away inside the safe confines of the United States of America, the war in Europe resembled a rather large chess game played out on a grand scale. The black-colored king, queen, rooks, knights, bishops, and pawns, otherwise known as the Nazis, were having a field day as they blitzkrieged across Poland, Denmark, Norway, Belgium, Holland, and Luxembourg and, finally, into France. It seemed that no country—no army, air force, or navy—could stop the German war machine as it set its sights on the island nation of Great Britain.

By all accounts, the lone white knight known as England stood firm and stoic as the early summer of 1940 brought with it much uncertainty and growing apprehension. The situation looked rather grim with the capture and occupation of fellow European countries by the Germans almost a year earlier. The German High Command and its well-trained Luftwaffe were held at bay at very close quarters as they watched and waited across the English Channel, enjoying the spoils of French cuisine and wine and waiting for England to drop to her knees and beg for mercy. But the Germans, in their infinite wisdom, failed to take into account the undying spirit and never-ending will of the free people living, breathing, and resolved to fight to the last man just a stone's throw away across the channel.

The final stage had been set as the curtain drew slowly open and the greatest air battle known to man was about to begin over the skies of Great Britain. The Battle of Britain would take place between the highly trained and superior numbered Luftwaffe fighters and bombers and the vastly outnumbered, but equally nimble, Hurricane and Spitfire fighters of the RAF.

When the German commander, Hermann Göring, finally unleashed his hounds of the Luftwaffe in July of 1940, he had at his disposal more than 1,200 bombers, 300 dive-bombers, and almost 1,100 fighters to swarm over England at will and annihilate the British aircraft industry and massive ground infrastructure. But Göring, along with his superior, Adolf Hitler, realized that if they caused a panic among the British people through intimidation and terror, they would then be able to force England into an unconditional surrender. What Hitler and his cohorts didn't count on was the 2,440 British RAF aircraft and over 500 pilots from various free and occupied countries joining together as one to form an impenetrable wall of fighters.

As the rest of the free world watched and held out hope, praying for the island nation, swirling dogfights between Spitfires, Hurricanes, and Bf 109s took place in the skies over England as wretched black contrails poured out from burning, twisted aircraft. Fighters and bombers from both sides fell from the English sky in great numbers and losses of men and aircraft to both sides began to mount.

603 SQUADRON

PILOT OFFICER LUDWICK MARTEL, RAF
SUPERMARINE SPITFIRE

Ludwick Martel was born in Piotrków in central Poland in 1919 and grew up yearning to fly. Like many Europeans, he saw the war clouds forming well before Poland was invaded in 1939. With broken treaties, empty promises, and the scars of World War I still fresh in the minds of many, the word "blitzkrieg," the bone-chilling sound of Stuka dive-bombers, and the sight of panzer troops pouring into their country would forever be etched in the minds of the citizens of Poland.

When I arrived on English soil in early 1940, I was a man without a country, as I had fled south from my homeland in Poland to avoid the Nazi occupation. Now I was welcomed with open arms by the British people, treated like a long-lost son and accepted into the RAF brotherhood. My hope was to someday return to Poland and rid her of the German menace, but first, a greater challenge lay ahead—not only for me, but for the entire RAF—as the Luftwaffe prepared to begin their aerial assault on England from occupied French aerodromes.

After receiving some refresher and primary training on de Havilland Tiger Moths, I was entrusted with flying the sleek and beautiful Supermarine Spitfire. I now had two separate things to learn: how to speak English and how to fly this wonderful elliptical-wing, enclosed-cockpit, inline-engine fighter. The language part came rather slowly, but the flying, especially in the Spitfire Mk I, was most enjoyable. The most unusual thing I found early on while flying the Mk I was that it had a retractable undercarriage. This was something I was unaccustomed to, having never flown an aircraft with landing gear that went up and down. All of my previous fighter experience had been in fixed-landing-gear, open-cockpit Polish fighters, most of them annihilated by the Luftwaffe during the opening weeks of fighting.

In the air I found the handling of the Spitfire to be a most pleasant experience. It was very quick and could turn and maneuver very tightly with just a small amount of stick input, as it was light on the controls and extremely nimble. I received about twenty hours of training in the Spitfire Mk I, and I found the entire process to be most educational, except for one small item. The RAF way of flying tactical formation was something I was not very comfortable with. We were taught to fly in a very tight, close formation of twelve Spitfires, with the leader out front. It was very difficult to look around, either up or down, for enemy aircraft and still try to keep one eye on the flight leader. Back in Poland, we had been taught to fly a more loose formation, giving ourselves enough room to look around for enemy aircraft. But now in this RAF tight V formation, I thought it was no wonder the Germans called our flights *Idiotenreihen*, which meant "rows of idiots."

After my operational training was complete, I was sent to 603 Squadron, which was part of 11 Group, and was welcomed like a family member by the other RAF pilots, who

Achtung—Spitfire! This is the scene many Luftwaffe pilots dreaded witnessing as a Spitfire roared in from behind them. *John Dibbs*

were thankful that I and the rest of the replacements were there to join the fight. By the time I joined the group, the Luftwaffe was concentrating its efforts on knocking out our airfields in hopes of destroying fighter command. This was a most hectic time for us in the RAF, with many of the replacement pilots having less experience and fewer hours in the air than I did; needless to say, many did not survive very long. Our one saving grace in the squadron was our CO*, Squadron Leader George Denholm, whom I affection- ately called Uncle George. Squadron Leader Denholm was thirty-two years old and had accumulated a vast amount of experience flying and fighting against the Luftwaffe, and he tried to pass on his knowledge to the rest of us.

As our squadron slugged it out in the fall of 1940, I saw less and less of the German Dorniers and Heinkel He 111 bombers over the English sky but saw an increase in the number of Bf 109s that tangled with us daily. On October 5, 1940, I scored my first victory when I engaged a Bf 109 near Kent and shot it down. Combat flying was life and death, and most of the chaps in the squadron understood that disturbing fact. For me, though, I missed my country dearly, and I focused on that fact as I continued to fly and fight the Luftwaffe, whom I called the "bloody German bastards." I also had great faith in the Spitfires that I flew and knew I could stay with the 109s as we twisted and turned through the sky, each of us trying to bring our guns onto one another. The only advantage the 109s had over us was speed; we had the advantage of flying over our home- land and were not concerned about our fuel status or being captured by the enemy. My main priority was staying alive and shooting down as many German fighters as I could. Unfortunately for me, on a cold day in October, the Germans got to me first!

On October 25, 1940, I was scrambled along with the rest of the squadron and was flying in a Spitfire Mk II as we lifted off of our airfield at RAF Hornchurch in the south of England. Squadron Leader Denholm was leading us up into some very thick cloud cover, and it was extremely difficult to maintain formation as he picked his way around the building clouds. We all stayed tucked in rather close to one another for fear of losing sight of our leader. About thirty minutes into the flight, still climbing through thickening clouds, we received a report of enemy aircraft in the area. With one eye locked in on the Spitfire next to me, I tried to look around the darkening sky with the other, searching for the Luftwaffe fighters.

As our flight passed through six thousand feet, we received a second report that the enemy aircraft were directly over us—right on top of our squadron. At that moment, I looked up and saw a flight of Bf 109s descending on our squadron with licking flames streaming from their cannons and machine guns. In an instant, the hail of 109 cannon fire tore through the air and hit four of our Spitfires, including my own. I saw a large hole in my left wing, compliments of the Luftwaffe, as the cannon rounds con- tinued toward my cockpit area. It was every man for himself, and the chaps who hadn't been hit gave chase to the 109s while the rest of us fought to control our damaged fight- ers and assess our injuries. I felt a burning sensation running along my left side; as I

* Commanding officer

glanced down, I found that I had taken some shrapnel in the left side of my body. I was bloody well mad at the Germans, not only because they had torn my flying jacket and damaged my Spitfire but because now I had to go back down, alone, through the same bloody cloud layer I had come up in!

It was most difficult to ignore the pain and still concentrate on my instruments as I brought the Spitfire lower, not really knowing where I was or how I was going to land my crippled fighter. I was thankful I wasn't bleeding too much, but I felt myself slipping in and out of consciousness. In my delirium I thought I observed a windmill below, which caused me to believe I was on the wrong side of the channel! Thankfully it was just a mirage, as I came out of the cloud deck and found myself all alone with no other Spitfires or 109s around me. Up ahead I found a lovely open field near Hastings, where I decided to set my Spitfire down, wheels up as I coasted to a stop in the tall grass. Both the Spitfire and I were damaged but still looked no worse for wear, as we would both fly again another day.

My troubles in the air only continued on the ground when I was approached by a group of British Army soldiers who had witnessed my crash landing. As they began to question me, they became very suspicious of my accent and thought I was a bloody German spy! I thought I was going to be taken prisoner until one of the more clever chaps in the group saw the Polish insignia on my flying uniform and realized I was on their side. I was taken to a local hospital, where I stayed for the next ten days and was treated for my injuries.

I had flown over thirty combat missions during the Battle of Britain, as an adopted son of another country, since my own homeland had been taken over and occupied. Living, flying, and fighting for Great Britain was a pleasant experience for me because the British people were so nice and appreciative. I will forever cherish my time spent with the pilots of 603 Squadron, as I can think of no better men or company with whom I would have flown into combat. I was one of the lucky few.

After the war ended, Ludwick Martel was released from service as a flight lieuten-ant. He flew crop dusters in East Africa and then returned to London, where he ran a successful property-maintenance business. He died on April 25, 2010, at the age of ninety-one.

SPITFIRE FOLLIES

PILOT/OFFICER ROBERT "BOB" LARGE, RAF
SUPERMARINE SPITFIRE

Robert Large was like most young men in the RAF in 1940—wide-eyed and itching to fight. But before he could slug it out with the Luftwaffe, he first had to master the Spitfire.

During the summer of 1940, when the great air battles between the RAF and the Luftwaffe took place high over England, I was stuck in Scotland, having just completed my checkout in the Harvard trainer. Since I had survived training thus far, the RAF instructors had no other choice but to turn me loose on the Spitfire Mk I. Like everyone else before me, I found it a wonderful experience. There were no dual controls and no instructor screaming at me from the back to "Put in more rudder! Watch your air speed!" I was alone and relied on my training and luck.

The very first time I took off in the Mk I was the most exhilarating experience I had ever had. The power was enormous compared to the previous aircraft I had flown. I remember that flying in the Spit I, as you selected your undercarriage up with your right hand and then with your left hand, you pumped a large handle up and down to manually bring your gear up. It was an extraordinary thing as I went roaring into the sky, working this handle backwards and forwards, causing my stick to move in the opposite direction each time I pumped the handle. The Spitfire flew up and down with each rhythm of my pumping. What a sight it must have been for my poor instructor on the ground, seeing me on the verge of destroying an RAF aircraft. To make matters worse, I had left the hood open on takeoff, and my scarf began to billow and unravel from around my neck. The scarf flew out and twisted my helmet and oxygen mask around my face until I couldn't see anything at all. But that was how we learned; we were young and quickly sorted these things out. If we didn't, then we were dead!

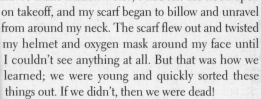

LEFT: A smiling Robert Large had an adventurous career with the RAF that included flying the Supermarine Spitfire, the Westland Lysander, and the Gloster Meteor jet. OPPOSITE: The Supermarine Seafire was a naval version of the Spitfire that had a tailhook installed for carrier operations. *EAA/Jim Koepnick*

In 1941, the tide of the war more or less turned, but it was a minimal effort because we in the RAF were still not that strong. Our group was used to escort bombers into France and Belgium. The problem, though, was our bombers were only little twin-engine Blenheims with a very small range and an even smaller bomb load. We used to escort six Blenheims at a time with a wing of thirty-six Spitfires split into three flights of twelve. One flight of Spitfires flew on either side of the Blenheims, and the third flight was stacked high above as top cover. The whole lot was called a "Beehive," and it did resemble a beehive, too, with Spitfires buzzing all around the slow-moving bombers. The whole lot would then fly to the French coast, which wasn't far away, and we'd bomb Dunkirk or Calais and gradually move a little farther inland to where we would find a German aerodrome about. The Blenheims had trouble right off the bat with terrible losses because these poor chaps had to fly straight and level during daylight. The Russians had still not entered the war, and that allowed the Germans to concentrate tremendous amounts of airplanes and machinery on the French coast. They merely waited for us to come across the channel to break up our escort flights and go after the bombers. The Blenheims took terrible losses without inflicting much damage on the enemy. It was a nominal operation at best, but this we did all the time because it was our duty. Getting to France was easy, but getting back home to mother England was another matter. At least in the Spitfires, we had a fighting chance. In a Blenheim, it was extremely tough and nearly impossible, especially with the well-seasoned Luftwaffe about.

In the early summer of 1942, on another mission, I was obliged to leave my bullet-riddled Spitfire Mk VI in the English Channel, about twelve miles from the White Cliffs of Dover. I had been up at high altitudes over France on a fighter sweep, but the German Bf 109s were up even higher and dove onto me, spraying my Spit with cannon and machine-gun rounds. Needless to say, I took a summer's swim in the channel and vowed to somehow even the score with the Jerrys.

In late 1943, I got my chance when I was assigned to a Lysander squadron. I would take off at night with an Allied spy and weapons stuffed in the back; we would fly across the channel and land in occupied France right under the bloody Germans' noses. I made countless missions supplying the French resistance with weapons and personal—it was my ultimate payback to the Germans.

Robert Large went on to fly covert night missions into occupied France, dropping off and picking up Allied spies. In early 1945, he was selected to fly the new Meteor jet aircraft, but the war ended before he had a chance to once again tangle with the Luftwaffe.

TALLY HO!

WING COMMANDER ROBERT W. "BOB" FOSTER (RET.), RAF
HAWKER HURRICANE

Robert Foster was born May 14, 1920. As a young man, he saw the clouds of war rising over Europe and decided to join the Royal Air Force Voluntary Reserve in January 1939 because he thought it would be much safer in the air than in the trenches.

In Hollywood's version of history, the Supermarine Spitfire, with its long, slender fuselage and graceful elliptical wing, was portrayed as the lone defender over the White Cliffs of Dover during the Battle of Britain. Although the Spitfire played an important role in beating back the daily Luftwaffe raids, it was the tenacity of the pug-nosed Hawker Hurricanes of the RAF that bore the brunt of aerial combat during England's darkest days. The Hurricane was slower than the Spit and it took longer to climb to altitude, but once it got there the stubby little fighter jumped in and out of scrapes like a backstreet brawler.

Although the RAF Hurricanes had their noses bloodied many times over by the German raiders, they were able to stay upright even as they absorbed many punishing blows. British estimates credit the Hurricane with four-fifths of all German aircraft destroyed during the peak of the battle—July through October of 1940.

One of the few: Battle of Britain Hurricane ace Bob Foster. *Collection of John Dibbs*

LEARNING THE ROPES

I joined the RAF in 1939 because I thought it would be more glamorous to be shot down in a fighter than to be shot or bayoneted as a foot soldier in a trench! By November of 1939, I had already accumulated over fifty hours of flight time in a trainer called the Avro Cadet and progressed on to the Hawker Hart, Audax, and Harvard. However, I only had five hours of retractable undercarriage time in the Harvard before I was kicked out of the nest in June of 1940 and sent on to a Hurricane operational-training unit in Norfolk. My first flight in the Hurricane was almost my last, as I tried to bust up a perfectly good flying machine.

There were no two-seat trainers and no pilot notes to study—just a seasoned Hurricane pilot standing on the wing, leaning into my cockpit and telling me to push this button, pull this lever, and turn this dial as I prepared for my maiden flight. I was able to start the Rolls-Royce Merlin engine under my hood with no problems and I waddled down the long grass runway trying to get my propeller into the correct pitch. I had it all backwards, and it seemed like it took me forever to get airborne. With my propeller out of sync, I wondered out loud how I could ever fight a German fighter in this wretched machine! My attitude quickly changed, however, when I figured out my mistakes and managed to get the plane into its proper flight régime. It was at that moment I began to appreciate the finer points of the Hawker Hurricane Mk I.

RAF armorers load belts of ammunition into the wing-mounted machine guns of a Hawker Hurricane. *Collection of John Dibbs*

It turned out to be a very easy airplane to fly and fight with. It had no real bad vices; it swung a little on takeoff and it would drop a wing if you got too slow, but both of these were easily corrected. Although you could get it to spin quite easily, you could get it out of the spin even quicker. I thought it was the perfect little airplane for the job we had to do.

Compared to the German Bf 109, the Hurricane was on an even playing field when it came to a turning, circular dogfight, but the 109s had us beat on all other fronts because they were faster and could fly higher. But the Germans' main weakness was the fact that they lacked the fuel capacity to stand and fight for any length of time. We in the RAF, on the other hand, flew over our homeland, so it was more or less a safe haven when our fuel gauges were low and it was time to land.

SO MUCH OWED BY SO MANY TO SO FEW

The Battle of Britain was in full swing when I joined 605 Squadron in July of 1940. The problem for me was that I was stationed up in Scotland and the battle was farther south, around London. We had no action at all, which turned out to be a godsend for me because I accumulated a total of eighty hours of flying time in the Hurricane. I think it was time well spent, and it helped me immensely later on in the war. The chaps that were flying in the battle straightaway only had about twenty hours of flying time on Hurricanes, and many of these poor chaps didn't survive more than a few weeks in combat.

In early September, our squadron was brought down to Croydon, in the South London area, to replace a very tired and worn-out group. When we arrived, the Germans had been targeting the docks around London. As I approached our airfield for the very first time, I watched London burn from the cockpit of my Hurricane and knew I wasn't in training anymore—I was in a bloody war. Our combat was straightaway as we began to fly multiple missions per day.

On my first combat, we had been scrambled to attack a formation of German bombers. The problem for us, though, was that our CO didn't see the bombers, and he led us right into a collision course with them. Aerial combat is a funny thing; you can train months and months for it, but the first time you attack another airplane, your survival instincts take over. For me, this was the first time I had seen more than fifty enemy airplanes in the sky at once. As our flight of Hurricanes flew into this crowd of German He 111 bombers, the whole thing turned into a ball of confusion on both sides. I got away with it by closing my eyes, firing my guns at the pack, and diving straight through the middle of them. Whether I hit any of them, or anything else for that matter, is worthy of debate. My attack wasn't very straightforward, and it was more or less a haphazard thrust, but you learned from experience and hoped you survived for a next time.

Although the Hurricanes and Spitfires more or less were the aerial defense of England, the thing that really saved us was radar. Dare I say that without it, we might not have survived the continuous German onslaught? We seemed to be placed in the right positions at the right time as we slugged it out with the Luftwaffe on a daily basis.

LUFTWAFFE LUFBERY

On September 27, 1940, we had been vectored above Sussex and found a group of German Me 110 bombers that were either lost or were waiting for their Bf 109 escorts to show up. The 110s were flying at eighteen thousand feet in a defensive circle, going around and around. During my attack, I had opened fire with my machine guns when all of a sudden there was a horrendous bang that came from under my hood: the Hurricane's engine blew up! With hot glycol pouring out of my stricken fighter, I knew it was time for me to leave the party. No one stayed with me, as they were quite busy with other things, so I pushed my nose downward and headed for the deck.

At first I thought I had been hit and had to bail out, but after seeing no fire, I thought, "I'll stay with the Hurricane for a while and see if I can do something about this." I shut off the petrol and the engine and turned my oxygen all the way up. As my fighter turned into a glider, I glanced down and saw a large, lovely green grassy field below me. I knew I could easily make the field, but I wasn't keen on the fact that I might have to belly in my Hurricane. I tried my flaps and they wouldn't work. I hit the undercarriage lever and the wheels came down like a piece of cake! After I made a smooth dead-stick landing, I hopped out and saw that my engine was literally blown apart—although it wasn't from enemy fire, the effect was just the same. Still, I can't say enough about how tough the Hurricane was.

JU 88 CLOUD CHASE

I was back at it on September 28 and flew four patrols that day. Most of them were less than an hour in length. On my last flight of the day, I was sent along with two other Hurricanes to swing out towards the south coast of England. As we began to patrol, we lost our number-three man in a cloud. As the two of us came out of the cloud together, we spotted two Junkers Ju 88s making a fast exit back across the channel to France. These Ju 88s had been on a hit-and-run mission—they came in together, dropped their bombs, and were now trying to make a mad dash for home.

We picked out one of the German bombers and dove down on him as we both fired our eight .303 machine guns at him simultaneously. We got one of his engines to burn, and he began to trail smoke and flame as he ducked back into a cloud. We knew he had to come out sooner or later, so we puttered about until his safety cloud disappeared. He was easy to spot with that engine on fire. We made another go at him as he disappeared below us. Our job was to hit the bombers hard and get out of there quickly; you didn't want to linger about too long to see whether or not these chaps crashed, because you never knew if a 109 was right around the corner waiting to do the same thing to you.

TURNING THE TABLES ON A 109

We were up near the south of England in early October and got ourselves into a running fight with some bloody 109s. One minute we were stooging along, being vectored by our radar contacts to incoming bandits, when all of a sudden someone yelled over the radio, "Break!" I pushed my Hurricane towards the deck while my number two pulled his nose upward and climbed. When I finally leveled off, I thought I was all alone; that is, until I spotted the 109 flying straight and level below me.

It was almost surreal for me to see my adversary flying as if he was on a pleasure flight a mere two hundred yards ahead of me. As I inched the Hurricane forward, I had my head on a swivel looking for other 109s because I thought this had to be some sort of trap. As I closed to about one hundred yards, I opened fire on the 109 and immediately hit

A Hurricane bearing Battle of Britain Eagle Squadron markings. *EAA photo*

him. He began to burn as he arched downward to the channel below. This chap had paid the ultimate price for being foolish and breaking the golden rule: there is no time to relax when you are involved in aerial combat.

NUISANCE RAIDERS

By late October, the massive German raids that had occurred throughout the summer of 1940 had now been whittled down considerably to more hit-and-run, nuisance-type attacks. Sometimes it would be just bombers, and other times it would be 109s carrying a small bomb load. Nevertheless, it kept the RAF on its toes as we tried to intercept these bandits.

In early November, we were scrambled to intercept some very high-flying bomb-carrying 109s that were interested in trying to get us into the air to fight on their terms. It was a typical cloudy English day as we rattled around with the 109s in a running dogfight over the channel and chased them back towards France. With their fuel becoming low, the 109s turned for home; we did the same and dropped below the clouds, making our way for the southern English coast. When I finally came out of the clouds, I turned north and glanced at my instruments and thought I had fouled them up during our swirling dogfight because my compass said I was heading south. I could clearly see the English coast up ahead of me, and, as I crossed over it, I was met with a barrage of black-colored flak.

I instantly became infuriated with our gunners for shooting at me and my Hurricane— they must have thought I was a 109! It only took me another second to realize that not only was I not over England, but I was on my way to Paris! I quickly turned my Hurricane around and made a mad dash across the channel. Lucky for me the 109s were long gone, and my own British gunners welcomed me with a friendly wave as I passed overhead.

CHANGE OF SCENERY

In early February, our squadron was sent to Martlesham Heath on the east coast of England, where we received a new and improved version of the Hawker Hurricane. The Hurricane Mk IIs were a vast improvement over the Hurricane Is because we now had superchargers, which gave us more height and speed. The Hurricane II also carried heavier guns in the form of four twenty-millimeter cannons. It didn't take us long to utilize and exploit these refinements against the German Luftwaffe.

During a cloudy, dreary day in early March of 1941, we sat in our Hurricanes on the airfield in a readiness state. As my mind began to wander, thinking of the breakfast that awaited me, a large formation of low-flying He 111s came roaring across the air-field. They dropped their bombs on some of our buildings and caused quite a ruckus as they thundered on by. We were scrambled individually to have a go at them as they disappeared back into the clouds and made their way out across the North Sea.

I really didn't think we would ever see them again, or even catch them for that mat-ter, as I pointed the Hurricane's nose through the low, gray clouds. I was droning around boring holes through the clouds for over twenty minutes and was thirty miles out over the North Sea when I popped out on top. I began to daydream again about my hot breakfast back at the airfield and was enjoying the splendid view of the clouds around me when I suddenly sensed I was not alone. I turned around and looked over my shoulder, and sitting there right behind my tail, larger than life, was an He 111.

In an instant, I snapped the Hurricane over as the He 111 gunner opened up on me, trying to plug my Hurricane. Fortunately, he missed, and it now became my turn to have a go at him as I quickly maneuvered my plane into a firing position. The He 111 tried to make a run for it and dive back into the clouds, but he wasn't quick enough, and I raked him over with my twenty-millimeter cannons. The last I saw of the He 111 was him smoking badly as he reentered the clouds. I still don't know to this day why I turned around; had I waited another half second, I trust I would have missed my breakfast altogether!

Bob Foster continued to fly and fight with the RAF and eventually became a Hurricane instructor pilot before being sent to the South Pacific as a Spitfire pilot tasked with fighting the Japanese. His total wartime credits include six air-to-air victories and one shared destroyed, three probable destroyed in the Hurricane, and six air-to-air victories and one shared damage in the Spitfire. Although he flew a variety of British fight-ers, he always had much affection and admiration for the Hawker Hurricane, as he considered it his first love. He passed away on July 30, 2014.

1941

OUTGUNNED
AND
OUTNUMBERED

As the fires of war raged across Europe, the Japanese, who had already begun their own campaign of imperial expansion in 1937, were making a mad dash south toward Australia and east across the Pacific on an island-hopping campaign. Unfortunately, there wasn't much that could stop a military force composed of superior equipment and weapons. A glaring example of this fact was the well-planned and well-orchestrated surprise attack on Pearl Harbor during the early morning hours of December 7, 1941.

JANUARY 1941–FEBRUARY 1942

WHERE THE BUFFALO ROAM

SERGEANT PILOT GEOFFREY B. FISKEN, RNZAF (RET.)
BREWSTER BUFFALO

Geoff Fisken was born on February 17, 1918. The son of a New Zealand farmer, he took up his father's trade. Before the war, Geoff was able to get some flight time in a de Havilland Gipsy Moth, but when the war broke out, he was unable to join the service because farming was considered vital for the war effort. In 1940, however, he convinced his boss to release him, and he quickly joined the Royal New Zealand Air Force (RNZAF) before his boss could change his mind.

Much has already been written about the attributes of the Brewster Buffalo, and, unfortunately, most of those words have not been favorable to the stubby-winged fighter. Some called it an outcast, while others called it worthless and weak. The Buffalo has never really been spoken about with flattering comments during its short tenure in the Army Air Force and US Navy front-line inventory. Even the British, whose backs were against the White Cliffs of Dover while they slugged it out with the Luftwaffe during the Battle of Britain, were less than impressed with the anemic flight characteristics of the Buffalo. Although the British had placed a large order—170 Buffalos for its RAF squadrons in England—they were deemed unsuitable for aerial combat against the Luftwaffe even before they arrived.

The Buffalo was far from extinct, however, at least for the moment. All of the RAF Buffalos were transferred and shipped to the Far East, where they would operate with Commonwealth squadrons from Australia and New Zealand in the Singapore, Malaya, and Burma regions against the Japanese. Unfortunately, when the war broke out, these Buffalo squadrons were quickly outnumbered and outgunned by the superior Japanese aerial armada. Although the plane's days were numbered, there were a few shining moments in its disastrous career.

RZNAF Buffalo ace Geoff Fisken also earned ace status in the P-40 Warhawk. Geoff is shown here standing next to his P-40, which he nicknamed after his hometown, Wairarapa. *Collection of John Dibbs*

BUFFALO TAMER

I had always been intrigued by airplanes, for as long as I can remember, while growing up in New Zealand. When I was fourteen years old, in 1932, all I had known up until that time was sheep farming. That all changed when I met a World War I pilot from Canada named "Tiny" White, who taught me how to fly a Gipsy Moth. Although he let me solo the Moth after six hours of instruction, I was still too young to get my pilot's license; I had to wait until I was old enough to enlist in the RNZAF. When I earned my wings in late 1940, I was initially posted with 205 Squadron in Malaya. I didn't particularly care for my assignment because I was stationed with a flying-boat squadron, and we flew a four-engine push-pull job called the Short Singapore III.

I knew I hadn't joined the RNZAF to fly "boats"; I wanted to be a fighter pilot. I pestered the orderly officers on a daily basis, sometimes twice a day, to transfer me. I also knew I didn't want to be transferred to the Vildebeest squadron that I walked by on a daily basis to get to my flying boat. The Vickers Vildebeest was a big brute of a biplane that had a single engine and carried a large torpedo. You could also walk faster than they could fly! What I wanted was the new fighter plane that I heard the RNZAF was going to get, called the Brewster Buffalo. I really didn't know much about the Buffalo at the time; all I knew was that it carried six machine guns and was more advanced than what I was currently flying. I also knew that the Buffalos were a damn sight faster than anything else we had in the area. The flying-boat officers finally had enough of me and cast me off to be a Buffalo pilot with the recently formed 67 Squadron and 243 Squadron.

I had a total of 150 hours in the air by the time I met my first Buffalo in early 1941. I was considered "high time," and because I had a

RAF Buffalos await their next mission.
Collection of John Dibbs

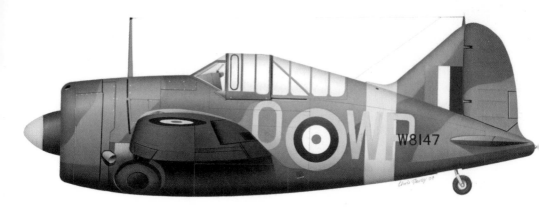

The Buffalo color scheme used by Geoff Fisken while stationed in Singapore. *Collection of John Dibbs*

few hours of retractable time in Oxford twin-engines, I was assigned to test-fly and deliver the newly assembled Buffalos to both squadrons that were based in the Malaya area. As I made my first flight in a real fighter, I thought that it was quite easy to fly and a real beautiful airplane. It landed as easily as it flew, and after a few hours of air time, I thought of it as an "old ladies' airplane." I thoroughly enjoyed doing aerobatics in the Buffalo, but I quickly found that it was underpowered, had poor turning capabilities, and climbed like a brick. It took fifteen to twenty minutes just to stagger up to fifteen thousand feet.

Although the Buffalo was not a suitable aircraft to fight the Japanese with, had it had another three hundred horsepower, I think things would have been much different. By the time our squadrons had received our full complement of pilots—we received four new men every month from New Zealand—I had amassed over three hundred hours in the Brewster. I had heard reports in those days that the Americans thought the Buffalos were awful. Most other people I flew with concurred with the Yanks and described flying the Buffalo as "bloody awful." I was different; I enjoyed flying it, even in combat.

We had almost twenty Buffalos to start with before the war began but just half as many pilots. The main problem we encountered right away was the God-awful climate we operated in. The Buffalos would be deemed ready to fly in the early-morning hours, but as soon as the sun came up, most of the crates would be unserviceable because of the stinking heat and humidity. I have to say, though, that my Buffalo—number 8147 with the call letters WP-O—was always ready to fly. I had a couple of Welsh mechanics along with a Welsh rigger, and these three were the biggest thieves on two legs! If something was broken or wrong with my Buffalo, they would have it off someone else's airplane in no time flat. I never asked, and they never told me how they fixed it. All they would say as I climbed into the cockpit was, "Now give that a try and see if that fixed your problem."

We also experimented with armor plates inside the cockpit, and these were placed behind the seat and on the side of the cockpit wall. We soon found that the side armor was too heavy and cumbersome, so that was removed. It was only on my last flight in the Buffalo that I wished I had left it in there.

BLOODY GOOD SHOW: DECEMBER 1941

I was one of a dozen or so pilots posted with 243 Squadron based at Kallang Aerodrome in Singapore while 67 Squadron was sent up to Burma and flew with the Flying Tigers.

RAF Buffalos close up ranks as they make their way to a target. Unfortunately, the Buffalo didn't fare well against more maneuverable Japanese fighters. *Collection of John Dibbs*

The war started for me the same day it did for America. We had heard that Pearl Harbor had been attacked during the day on December 7, and later that night the Japanese had flown over Kallang Aerodrome as they flew around Singapore while the searchlights tracked them in the sky. There must have been forty or fifty of them milling around up there as they let go with their bombs, not really doing much damage that we could see. The next day was when the shooting really started, as the Japanese invaded Malaya and began their push south to Singapore. I had been flying out of Kota Bharu; a few weeks earlier I had flown north just inside of Thailand at a place called Singora. When I overflew the aerodrome there, I realized that we were eventually going to get into a fight; I saw over two thousand Japanese aircraft parked on the tarmac. Needless to say, we were outnumbered sixteen to one.

Because I had more time than most in the Buffalo, I was sent to Ipoh in mid-December 1941 and was temporarily attached to 21 Royal Australian Air Force Squadron. It seemed to me that the commanders took great delight in attaching me and others from the RNZAF to Australian squadrons that were getting a bit downhearted. The Australians, in my mind, never really liked the Buffalos and would have given their eyeteeth for the Hawker Hurricanes that were, unfortunately, a scarce commodity on Malaya. As the advancing Japanese pushed further south, the Australians took one hell of a beating, so I was sent back to my old squadron.

Our main job was aerial protection of Singapore, but that became a daily struggle because we didn't have any early-warning system or radar to speak of. By the time we

A Brewster F2F Buffalo in US Navy colors flies over a Florida training base.

received word that the Japanese were on their way down, they would be over our heads dropping bombs on us as we taxied out in our Buffalos. There were several Buffalos that were blown apart as they tried to dodge the falling bombs on takeoff. Needless to say, we didn't have any replacements heading our way as our Buffalo numbers began to dwindle.

THE DEFENSE OF SINGAPORE: KALLANG AERODROME, JANUARY 1942

There were eight of us up one day in January, and we had been flying in some clouds at around twenty thousand feet. When we came out of the cloud, I looked down and saw at least twenty Japanese Type 97 fighters one thousand feet below us. I pushed the nose of the Buffalo downward because I knew that once the old Buffalo wound up while descending, there was nothing that was going to catch it. I started firing my six .303 machine guns at the group right away, as one of them turned towards me. I saw that he was shooting at me as well as we accelerated towards one another.

Just before we met, he burst into flames and blew up right underneath me. The concussion of that blast sent my Buffalo into a God-awful spin, and I tried to regain control. I was having a devil of a time, so I decided to jump out. I got one foot over the side but was yanked back into the cockpit because the snakeskin helmet I was wearing was sown to my oxygen mask, which was currently tangled up in my spring-steel oxygen tube. To this day, I have no idea how I got out of that spin. I had lost twelve thousand feet as my whole life flashed before my eyes. Things that happened on the farm, the fights I got into at school when I was a kid—all of them were as clear as day to me. But I was able to wrestle the Buffalo back and finally landed a half hour after the others in my flight.

I was swearing up a storm after I landed because I was so mad at myself for simply not undoing the straps in the back of my head that held my helmet in place. People have asked me if I was frightened. My answer is no—you don't have time to get scared because you are so busy fighting. The only time I was scared was when we were flying towards the enemy, because you knew you were going to get into a fight. And from that moment on the fighting only got worse.

I shot down my second airplane, a Zero, on January 14. On January 17, I was up again on patrol with three other Buffalos. We had been flying through cloud again, and when we came out of the big, white cumulus ball, there was only me and another Buffalo on my wing. The other two had got lost and turned for home. I looked down and saw close to two dozen G3M 96 twin-engine bombers four thousand feet below. They were coming back from a bombing raid and heading north. The two of us flipped our Buffalos over and dived straight down on top of them. I took one of the bombers that were on the out-side, and the gunners began to fire wildly at us as my rounds tore into one of his engines. The bomber began to smoke heavily before bursting into flames and diving straight into the jungle below.

I zoomed through the formation and pulled out of my dive at two thousand feet as I blacked out momentarily. In doing so, it gave me another chance to get right up underneath the guts of the rest of the bombers again, and I shot down another one on my way up. That one burst into flames as well, but instead of blowing up like the first chap, he dropped out of formation and glided downward until he crashed into the jungle. We were miles from our base, so we turned for home because we had pushed the throttles through the gate and were worried about running out of juice. On our way home, we caught another bomber in the middle of nowhere, and the two of us let him have it as well. By the time we left him, he was smoking very heavily and losing altitude. I received credit for two victories and one prob-able. I now had four victories in the Buffalo as the Japanese tightened their noose around Malaya.

I shot down my fifth airplane, another Zero, on January 21. On an earlier mission, I had come back with 143 bullet holes in the airplane, and I was fortunate that the Buffalo was such a tough old bird. I could not say the same for the outdated Vildebeests that were stationed nearby. The Japanese sent down a convoy of ships that included transports, cruisers, and destroyers to assist in landing their troops at a place called Endau, and on January 26 we were sent up to act as top cover for a dozen or so Vildebeests that had been armed with torpedoes. Those slow-moving biplanes never stood a chance, and they were mauled and chewed up by the antiaircraft fire from the ships and the Zeros that were waiting for them as they made their torpedo runs.

Most of the poor buggers that went out that day never made it back. I was able to latch on to one of them at the rendezvous point on the return to base but was having a devil of a time staying with him. Because the Vildebeest flew so slowly, I had to fly with full flaps and lower my landing gear. I was still faster than he was in that configuration. Unfortunately, they sent up another flight of Vildebeests in the afternoon, and it ended in a bloody massacre, as they were hammered to hell by the Japanese.

After this, there was not much left of our squadron, so we were disbanded. I was sent to RAAF 453 Squadron.

LAST FLIGHT OF THE BUFFALO: FEBRUARY 1942

The Australians had been hammered so much by the Japanese during that time that not many of them wanted to fly the Buffalo any longer. There were only two of us up on a patrol mission on February 1, just me and my number two, and I was flying Buffalo W8327. We had just come out of some thick cloud when I saw about twelve Zeros a couple hundred feet below us. We had the edge, even though we were outnumbered six to one, because we were on top of them and they hadn't seen us yet. We dived onto them, and I started to shoot at one Zero when I was less than three hundred yards away. It turned into me and began to fire as well, his machine-gun and cannon rounds tearing into my Buffalo.

I knocked down the Zero I was shooting at, but just as quickly I was attacked by two more. I took some more hits as I ducked back into the clouds. The Zeros hung around for quite some time— every time I poked my head out of the clouds, there was a Japanese fighter ready to pounce on me. One of my arms began to get sore, and I saw that I had taken a bullet in the arm, so I flew back towards Singapore. Although the Buffalo had been hit numerous times, it still flew just fine; unfortunately, I could not say the same about myself.

I knew something was wrong because after I landed, I stood up in the cockpit to undo my parachute and one of my mechanics fainted. We wore white flying suits in those days, and my rigger was pointing down at my leg. I was covered in blood from my hip on down. I saw a piece of steel sticking out of my hip about three inches. It turned out to be the remains of a Japanese cannon shell that had bounced off my armor plate and split up into two pieces, one of them tearing into my hip. I tried to wobble it to see if it would come out, but it didn't, so I asked the other mechanic to get pliers so I could pull it out. By that time, though, it was too sore, so I had to have it cut out. I wasn't much use after that, as I hobbled around walking on a stick with one arm in plaster. I was one of the lucky ones, though, because I left Singapore days before the Japanese captured the island.

The Buffalo had saved my life countless times, and although I have not met many pilots that have anything good to say about her, I still consider her a very nice and easy airplane to fly, even for an old lady.

> *Geoff Fisken continued to fly and fight after his wounds healed and scored an additional five victories while flying the Curtiss P-40 for the RNZAF. He was later awarded the Distinguished Flying Cross (DFC), and with eleven victories total he became the leading Commonwealth fighter pilot against the Japanese. In 1943, because of the injuries he had received while flying the Buffalo, Geoff was invalided out of the RNZAF. He quietly returned to farming in New Zealand and passed away on June 12, 2011.*

WAKE-UP CALL

PILOT SECOND LIEUTENANT BESBY F. HOLMES, USAAC
CURTISS MODEL 75/P-36 HAWK

Besby Holmes was born on December 5, 1917. As a kid growing up in San Francisco, he spent a lot of time fishing off a local pier. He was enamored when he saw Army Air Corps P-26 Peashooters roaring by one day, and from that day forward he was determined to become a fighter pilot. Besby earned his wings in November 1941 and was assigned to the 15th Pursuit Group, stationed on Hawaii.

Besby Holmes—kneeling in the front row, second from left, wearing sunglasses—also participated in the downing of infamous Japanese admiral and Pearl Harbor architect Isoroku Yamamoto.

One of the many casualties of the Pearl Harbor attack.

In late November of 1941, I arrived in Hawaii and was as green as the vegetation that covered the islands. The biggest and fastest airplane I had ever flown in my short two-hundred-hour fighter-pilot career was the North American AT-6, but that all was about to change when I moved up to a real front-line fighter. It was called the Curtiss Model 75, or P-36 Hawk. Good God—here was an airplane with retractable gear, a cockpit that opened and closed, and, best of all, machine guns that fired through the nose. A real fighter plane in the eyes of a naïve second lieutenant!

Our squadron, the 47th Pursuit Squadron, was posted at Haleiwa Field, which was a 3,500-foot grass strip. On December 6, we had been on alert, and when it was finally decided that there was no threat that day, I was allowed to take a P-36 up for some touch-and-go's as long as I promised to bring it back in one piece. If something happened to me, I could be replaced, as there was a pool of pilots to choose from; the fighters, on the other hand, were a bit scarce and were treated as such. I was on cloud nine as I roared down the grass strip into the air. The P-36 was a quantum leap from the earlier planes I had flown. It had the same fuselage as a P-40 Warhawk, but it had a radial engine instead of the inline Allison found on the P-40. After three touch-and-go's, I taxied back to the hangar and put the Hawk to bed. Because the alert was now cancelled, most of us went into town to celebrate. Little did we know that it would be the last time in a long time that any of us would have a reason to celebrate.

The next day, December 7, 1941, I awoke with the most God-awful hangover, brought on by sweet rum drinks. I went to Sunday mass dressed in my favorite pinstripe suit in hopes I could pray my headache away. As I sat in church, the explosions in my head mirrored the sounds outside; bombs were falling all around! I ran outside to see army six-by-six trucks racing down the street and Japanese airplanes in the sky. After hijacking a civilian car, I made it back to Haleiwa Field, where I was handed a cloth helmet, a .45-caliber pistol, and a parachute. I was shown to a waiting P-36 off in the distance, and as I made my way to the fighter, a Japanese dive-bomber came down and started firing at the P-36. I got kind of mad at this guy, and I unloaded my pistol on him, never knowing if I hit him or not. We were now at war, and I was not about to be left out on the sidelines!

I hopped into the P-36 and had to have the line chief show me how to work the guns. I roared off into the unknown and flew over Wheeler Field, where I saw the charred remains of P-40s still smoldering on the ramp. I flew on to Ford Island and Pearl Harbor, where I saw nine to ten battleships on fire; some of these were still sinking while others were sitting on the bottom of the mud. Everywhere around them, though, was death and destruction. I flew over another naval air station, where I attracted the attention of every man with a rifle or machine gun and they began to fire at me.

A Japanese Zero launches from one of several carriers used in the Pearl Harbor raid on December 7, 1941.

A US Army Air Corps P-36 Hawk, built by the Curtiss aircraft company, had a radial engine installed up front instead of the inline Allison that was found on the P-40.

Pearl Harbor, Hawaii, before the Japanese attack on December 7.

It was time to get the hell out of there! I decided this was no place for me and went back to Haleiwa to land. When I got out of the P-36, some soldiers gathered around the airplane. All I could say standing there in my non-fighter-pilot-looking pinstripe suit was, "Hey fellas, it's a mess out there!" The world as we knew it would never be the same.

Besby Holmes continued to fly and fight. In 1943, he was part of a flight of P-38 Lightnings that intercepted and shot down Adm. Isoroku Yamamoto, commander of the Japanese Pacific Fleet and planner of the Pearl Harbor attack. Holmes passed away on July 23, 2006.

WORLD AT WAR: In Europe, Adolf Hitler, frustrated by his top aerial commanders, had to switch gears on invading Great Britain and instead continued a terror war involving the night-bombing of civilian targets. Hitler also understood that in order to keep his war machine moving, he needed oil and resources located on Russian soil.

When it came to calling in some serious firepower during World War II, especially in the European theater, the Allied troops on the ground relied heavily on either the zebra-striped Piper L-4s or the whale-tailed Stinson L-5s. Operating over the enemy front lines, the tandem team of pilot and observer had a front-row seat to the action below as they relayed the enemy's coordinates back to their artillery firebases. As artillery shells rained down on Tiger tank–infested forests and other Axis strongholds, the slow-flying, unarmed "Grasshoppers" were capable of delivering more death and destruction than an entire squadron of B-17 Flying Fortresses. But the Allies weren't the only ones lucky enough to have liaison aircraft at their disposal.

The Axis powers, specifically the Germans, utilized one of the most versatile short takeoff and landing (STOL) aircraft ever developed—the Fieseler Fi 156 Storch. From the deserts of Africa to the hedgerows of Western Europe and on to the frozen tundra of the Eastern Front, the Storch was a jack-of-all-trades. Although it couldn't hover in midair like a helicopter, it came pretty darn close. Able to take off and land from postage stamp–sized fields, the Storch was tasked with a variety of duties. Whether delivering German officers to the front lines, performing reconnaissance missions, or carrying multiple litters of wounded soldiers from bomb-cratered battlefields, the Storch could do almost anything it was tasked with.

RUSSIAN ROULETTE

FLYING A STORCH OVER THE RUSSIAN FRONT

GUNTHER VOLTZ, LUFTWAFFE
FIESELER FI 156 STORCH

STORCH TRAINING

I easily mastered the Focke-Wulf Fw 44 trainer because of my previous glider time*and became the first in my class to solo. But as I progressed into heavier aircraft, I found that I had a serious inner-ear problem that caused me great pain at high altitude. Actually, the altitude wasn't the problem—it was the rapid descents during dive-bombing practice that caused me so much grief. My dream of becoming a bomber or fighter pilot was quickly snuffed out, and I was given one last choice: either I could become an infantry soldier slogging through mud and snow or I could push for a chance at becoming a reconnaissance pilot flying the Fieseler Storch, which, by the way, always operated down low.

I was sent to a Luftwaffe training base in central Germany and was immediately impressed with the flying characteristics of the Fieseler Storch. One of the nicest things about it was that you could fly it slow—almost as slow as a man could walk. With a slat built into the leading edge of the wing and the big flaps that hung down from the trailing edge, the Storch wing was like that of a Junkers Ju 52 trimotor. But to me the greatest advantage of flying the Storch was the amount of weight that could be stuffed inside of it. This was a fact I would prove over and over again when I airlifted wounded troops off the Russian front later in the war. But first, I was assigned as a Luftwaffe reconnaissance pilot attached to an army unit.

BAPTISM BY FIRE: SEVASTOPOL AND LENINGRAD

In September of 1941, I was assigned to accompany another Storch that was carrying Gen. Eugen Ritter von Schobert, commander of the Eleventh Army, to the front lines as he prepared to invade the Crimean Peninsula during the advance into Russia. As I flew just behind the general's Storch, I watched as it prepared to land. As the Storch settled in for a smooth landing on the Russian soil, I began my own approach for landing right behind it. Then, a flash of light in front of me caused me to jerk my Storch upward as the general's Storch disintegrated into a black, oily fireball—it had landed on a Russian minefield! I pulled up and away to avoid the shrapnel and flew on ahead to what I hoped was

*See page 11

This photo taken from the rear observer's seat showcases the slanted side windows that afforded both pilot and observer an unobstructed view of the battlefields below.

a mine-less field. Although the Storch could take a lot of punishment, it was no match for a Russian land mine. General Erich von Manstein was appointed our new commander, and I stayed with him for the majority of the war as we invaded and retreated in and out of Russia. The general's first order of business, however, was to capture the Russian port city stronghold of Sevastopol.

Both the German navy and the Luftwaffe hit the defenders of Sevastopol with everything they had, and still the Russians held on. General von Manstein even called in some very heavy firepower in the form of the eight-hundred-millimeter Gustav railway gun. I was sent up in my Storch to observe and report back the destruction these heavy guns caused. Thankfully, the Russian antiaircraft had been annihilated and silenced as I flew nearby when the firestorm erupted below. Shells as big as trucks exploded into the fortified city as the Russians struggled to survive. With the Russian Air Force out of commission as well, we were soon inundated with a new problem—"desk-chair fighter pilots" from Berlin. Most of them were Luftwaffe officers who had never seen combat, and they flew German fighters and bombers over Sevastopol at will just to say they had flown in combat. After their flight, they would receive their air medals and then fly back to the safety of Berlin with their claim of combat experience on the front. Had the Russian Yaks and LaGGs been around, they would have had a field day with these armchair warriors!

In early July 1942, Sevastopol finally fell to von Manstein; He quickly became Hitler's darling and was promoted to field marshal. Because of his conquest of Sevastopol, we were sent from the south end of the Crimean Peninsula all the way north to the Baltic Sea so we could capture the city of Leningrad. I flew the entire length of the Russian front in my Storch and was pretty much on my own, even having to cut my own wood to make a simple fire. Although I was assigned to an army group, I was still attached to the Luftwaffe, and my primary role was to fly army officers to the front lines so they could figure out whether they should attack or retreat. I was the only Storch assigned to von Manstein, and I got the feeling from him that he never liked the Fieseler very much. I know he was relieved when Hitler sent down an order stating that no field marshal was

Gunther in front of his Storch while on the eastern front near Sevastapol.

allowed to fly in anything with fewer than three engines. At that stage of the war, the Russian army was not that well equipped with antiaircraft guns, so I felt lucky just to be shot at with small-arms fire—but some of my buddies in the other units weren't so lucky.

WHEN HELL FROZE OVER: THE BATTLE OF STALINGRAD

In November of 1942, Hitler ordered General von Manstein to organize and lead a rescue effort of the Sixth Army, which was encircled and trapped near the Russian city of Stalingrad, situated on the Volga River. Earlier in the summer of 1942, the German army had blitzkrieged their way across southern Russia, setting their sights on the oil-rich fields near the Caspian Sea. By the time we arrived in the Stalingrad area, the brutal Russian winter, along with a more organized and tenacious Russian army, made our advance impossible. Our airfield was no more than a sheet of ice, and the cloud layers were so low and full of icing conditions that the Luftwaffe bomber pilots proclaimed their missions suicide runs. They told their commanding officers, "If we fly, we die," and the officers would say, "You fly anyway." More often than not, those poor bomber pilots went up, flew into the clouds as heavy ice built up on their wings, stalled out, and spun in before they reached their target.

Thankfully, in the Storch, I never had to fly into the cloud base, and landing on ice wasn't so bad either, especially with those slats and flaps getting me slowed down. That's why my Storch and I were selected to fly a local field commander into Stalingrad so he could replace an officer that had fallen. I was told we would be going in a back way to Stalingrad, and that morning I had the Storch's engine warming on our airfield as I waited for the army officer to arrive. Unfortunately, the Russians had other plans. Suddenly, out of nowhere, our airfield was attacked by American-built twin-engine Douglas A-20 bombers flown by Russian pilots. They came in low and fast as I ran, slipped, and slid away from my Storch as fast as I could. The A-20s scored a direct hit near my Storch, and I was hit as well—not by shrapnel but by flying shards of ice, which, by the way, hurt just as much!

Although the rips and tears in the Storch's fabric covering could be easily repaired, the Argus engine that powered it was leaking oil like a sieve. I called back to the Luftwaffe headquarters in Germany and they told me to stay put, as they would be sending me a new engine and a mechanic in a few days. As if on cue, a Ju 52 trimotor flew in and landed on our sheet of ice. I was a little confused, though, when the big transport pulled up next to me in the middle of the field with all of its engines still running at a high speed and the pilot motioned me to the side door. At least they could stop for an hour and chat with a fellow Luftwaffe pilot, I thought. Suddenly the side door opened, and a new Argus engine was kicked overboard at my feet—but no mechanic followed it out the door. The Ju 52 revved its engines and took off as fast as it had arrived, heading west, back to the safety of Germany.

Thankfully, some of the army soldiers helped me push the engine closer to the Storch, and I was able to convince some of the guys in the mechanized repair shop on the field to install it. I was lucky to get out of the Stalingrad area when I did, because right after I left, an order came down stating that every able-bodied German soldier was supposed to go into the trenches, as the Russians were pushing through our lines and advancing. I flew my tattered Storch back to Germany and picked up a new one. But this time I was not returning to the Russian front as a reconnaissance pilot; instead, I became an ambulance pilot, flying wounded off the battlefields. I was sent wherever there was a "real bust-up" to pull the wounded out of harm's way, and one of those places was the large tank battle at Kursk.

KURSK: HEAVY LOADS AND SHORT FLIGHTS

Lucky for me, there seemed to be Panzer tanks everywhere along with Stuka dive-bombers and Fw 190s, so the Russian fighters paid little attention to my Storch as I flew in and picked up wounded soldiers from the battlefields. I had about four hours' worth of fuel endurance and could carry two wounded soldiers at a time on litters as I flew back and forth from the field hospital to the battlefield. When I landed back at the field hospital, I would offload my wounded, and they would be placed on waiting Ju 52s and flown back to Germany. I flew about twenty to twenty-five wounded guys a day, but as the battle progressed, the Ju 52s couldn't keep up with the never-ending stream of wounded soldiers. Things only became worse at the field hospital. When I would try to enlist some help from the orderlies with the wounded lying in the back of my Storch, more often than not, I would be told, "What makes these two guys so special? There are hundreds of wounded men ahead of them!" I had to scrounge around for help; otherwise I would be stuck with two bleeding soldiers in the back of my Storch. I wondered if this war would ever end.

OUT OF GAS: 1945

I continued to fly the wounded from countless battlefields in and around the Russian front as the German army advanced to the rear, back toward Germany. By early 1945, I found myself back on German soil with the Russians hot on our heels. I was completely exhausted and out of gas—both myself, physically, and in the Storch's fuel tanks as well. Because of the fuel shortage, during the last two years of the war we had to resort to using a 30 percent alcohol mixture with our gasoline. During the first few months of 1945, my Storch was grounded at the last aerodrome I flew into because the fuel in my tanks was needed for the fighters, but even that was short lived. As a precaution, I removed the propeller and hid it so no one else could take my Storch and escape with it. Because I was only a sergeant, the possibility of a higher-ranking officer taking my airplane and fleeing toward the American lines was almost a given. Thankfully, my luck changed when Hitler's escape transports arrived.

Near the end of the war, two Junkers Ju 290 four-engine transports had flown into our aerodrome, each of them loaded with fuel. They were originally supposed to fly into Berlin, pick up Hitler and his entourage, and fly them to Japan. Lucky for me, a General Seidemann, who was a long-time friend of my brother's, was at the aerodrome when the 290s came in. General Seidemann had been an early glider instructor pilot before the war and had even trained at a secret facility in Lipetsk, Russia, between the wars. He knew that Hitler would never leave his bunker, so he ordered all of the airplanes on the field to gas up and fly westward, away from the

This Storch, owned by Kermitt Weeks of Florida, shows off its high angle of attack on takeoff, only one of its many attributes during World War II. *EAA/Jim Koepnick*

With full-span ailerons and forward slats, the Storch was one of the most manuverable airplanes ever producded during the war. *EAA/Jim Koepnick*

advancing Russian army. I was one of the first airplanes to leave, and I flew toward my hometown of Erfurt.

I was amazed when I crossed over the American lines and saw the mass movements of tanks that filled the autobahn below. I had never seen so many tanks, not even in all the battles on the Russian front, and never realized that the Americans had so much firepower. I was attacked suddenly by an American fighter as tracers whizzed past me. Two P-51 Mustangs flew alongside me as slow as they could, pointing to an airfield near my hometown—it was very exciting for me to see these fighters, and I knew I had to surrender. I landed the Storch, and the Mustangs continued to orbit above me until I shut my engine off. I noticed some American troops nearby who were celebrating the war's end, and they never gave me a second look. I restarted the Storch, quickly took off, and flew the short distance to my mother's house, where I became a civilian again. A few days later, some Americans found my Storch and flew it off my field. I only wish I could have left them a note warning them about all the alcohol that was still in the fuel tanks.

Looking back, the Storch was an ideal airplane for the variety of missions I flew. But I really think it prevented the further development of German helicopters. We did have some primitive models, but the thinking back then was, "We already have the Storch, so why should we keep going with helicopters?"

Gunther Voltz ended the war with over 1,500 hours of flight time in the Fieseler Storch, which included over 250 casualty flights from the Russian front. When the war ended in Europe, he was hired by the US Army as an interpreter and traveled along with them throughout occupied Germany. Eventually he made his way to the United States, where he became a glider instructor and was enshrined in the Soaring Hall of Fame in Elmira, New York, in 1994. Gunther passed away on June 8, 2011.

1942

WE FOUGHT
WITH WHAT
WE HAD

With America's entry into the war, the US military needed to get men and supplies safely to the war zone. Unfortunately, the North Atlantic Ocean was swarming with Nazi U-boats that formed wolfpacks and hunted Allied shipping at will. If Europe was ever to be freed from the Axis stranglehold, England was the logical place to create the world's largest bomber and fighter base from which to operate. But getting airplanes there safely was a herculean task that was fraught with many obstacles.

ARCTIC ICE CAPADES IN A P-38

COLONEL JOSEPH BRADLEY "BRAD" MCMANUS, USAF (RET.)
LOCKHEED P-38 LIGHTNING

Joseph Bradley McManus was born in 1919 and earned his wings on December 12, 1941. He eventually joined the 1st Fighter Group, with whom he learned how to fly P-38 Lightnings.

As America's entry into the war was in its infancy, and with President Roosevelt's insistence on a "Europe first" policy, war material and goods were being sunk at an alarming rate. A faster, safer means of delivering fighter aircraft and bombers to England was needed in a hurry. General "Hap" Arnold, chief of the Army Air Corps, and Gen. Carl Spaatz, commander of the Eighth Air Force, devised a plan to send the B-17s and the new long-range P-38 Lightning fighters on an arctic cross-country.

Nothing in war was easy or foolproof. Risks had to be taken in order to defeat the Axis, and with these thoughts in mind, the Allied generals gave the go-ahead for Operation Bolero to commence immediately. I was posted with the 1st Fighter Group, 94th Fighter Squadron. A proud history and lineage going all the way back to World War I, coupled with the exploits of Capt. Eddie Rickenbacker, enabled our "Hat in the Ring" squadron to be chosen for Operation Bolero, and our first task was to fly our P-38s from California to Maine. The combat air patrols we performed up and down the sunny California coast, on the lookout for invading Japanese forces, would now be a distant memory.

Out of options and out of fuel, this B-17 joined the rest of the flight on the frozen Greenland ice cap. The plane also acted as a warming shelter for the group of stranded pilots.

Brad McManus, standing at left, is all smiles after flipping his P-38 on a snow-packed Greenland and surviving.

The P-38 was a beautiful airplane to fly. With its counter-rotating props, it felt perfectly balanced in a dive, climb, or loop. There was no notice of torque at all. With drop tanks attached, our Lightnings were well suited for the long arctic journey ahead. We were trained on fuel management and how to get the most out of the airplane in terms of distance—knowledge that would later save my life.

In June 1942, our group began to train with our B-17 "mother ships," and it was quite an adjustment flying alongside the lumbering Flying Fortress. A tactical formation of bombers and fighters was established for our journey to England. A P-38 leader and wingman would fly on either side of the fully crewed B-17, although the navigating and communicating was done inside the B-17s. As we were totally dependent on them, they had to consider us in whatever decisions were made. We were all eager and adventuresome, looking forward to combat and to test our skills and training against the seasoned Luftwaffe. We were also young and foolish!

July 4, 1942. Leaving the safety of American shores, two B-17s and eight P-38s began their journey to the European combat theater. Departing Presque Isle, Maine, we flew a very trouble-free flight to Goose Bay. For two days we sat and waited out the weather. Finally it broke and we departed Goose Bay. Our next leg was to take us to a secret base on the soutern tip of Greenland called BW-1—Bluie West One. Two separate elements of one B-17 and four P-38s each lifted off with an assurance by weather forecasters of good weather. We soon found out there was nothing "good" about it!

Our flight was code-named "Tom Cat Green" and the other element named "Tom Cat Yellow." Our flight of four P-38s and one B-17 shadowed Yellow Flight by about five miles. As our flight proceeded on, we ran into some nasty weather. Visibility was reduced considerably, causing us to tighten up the formation. We also lost sight of Yellow Flight. This was not what the forecasters had promised!

We received word from Tom Cat Yellow that the weather was much clearer up ahead, below ten thousand feet. Pointing our noses downward into the soup and clinging to the wing of the aircraft next to us, only feet away, we began our descent. Although I was freezing inside my cockpit, I never thought about the cold because I was so damn busy maintaining my position on my wingmen. If I lost him, I had a strong chance of going for a cold dip in the North Atlantic.

We were approaching two thousand feet and still in the clouds. We were also reaching a halfway point in the flight. With all the throttle adjustments and jockeying around, our fuel status was becoming critical. I, along with the rest of the P-38 pilots, began to have a discussion over the RT. A 180-degree turn was ordered, and we flew back to Goose Bay. About an hour later, we reached clearing skies. On any other flight, I would have been relieved, but in the frigid waters below were icebergs—none of which contained a runway for a fuel-starved P-38! After flying for almost eight hours with barely enough fuel left in the tanks to go much farther, we landed safely at our starting point: Goose Bay. Yellow Flight also made it safely to its destination. The aircraft landed at Bluie West Eight; they had tried for BW-1, but because of the harsh weather conditions, they diverted to Greenland's west coast and landed at BW-8.

Some of the P-38 and B-17 crew pose before going out on their ill-fated mission.

On July 12, Tom Cat Green Flight made another stab at trying to reach BW-1. This time the flight was trouble free and the weather forecaster's prediction right on. Although both Tom Cat flights were separated, now they were at least on the same continent. A storm front moved across the area, and for two more days the men in the planes of Green Flight at BW-1 sat it out. Finally, on July 14, 1942, Green Flight joined up with Yellow Flight at BW-8. It was also the first time in over a week that I took a shower. No one seemed to notice, as we all smelled the same!

One July 15 at around two o'clock in the morning, we were awoken and told the weather had cleared on our route to Iceland. I had heard these weather assurances before, but with a war to be fought, no one argued the point. With drop tanks and internal tanks completely full of gas, and us fully briefed and fed, we began to crank the cold Allisons up in the early-morning hours. Eight P-38s and two B-17s roared down the frozen terrain at BW-8. One by one we lifted off, and our flight began its estimated six-and-a-half-hour trip to Iceland. Things began to unravel early—two P-38s aborted the flight due to mechanical failure and returned to BW-8. Six P-38s and two B-17s continued on into the frigid unknown.

As we progressed eastward, the clear weather we had been promised was nowhere to be found. In its place were swirling rain and snow clouds. Another fun-filled flight was in the making! We climbed higher and higher, trying to get over the clouds. As we did this, the outside temperatures dropped lower and lower.

ABOVE: The distinctive twin tails of the P-38 Lightning are showcased in this photograph. *EAA*
LEFT: *Glacier Girl* takes to the skies once again. This P-38 is one of the original ones forced down over Greenland.

Climbing to twenty thousand feet, we found ourselves still in the overcast. For over an hour, we flew blind. Through snow and rain we flew on, never observing the sea below. We were already one hundred miles east of Greenland, flying through thickening clouds with ice beginning to build on our wings, and our gas consumption was quite high due to our throttle movements to keep our planes flying. It was decided that we would make a letdown to see if we could get under this gauntlet of clouds. We tightened up the formation and latched on to our B-17 mother ship, flying mere feet off the lumbering bomber as we made our headlong descent toward the unknown below. Breaking out at 1,500 feet, we saw rough seas and icebergs. No one was comfortable at these low levels. A quick glance at the fuel gauges only added to our anxiety: we were approaching the point of no return.

After electing to go back upstairs, consuming more precious fuel on the way, we received word that Reykjavik, Iceland, was weathered in and closed. As we instinctively turned our planes 180 degrees, I wondered out loud if I would ever make it to England before the war ended! We flew through the same snow, rain, and clouds on our way back to BW-8. After almost seven hours of flying, with my drop tanks long since dried up and punched off, we received a sudden change in course from one of the B-17s: BW-8 was at minimums and closing fast; we were now diverted to BW-1. I was convinced at that time I could not hold on much longer and I would not make our new destination.

Sunlight appeared out of nowhere and reflected off the icecap below. What a wonderful sight it was! My joy was short lived, however. No matter how hard I tapped the fuel gauge with my finger, the needle showed I was almost out of gas. After what was now eight hours and five minutes of continuous flying, I called the flight leader and advised him that I was going downstairs. I peeled off from the formation and buzzed the icecap. The terrain was level and flat, almost concrete-like in appearance. I figured that if I landed with my wheels down, I could save both the airplane and myself. Once safely on the ground, I would just have to sit and wait for a fuel drop. With full fuel tanks, I could then take off and fly to Iceland. Besides, no one ever said it couldn't be done. Then again, I was the first one to try!

I lowered my gear and flaps and throttled back, flying low over the ice to test the firmness. I let the mains touch for a second or two and the ice seemed hard packed to me. I let the P-38 settle in as I reduced power, feeling pretty good about myself as I rode in on the mains. My nose wheel was still off the ground as I held the tail down. I gently eased the nose wheel down, and that's when it bit me! The nose wheel sheared and bent backward. The nose of the P-38 fell digging into the not-so-hard ice, flipping me on my back.

I was now hanging upside down, still connected by my harness straps. I was completely buried under snow. To make matters worse, the cockpit began to fill with smoke. Thank goodness that didn't last long, as there wasn't any gas left to burn. I wrestled and twisted my way out of the straps, kicking my way out of the Plexiglas canopy. I cut my arm. I was more upset about the tear in my flight jacket than my bloody arm! I tunneled through the snow and came to the surface near one of the wings.

All the other guys flying overhead thought I was dead. And for a second or two, so did I! Shaking the snow off and pulling myself upright, I waved to my fellow pilots above. They did loops, rolls, and buzz jobs over my head, glad that I was alive and OK. Seeing my display on how not to land on the ice, they all decided to leave their wheels up and belly-land. As the B-17s circled overhead, sending out distress messages with our location and status, the P-38s began to land—it was more of a controlled crash, and Lightning after Lightning skidded past me on the ice. It was a real shame to see these brand-new fighters succumb to this treatment. At least all the pilots were safe and unhurt.

The only P-38 I saw belly-land without his props turning was being flown by Harry Smith; his engines were absolutely stopped and his props still. But try as he may, the P-38 was not meant to be a glider! Harry, nevertheless, kissed the frozen turf and slid to a stop. Most of his propeller blades appeared unscathed. Little did I know at the time, but these same propellers would turn again sixty years later!

For over an hour, the aerial B-17s continued to send out SOS messages to whomever might be listening. Everyone hoped that the signal got through to someone, but we also knew that with all the magnetic interference in the area, there was a greater chance no one was hearing our call for help. As fuel became low for the Flying Fortresses, they, too, made controlled crashes on the icecap.

With the majority of the bombers and fighters on their bellies and one on its back, we began to set up camp. It is really amazing to see, when a group of guys are stranded in the middle of nowhere, what kind of ingenious inventions they can come up with. The B-17s would become our main shelters, and some of the crew rigged up "space heaters" that glowed red. Using an oxygen tank, they cut a hole in both ends of it and using siphoned gas and a wick, the heater kept the temperature inside the bomber at a comfortable level. We also sawed the props off one of the B-17s, then started the engine and that kept the generator running, which in turn charged the battery. The radio operators were then still able to transmit a distress signal. After three days of attempting to contact our people with no luck, we began to become somewhat alarmed. We all pooled our resources together, and for three days we didn't eat much. Finally, our radio operator began to receive a Morse code signal. We had made contact! Later that day and in the days to follow, it looked like LaGuardia Field, New York, as C-47s and PBYs flew overhead, dropping supplies to us.

We were seventeen miles from the east coast of Greenland, and for the next twenty hours we began our snow-covered cross-country trek. As we plodded along, our feet sinking into the snow crust, I looked behind me. There was a trail of equipment the guys were throwing away to lighten their load: uniforms, extra shoes, Colt .45 guns, gifts, and anything else they didn't need. There were brief stops of no more than five minutes' rest. When we reached the coast, we were so tired that we collapsed onto the rocks. They felt like mattresses as we slept!

Initially, I was sent back to sunny California to train P-38 pilots, and I did this for eight months. I received orders that I was to report to England for combat and was one of twenty thousand GIs—men and women, including my future wife, Lois—who sailed aboard the *Queen Elizabeth* as we zigzagged our way across the North Atlantic. When I arrived, I was eventually posted with the 364th Fighter Group, 383rd Squadron, and, as a captain, I was in charge of the squadron. Based out of Honington, we started out flying P-38s, mainly in support of bomber escort. I scored one victory in a Lightning when I shot down an Fw 190 in July of 1944 while protecting a box of bombers. Later that month, we traded in our P-38s for the North American P-51 Mustang. I really missed flying the Lightning and was somewhat saddened to see her go; after all, she had saved my butt countless times. However, I am very thankful now, sixty-five years later, that one of the original P-38s will finally complete her mission to England. I only wish I were young enough to be the one landing her on English soil.

Brad McManus married his shipboard sweetheart, Lois, in London on December 26, 1944. He flew a total of eighty-five combat missions in both the P-38 and P-51 until war's end. One of the P-38 Lightnings that crash-landed on Greenland with Brad's flight was eventually unearthed from its frozen tomb and brought back to the United States, where it was restored. It is now owned by Rod Lewis of Texas and flies as Glacier Girl in honor of these brave men. Brad passed away on March 21, 2011.

WORLD AT WAR: The German army area of operations was not measured in miles but by continents. At one point, it literally stretched from the frozen lakes of northern Russia to the hot, arid deserts of North Africa and beyond. It was here that the great Erwin Rommel, and his Afrika Korps attempted a dash across the sand while prowling Luftwaffe and Italian fighters protected them from above.

FLYING TANK OF THE DESERT

SECOND LIEUTENANT THOMAS ANDERSON, USAAC (RET.)
CURTISS P-40 WARHAWK

The German field commander could only stare in disbelief as Curtiss P-40s began high-speed bomb and gun runs on his position. Ferocious-looking shark mouths were painted prominently on their noses. With fixed gun sights out ahead of the pilot, machine guns erupted as tanks, trucks, and personnel were sprayed with hot lead. The P-40s were flying less than fifty feet off the desert sand as they flashed over the now-burning convoy.

It was the beginning of the end for the blitzkrieging Afrika Korps. American "flying tanks" were being flown by experienced British pilots. Field Marshal Erwin Rommel, the brilliant military tactician commonly known by both allies and enemies as the Desert Fox, knew that with America's entry into the war, it was only a matter of time before more and more of these menacing Warhawk fighters would arrive in the deserts of North Africa. Rommel also knew they would be flown by an endless supply of American pilots.

Although new to the war and hurriedly trained, these desert aviators made quick use of one of the only available fighter aircraft in the fledgling Army Air Corps inventory. The P-40 was less maneuverable than the German Bf 109s it encountered, but as a ground strafer it decimated the Afrika Korps, contributing to its defeat.

As a second lieutenant in the armored division, I always marveled at the planes flying overhead. Especially the fighters, as they made practice strafing runs at us, dropping flour sacks to "bomb" our tanks. I was stationed at Fort Knox, which had a monstrous reservation on which to train and conduct war game maneuvers.

In mid-1941, I decided to put in for pilot training. I had not heard anything from the air corps for a few months and thought that I would have to spend my time on the ground, buttoned up inside a tank. In early December of 1941, I had an allergic reaction to medication I was taking, and I ended up in the hospital at Fort Knox. I mentally kissed my flying days goodbye for a while.

Recovering quietly in the infirmary, I was told by some nurses that the Japanese had just bombed Pearl Harbor. I felt anger and helplessness as I lay on my bunk, unable to assist the war effort. I also knew that everything in Washington would be frozen, including my orders to report to flying school. Now I was really mad!

War does some pretty strange things to get bureaucrats moving. At two o'clock one morning, shortly after Pearl Harbor was bombed I was awoken and told, "Pack your things—your orders came in for flight school." I was dumbfounded! Neither fully recovered nor fully dressed, I was sent to Montgomery, Alabama, in the midnight hours to begin flight training. I just hoped I could fly an airplane as well as I drove a tank.

Six months later, after earning my wings, I was introduced to my "flying tank." The P-40 was a sight to behold; a true fighter in its own right, it had already proven itself with the British in North Africa, and the American Volunteer Group (AVG) in China. The P-40 would become my front office during my combat career—but not until I learned the little secrets and nasty habits of flying this gunfighter.

After a few dry runs and a blindfold checkout, I was deemed ready to fly, and I was selected first out of my class to go up and "ring out the P-40"—not because of my superior flying skills or my higher rank of second lieutenant, but because my last name started with an A. I didn't mind going first; I just didn't want an airfield named after me!

Startup was easy, and the big Allison engine roared to life. I was trying to remember everything my instructors had told me about the care and feeding of a P-40. One item of importance was a manual button on the dash; this magic button would automatically control your prop if it "ran away." I quickly tested it and went ahead with the preflight tasks. I nervously did my run-up, glancing on ahead, noticing my fellow classmates on the sidelines looking more like a row of vultures waiting for their first victim. I eased the throttle forward, picking up speed. Pushing the stick forward brought my tail up as flying speed was reached. I lifted off the ground, expecting to rocket skyward, but the P-40 just wanted to settle back down as the runway length decreased. I glanced at the panel and found my problem: when I had ground-tested the prop button, I didn't push it in all the way. It was now telling my engine to decrease rpms! I punched the button hard, the automatic took over, and I struggled into the air.

With the prop at full speed, I sucked up my gear. I flew straight and level for most of the flight, just acclimating myself to the handling of the P-40, then began to set up for landing. My only previous landings in aircraft with high horsepower had been in AT-6s, and those had far less than the P-40. I made the turn to final, and I was moving a lot faster than I was accustomed to. I was well behind the curve—I was too close, too high, and too fast. I went around and tried it again. Same thing: too damn fast!

A bomb-laden P-40 taxis out for another low-level mission while a P-47 Thunderbolt stands ready in the background.

On my third pass, I finally got it lined up and realized I better do things now and not wait five seconds or I was gonna get my ass in trouble! I had everything lined up, gear down, flaps down, and touched down with no other problems. My CO had been observing my trials and tribulations of P-40 flying from a tower built atop a tree; I was just climbing out of the cockpit when I saw him walking toward me. With all the other "virgin" students standing nervously by, I thought I was about to get an ass chewing. The CO looked at me and with tongue in cheek said, "Each time you came by, I thought I was gonna have to shoot you down! Good job! Next guy, get your butt in the air!"

Suddenly everyone around me wanted to know what mistakes I made up there so they wouldn't repeat them. We were all learning as quickly as we could; the war was progressing at a very rapid rate, and we were badly needed to help stem the tide. As I progressed through my training, becoming more aggressive in flying the P-40, I learned the hard way of grabbing a tiger by the tail.

Newly posted with the 79th Fighter Group, I began intense training in aerial combat. I thought the P-40 was a very maneuverable airplane—that was until I was in a death spin over the ocean. I was up at about ten thousand feet, chasing tails with a guy who had a lot of P-40 time. I was trying my damnedest to get on his tail when all of a sudden I went into the screwiest spin I had ever encountered. I must have overcontrolled, because I began to tumble downward.

The gear horn was blowing in my ear, adding to the excitement inside the cockpit. I chopped the throttle and tried to recover. Everything I did just made the spin intensify, and that nagging horn blew louder. I was losing a lot of altitude and decided to bail out; I tried to get the canopy off, but it wouldn't budge. No matter where I looked, trying to orient myself in the cockpit, my eyes couldn't keep up with the spinning instruments inside.

I let go of the stick and tried the canopy again. Still jammed. Time seemed to stand still for a moment, and I thought, "I'm gonna make one helluva splash when I hit!" Suddenly the nose dropped a bit and I caught it. I popped my stick forward and pulled out less than two hundred feet over the water.

With very minimal flight hours in the P-40, I, along with the rest of the 79th Fighter Group, was ordered to North Africa. I was with the 85th Fighter Squadron and we were known as the "Flying Skull." I was beginning to wonder if I had a cracked skull, trading tanks for airplanes! The 79th was to become part of the desert air force, which was made up of British, Australian, New Zealand, and South African wings already in combat against the battle-hardened Afrika Korps.

Just getting into the combat theater in October 1942 was an adventure in and of itself. We left Miami on C-54 Skymasters and traveled to South America. The squadron then boarded Pan Am Clippers for the 2,800-mile trip across the Atlantic. After arriving in Africa, we were taken to a well-hidden P-40 assembly plant, where we picked up brand-new desert-camo P-40s and began our long journey across the width of Africa.

Our "tour guide" was a French-Canadian pilot who probably could have flown the route blindfolded. We, on the other hand, wouldn't have lasted five minutes. Needless to say, no one took their eyes off our flight leader! The country below was very desolate. If you had engine problems and had to put your plane down, no one would have ever found you. Apprehensive at first, we became a little more relaxed as we drew closer to

A desert P-40 pilot, second from left with the shoulder holster, stands with the crew that kept the Warhawk flying.

our destination. As we approached Cairo, we made a "hard left turn" at the Suez Canal, descending to five hundred feet above ground level.

I was with a flight of four P-40s as we neared Cairo, and one of the guys I was flying with was kind of a screwball. Below us was a large column of British trucks coming out of Cairo. This idiot peels off and decides he's going to buzz the truck column. Sort of an American way to say hello, I guess. I watched him go down and down, right over the tops of the trucks. After we landed at our new base, this guy comes up to me with a funny look and says, "I think my flight jacket got sucked out of the cockpit." As I neared his plane, my jaw just dropped. He'd lost not only his jacket, but also eight inches off of two propeller blades—the moron had flown his P-40 right into the cab of a truck and bounced off it! That he managed to keep the thing in the air was a testament to how tough the Warhawk was. I had a long talk with him and convinced him to report what happened before the British found out and kicked our asses. No one ever complained and we never heard a word from the British. These guys had been through so much already that it was just another happenstance to them.

Our new home was designated Landing Ground 174, or just LG-174. Out here in the blue, as the British called the desert, were some of the most God-forsaken, desolate pieces of land I had ever seen, and adding to the fun were sandstorms, heat, and the menacing flies that seemed to be everywhere. Bathing once a week was a luxury. At least we had food, which was terrible at best, but you ate what you got!

Our group was placed on reserve status until we had been properly trained in desert tactics. Flying off the hard-packed sand in 120-degree heat, we learned how to survive and fight the Afrika Korps. Our instructors were all high-combat-time British officers; many of them had fought in the Battle of Britain. The Luftwaffe and Italian pilots we were up against were all seasoned veterans, too.

The other enemy we encountered was sand. It filled engines, guns, and anything else that had an opening larger than a pencil tip. Maintenance performed on our birds was a never-ending battle for the crew chiefs and personnel. Engine changes were done in the open, in the blistering heat. My hat really goes off to the mechanics that kept the desert air force flying.

In late February 1943, the 79th Fighter Group moved once again—this time to Mussolini's pride and joy, the Castel Benito airdrome, situated less than fifteen miles south of Tripoli, Libya. The Italians and Germans, in a hasty retreat, had left a large amount of aircraft behind, though most of these were nonflyable. The airfield was a welcome sight, with green vegetation growing nearby. This would be a short stay, as we were now combat-ready and ordered to the front.

Our primary mission was in support of Gen. Bernard Montgomery's Eighth Army, whose ground troops were slugging it out with Rommel as they pushed the retreating Afrika Korps west. Very few of our missions were bomber escort, and the majority of our Warhawk flying was done at low level. Extremely low level! Striking and blowing up convoys, troops, and rear airfields of the Afrika Korps was an everyday occurrence. German Ju 88s seemed to be everywhere we flew, and the German gunners were deadly expert marksmen—a brutal fact I was about to encounter firsthand.

By April, the "big squeeze" was really being placed on Rommel, with British ground forces punching through and attacking the Afrika Korps head-on. In an attempt to stall the British advance, the Afrika Korps dug in at a place called the Wadi Akarit line in Tunisia. Mountainous terrain and manmade German obstacles slowed the advancing British. The desert air force was called in to soften up, confuse, and deny the Germans the ability to resupply themselves. It would also be the last mission I flew.

On April 8, ten P-40s kicked up sand and dust as we roared across the hard-packed desert floor. Normally we would climb to just above the deck and fly to our target. Today, however, some brilliant planners back in Cairo ordered our flight to climb to twenty thousand feet. Upon reaching German territory, we were then to overfly the target, turn around, and point our noses downward, leveling off at two hundred feet and going balls to the wall. The trouble was that at fifteen thousand feet, the Germans picked us up and tracked our flight. Hell, they knew where we were going and they just set up and waited for us, using a truck and tank convoy as bait. We pushed our noses over and went screaming for the deck below. Leveling out at less than two hundred feet, the trucks and tanks ahead grew larger in my gun sight. The Desert Fox and his cronies still had some deadly tricks up their sleeves, and hidden German antiaircraft opened up on us from the front and sides. Hundreds of thousands of antiaircraft rounds streaked our way. They looked like white-hot burning golf balls but felt like bricks as we flew through the gauntlet. I was flying right next to my flight leader less than one hundred feet off the desert. His P-40 looked like it went through a shredder as the German gunners zeroed in on him; small, twisted pieces of burning metal fell to the desert floor below as my flight leader disintegrated before my eyes.

CURTISS *WARHAWKS*
STRIKE WITH GUN *AND* BOMB!

To destroy the enemy in the skies and to demolish his armored forces and services of supply on the ground is the dual mission which is bringing new fame to bomb-equipped Curtiss P-40 Warhawks. These pursuit planes give the United Nations a new and deadlier type of weapon.

For outstanding accomplishment, Curtiss-Wright Buffalo workers are now proud possessors of the new joint Army-Navy Production Award.

CURTISS WRIGHT
Corporation
AIRPLANE DIVISION

Send 10¢ for your copy of "Men and Wings"—a fascinating 96-page history of aviation by Assen Jordanoff, Airplane Division, Curtiss-Wright Corp., Buffalo, N. Y.

FIRST
Since the Birth of Aviation

1932 · The first Curtiss plane designed specifically as a fighter-bomber... a single seater, it was used by the U. S. Navy for operation from aircraft carrier.

1937 · First fighter-bomber to use retractable landing gear—used by the Navy and by China, Argentina and Siam. Wing bombs were also carried.

1938 · The Hawk 75... a monoplane fighter-bomber, incorporating heavier defense armament, increased maneuverability and carried a greater bomb load.

1940 · Curtiss P 40 Tomahawk... equipped the R. A. F. in the middle East and the American Volunteer Group in China, Java and Burma.

World War II advertisement placed by the Curtiss Aircraft company showing the devastating effects of a P-40 Warhawk.

A P-40 Warhawk is silhouetted against the rising sun. *Jim Koepnick/EAA photo.*

The Germans weren't the only ones doing the shooting—I opened up with my six .50-calibers. There didn't seem to be a spot in the air where there wasn't a bullet going somewhere. Unfortunately, "somewhere" was my Warhawk. I was hit so fast and in so many places that I was instantly flipped over on my back. Upside down one hundred feet off the ground was not a good position to be in! I felt as though I could slide the canopy back, reach outside, and grab a handful of sand.

My P-40 became lighter as pieces of wing and fuselage were ripped away. It was shuddering something terrible, and I glanced at the big hole in the wing. The stick seemed to go round and round as I tried to control and right my stricken bird. I was able to turn right side up; how I'll never know. My engine was smoking and vibrating like hell. But I was still flying! I knew if I put it down here, the Germans would shoot me for sure—especially after I had strafed them.

I tried to climb, but my poor P-40, missing pieces of its elevator, wouldn't respond. I just resolved to fly as long as it would let me and get the hell out of there. Fifteen minutes later, over no man's land, my Warhawk gave up. I chopped the throttle and skidded along the desert for about one hundred yards. I began to congratulate myself for such a smooth paste job and began to relax, when suddenly I was flying again! I shot off an embankment and dropped into a ravine. That is the last thing I remember for a while.

When I awoke, I was being pulled from my cockpit by some New Zealand troops. These "Newzies" had seen me go in and worked their way to the crash site. I was taken to a British dressing station and eventually flown to Cairo. My back was broken in three places, and I was in a body cast for over five months. For me, the war was over.

During Tom Anderson's recovery period, Rommel's once-proud Afrika Korps was routed and beaten in the sands of North Africa. At the forefront were the P-40 Warhawks, bombing and blazing away at the retreating Germans. These flying tanks, although soon to become outdated thanks to more advanced Allied aircraft, proved just how tough they were. And for one tanker-turned-pilot, the P-40 Warhawk, though badly broken and shot up, flew on to deliver him to safety. It also prevented an airfield being named in his honor. And that's just fine by him!

DUEL IN
THE DESERT

COLONEL J. D. "JERRY" COLLINSWORTH, USAF (RET.)
SUPERMARINE SPITFIRE

Jerry Collinsworth was born on December 23, 1919, in Dublin, Texas. His interest in flying started when he was a kid in the 1930s.

As a kid growing up in Texas, the allure of flying bit me real bad. In the early 1930s, after saving up a small fortune in nickels and dimes, I took my first airplane ride and knew right away that I wanted to be a fighter pilot. I enlisted in the air corps before the war, and this gave me the opportunity to experience two things I had never done before. One was to leave the great state of Texas for parts unknown, and the other was to get rip-roaring drunk for the first time. That champagne bug was a nasty little critter!

I joined the 31st Fighter Group in early 1942 and checked out in the lousiest fighter plane the United States ever built: the P-39 Airacobra. They told us it was the fastest tricycle in the world. After flying it some and realizing its weak performance and unimpressive flight characteristics, we found out you can't win wars on tricycles. Unfortunately for us, it was all we had.

In May of 1942, our group was chosen to make the first attempt flying our P-39s across the Atlantic to England, flying from Maine with 150-gallon gas tanks strapped to our bellies. They didn't tell us that our projected loss rate would be 25 percent. This great plan also called for us to follow B-17 mother ships over iceberg-infested waters and through blinding snowstorms and fog. I would have stood a better chance surviving a kiss from a rattlesnake than making this crossing. That's when the Japanese saved my life.

Half a world away, off the coast of California, some Japanese subs snuck in and shelled Santa Barbara. Our

This rare wartime photograph shows American Spitfire pilot J. D. "Jerry" Collinsworth having just returned from a fighter sweep.

B-17 escorts were now needed on the West Coast to fly anti-sub patrols. Our tricycles were left behind, and we boarded ships taking a slower, safer route to England. It was here where I met the airplane that saved my life over and over again.

When I first saw my new mount, I was completely dumbfounded. The British called it the Spitfire V, and they told us this plane helped win the Battle of Britain. I was concerned right away when I saw the three-blade wooden propeller. A wooden prop on a fighter? Man, what have I gotten into! I grabbed the wingtip with both hands and shook the hell out of it, twisting it up and down. Boy, this thing was fragile. The British gave us a real thorough checkout. As I squeezed into the cockpit, an RAF pilot sat on the wing and gave me the rundown.

"Here's the throttle; here's the stick. That's your gun and cannon buttons. Now start it up. Oh, one more thing: be very careful when you land, because with this narrow gear it wants to ground-loop. Now go up and give it a whirl, Yank!"

It was real tough to taxi and I had to "S" that long nose constantly. I poured the coals to her and shot down the grass runway. As soon as my gear came up, that Spitfire became all business. This was one hot fighter! Agile and responsive to the touch, the plane was meant to fight. That old Spit could turn on a dime, and I cranked one around so fast and hard that it would have snapped the wings off a P-39—but in the Spit it was effortless. After my checkout, which was only a couple of hours, my squadron, the 307th Fighter Squadron, was sent to Biggin Hill south of London to begin combat operations. On our first flight, RAF Wing Commander Thomas led us into battle on a sort of combat/training flight. We failed miserably but got high marks for playing follow the leader.

Commander Thomas took us up in a twelve-ship trail, one Spitfire behind the other, and made it perfectly clear to all of us that no matter what happened, we had to stick together and not break for any reason. As we approached the French coast, our Spitfires flew on an invisible string right behind our leader. We weren't looking for a fight because we didn't know how to fight, but the four Fw 190s above us sure knew how. They came out of nowhere and dove through our string-bean formation. Commander Thomas dove after one of the Fw 190s and gave chase. It was a valiant effort, but the 190s had such an advantage over us that it was futile. The Focke-Wulf could outclimb us, outrun us, and outdive us. The only thing we could do better was outturn them.

After we landed back at base, the good commander was mad as hell. He tore into us like a prairie wildfire. "What the hell's the matter with you Yanks?! I looked back and saw eleven Spitfires all in a row following me down after that 190. Why didn't you mix it up with the other 190s?" He'd told us to stay glued to his tail, and by God, that's what we did. He just threw up his hands and muttered something to himself about how long this war was going to last.

On August 19, 1942, with a whopping thirty-five hours of combat time and the ink still wet in my logbook, I was sent out to cover the invasion of France. Actually, they told us this was a practice run to see if the Germans could hold off six thousand Canadians who tried to storm the beaches of Dieppe, France. It was good practice for the Germans, as they annihilated over three thousand Canadian troops.

While our allies on the ground took a horrible beating, we didn't fare much better in the air. We started out at eight thousand feet, and the Fw 190s were at ten thousand feet. When we moved up to their level, they climbed another two thousand feet above us.

When the time was right for them, they just rolled over and went through our formation, picking a couple of us off on their way down, then hightailed it for the deck. This was our introduction to the scary business of fighting a war.

I survived three missions that day over the beaches of Dieppe during Operation Jubilee. I was one of the lucky ones, compared to the poor Canadians on the ground and the eight Spitfires from our group that fell to the battle-tested Luftwaffe. A short time later, having just received our baptism of fire, our group was pulled off combat status and ordered to stand down.

We had hardly unpacked our footlockers in England when we were transferred to the Twelfth Air Force and ordered to the deserts of North Africa in October of 1942. I went out ahead of my squadron and began test-flying brand-new Spitfires as they arrived in Gibraltar. I rejoined my outfit in early 1943, and that's when I began my steady diet of one Fw 190 per month for the next half year.

On February 15, 1943, I was in a flight of four Spitfires as we escorted some P-39s across the desert at a place called Sidi-bou-Zid. As the P-39s attacked German armor, we stayed low on the deck to keep the Luftwaffe off their backs. It didn't take long for those SOBs to show up, and I called a bunch of them out at four o'clock high.

The Fw 190s dived onto us as I yelled for my leader to "break right!" It was obvious to me that if I stayed in trail in my number-four position, I would give that 190 behind me a perfect curve of pursuit. Instead, I racked the old Spit around and was now below the 190 at his twelve-thirty position. I knew damn well he could see me because his guns were blinking on and off and he was planting rows of bullets in the sand beneath me. The funny thing is, in combat you really don't know how you're going to react until it happens. I didn't have time to get scared because I was so damn mad at this guy—he was trying to kill me! Well, if he can dish it out, then I can, too!

I pushed all the buttons on that Spit and wrestled my way behind the 190. I began to talk to myself: "Lead him, Jerry, lead him!" I put my gun pipper way out front and let it drift back toward his nose. I fired at him, and for an instant I thought I missed—that is,

An early-mark Spitfire taxis out for another mission. Note that the British and Americans used similar camouflage schemes while flying Spits.

until the ammo box in his left wing exploded. At eight hundred feet, the 190 coasted by me on fire and slid into the sand below.

My next victory came on March 8, 1943, and that was the scariest day of my life. That old Desert Fox, Rommel, had sent some of his boys up to the Kasserine Pass. Our base was only forty miles away, and we had to hightail it out of there before we became guests of the Luftwaffe. Four of us were sent out on patrol near a place in the sand called Pichon.

The weather was miserable, with light rain and low clouds. Lieutenant Merlin Mitchell led the flight with his number two wingman from the 309th Fighter Squadron. I was an element leader with my number four, Woodlief "Woody" Thomas, as my wingman. As we cruised over the desert at five hundred feet, holding a perfect box formation, a German tank below began to fire vertically into the air near us, but not at us. That should have been a wakeup call for all of us, but we missed the bell.

I called our flight lead and told him about the tank, and he ordered us to "break hard left." If I had followed his lead, I would have flown directly over the tank. Instead, I flew straight ahead around the tank as the other three Spits made their turn. When I rejoined the flight, I now became the number four man.

I noticed Woody out ahead of me begin to throttle back and S-turn from side to side. Woody was as qualified as I was to fly the number-three position, but if he was assigned number four, then, by God, that's what he was going to fly! That action cost Woody his life and saved mine. None of us saw the three Fw 190s coming in fast below and behind us.

As I passed by Woody, I heard gunfire and snapped my head toward his Spitfire. Woody never said a word as red flame and brownish-black smoke poured from his cowling. It was almost surreal, and it seemed like I was moving in slow motion. Woody's Spitfire slowly rolled over, and—bang! He blew up in the desert below.

The Fw 190 that shot him down zoomed up underneath me. He had so much overtake speed and energy that he pulled up in front of me and went into the base of the clouds, rocking his wings at us. I didn't know how many more there were, and I wanted to go into the clouds, too. I called Mitchell over the RT, and Mitchell replied, "Hell no! I'm going to fight these SOBs!"

I shot up after the 190 that got Woody as it broke hard left, still rocking his wings. I saw another Spitfire go into the low clouds, and I thought it was Mitchell leaving the fight, so I followed him into the scud. I was in the cloud deck for a few seconds, and when I popped back out, I saw Mitchell below me, banging around on the deck with two Fw 190s hot on his tail. I saw a third 190 trying to join the fight below; this was the same guy who had shot Woody down. I knew who I was going after!

I firewalled everything I had, pushed my nose over, and went hell-bent for leather trying to get this guy. I knew he saw me coming because black puffs of smoke poured from his BMW engine as he bent his throttle forward. That 190 dived until he could dive no more and pulled up just above the desert floor. He was like a scared jackrabbit looking for its hole.

I had altitude and speed as I pulled in right behind him. Just as I was about to unload on him, he pulled into a steep left bank turn. It cost him his life. Cannon and machine-gun rounds tore into him as I avenged Woody's death. That 190 must have been doing over 350 miles per hour when he snap-rolled into the desert. As I flashed over the carnage, all I saw was a great big ball of fire, black plumes of smoke, and tiny pieces of German aircraft scattered across the sand. My heart was beating like a trip-hammer! In an instant, I was alone with no other aircraft in sight. I had no idea where I was and began to worry about finding my airfield. I had just about an hour's worth of gas left when I saw the inline fighter above me heading east. Maybe this was a fellow Spitfire?

As I flew underneath him and got closer, I saw the swastika on his rudder—a Bf 109! I had one good cannon left because the other one had jammed when I got into it with that 190. I was so damn mad about losing Woody that I wouldn't have cared if I'd only had a slingshot; I was going after this guy. I stayed on the deck and got behind him. I kept one eye on the desert and one eye on him as I got into position, ready to attack. Then I heard a voice in my head.

A few months back, when I was England, the British told us, "Chaps, here's something you should never ever forget. Where there's one German airplane, there are quite often two of them." I cranked that Spit into a tight 180-degree turn and I looked up and saw the number two 109 pass right over the top of me. My old heart was beating so fast I thought the Germans could hear it. I turned back west where the odds were better, my cannons could be fixed, and I could get a stiff drink!

I got another Fw 190 on April 5, 1943, as I escorted some A-20s near La Fauconnerie. This was also the last time I flew a Spitfire Mk V and the last time I was scared. The Spit Mk IX changed our whole outlook on life.

This new and improved Spitfire made us turn from a defensive mind to an offensive one. We could still outturn the 190s and in some cases outclimb and outrun them as well. Most of the time, though, it was the Germans who were on the run! I went from scared looks to beating and thumping my chest and, in one case, thumbing my nose at the Luftwaffe.

On May 6, 1943, I was in a flight of Spitfires cruising over Tunisia and Algeria at ten thousand feet. Leading our finger-four formation was squadron commander Maj. George

American desert Spitfire pilots gather in front of their fighter.

LaBreche. I had flown with the major on one of the missions over Dieppe, France, where we both survived by the skin of our teeth. Times had changed, and we were now itching to fight.

It didn't take long to find a scrap to get into. My wingman and fellow classmate, Johnny White, spotted a pair of Fw 190s above us, and we got the OK to attack them. Johnny and I were a great team, and we always knew what the other was thinking. I got behind the number-two 190 and gave him a short squirt. When I saw his canopy come off, I stopped firing and watched him bail out. I broke to the right to clear my six and continued through a full 360-degree turn. I looked for Johnny and couldn't find him; all I saw was a billowing white parachute about a quarter mile away. Seeing no other German airplanes in the area, I decided to go back and give this guy the once-over.

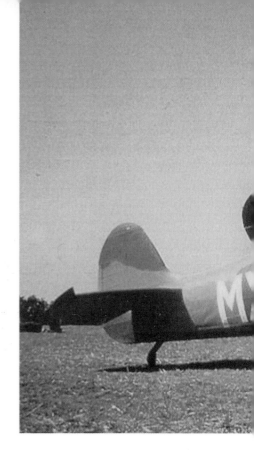

I pulled some power back and looked at the ejected pilot, floating down in his parachute through my open canopy. This guy had just made me one step closer to becoming an ace, so I wanted to thank him. I put my thumb to my nose and moved my fingers back and forth. It was a hell of an insult to him, but I'm sure he was glad I wasn't shooting at him as he hung in that chute. I split-S'ed out of there and headed for home.

In June of 1943, our group was busy slugging it out with the Luftwaffe over the heavily defended and fortified island of Pantelleria. On June 11, I claimed another Fw 190 and became an ace. My final victory came one month later over Sicily.

My wingman, Johnny White, and I were out over the waterside of Sicily doing some convoy cover at twelve thousand feet. I looked down and saw a glint from an aircraft canopy right on the deck. I rolled over and went right under Johnny, and he followed me down to investigate. When I got there, I found this lone Fw 190 doing a 180-degree turn twenty-five feet off the ground. I wondered what the hell he was doing here all alone. Maybe he was drunk or had lost one helluva bet! With Johnny tight on my side, I opened up on this guy and saw the spray of bullets kicking up off the ground under him. The guy panicked and put that old 190 into a steep climb. I stayed right there with him, firing my guns, until his canopy came off. I stopped shooting to give him a chance to get out.

We were close to two thousand feet when this old boy started to stand up. I pulled off to one side just a little bit and watched him depart that 190. This guy pulled the ripcord and his chute blossomed. What I saw next added to my concern of whether this guy was sober or not. He didn't have his leg straps fastened, and he slid right out of that chute at 1,200 feet. Drunk or not, it was a horrible way to die.

British built and American flown, the Spitfire was an excellent fighter, even in the deserts of North Africa.

In August of 1943, I was dealt a bad hand. I had volunteered to help put out a grass fire on our base at Agrigento, and as I was beating down the flames, an explosion went off in front of me. It felt like I had been kicked by a mule as shrapnel from a buried Italian hand grenade tore into my stomach and shoulders. I was down but not out. After my recovery, I returned to combat in the cockpit of my much-beloved Spitfire. After a half dozen more missions, my tour was over and I was sent back home. To this day, I still carry those Italian souvenirs in my shoulder and the wonderful memories of flying a Spitfire in combat.

In 125 combat sorties, Jerry Collinsworth shot down six Axis aircraft along with one probable and one damaged. In September 1943, he returned to America, finishing the war training pilots in the Republic P-47 Thunderbolt. He passed away on May 12, 2010.

WORLD AT WAR: It seemed like the momentum of Hitler's Russian "land grab" campaign, which had begun with a swift thrust toward Moscow, would never end—at least, until the Russian winter set in.

BEAR BAIT OVER RUSSIA

SERGEANT PILOT WILLI L. KRIESSMAN, LUFTWAFFE
HEINKEL HE 111

Willi Kriessman was born in 1920, joined the Luftwaffe in 1938, and began his flight training in March of 1939.

November 16, 1942. After two months of continuous combat in the Leningrad area flying the Heinkel He 111 twin-engine bomber and with fifty missions under my belt, I was now a seasoned Luftwaffe pilot. No longer looked upon as a greenhorn, I had learned my lessons from the never-ending Russian antiaircraft guns. Having earned a short break from the war, I hoped to enjoy it to the fullest. That was until the Russians went on the offensive.

The "Ivans"—Russian ground troops—poured through our lines at Welikije-Luki. It was controlled chaos as I flew with the rest of the group on mission after mission. Our He 111s attacked train stations, troops, and depots. We caused a lot of damage and destruction, but not enough to keep the Russian offensive at bay. They had us outnumbered seven to one.

Willi and fellow Luftwaffe pilots pose in front of an early German bomber.

Willi Kriessman at the controls of an He 111 during a bombing mission over the Russian front.

Our tanks and artillery units should have made these attacks, not our low-level heavy bombers. The He 111 was a very dependable aircraft and a relatively good bomber, but it was horrible as a strafer. We proved this theory day after day, getting chewed up by everything and anything the Russian gunners threw at us.

The war progressed at a very rapid rate, and I thought of having my He 111 painted a bright red, as it seemed we had become members of the Luftwaffe fighter brigade, putting out fires along the whole damn Russian front! The worst was yet to come with the deadly Citadel missions in Welikije-Luki. From late November 1942 through mid-January 1943, we flew in support of our besieged ground troops as they fought to hold their diminishing ground. Our cannons were loaded with tank-penetrating ammo, and our bomb bays stacked with 250- and 500-kilogram low-level, time-delayed bombs. One by one, we took off from our base at Korovje Solo and went hunting.

Diving down from cloud cover, we assaulted Yak positions, tank concentrations, troop gatherings hidden behind snow sheds, and small forest clearings. We operated from less than twenty meters above the treetops as we strafed these targets. The Ivans below shot at us with antiaircraft guns, and the Yaks above tore into us with deadly machine-gun fire. I quickly became very proficient in flying the He 111 on one engine while the other engine was on fire!

On Christmas Day 1942, a large-scale operation was planned to support the ground units that were completely surrounded by Russian troops at Welikije-Luki. Instead of the usual bombs and tank-busting cannon rounds, we now carried first-aid materials, food rations, felt boots, ammo for machine guns, and other supplies that were tightly packed into four 250-kilogram parachute containers. Our mission was to fly in low and fast, pull up to three hundred meters, drop the containers, push the nose back down hard to just above the

ABOVE: Luftwaffe ground personal pose on top of the bombs they will load into the Luftwaffe He111's.
LEFT: The Dornier Do 17Z was a twin-tailed German bomber that carried a crew of four and bristled with six machine guns for protection against Russian fighters.

ground, and then fly back to our base and do it all over again. A supply drop was one thing, but to fly against so much concentrated antiaircraft fire was horrendous. My He 111 was more like a flying magnet—I picked up most of the metal that was thrown at me.

The toughest days were between December 25, 1942, and January 11, 1943. I flew at least two missions every day and came back home more than once on one motor, with broken props on the other and large pieces of aircraft shot away. Adding to the fun was the weather, which was the worst we had seen in years—snow, ice, and fog. The planners back in Berlin picked the wrong winter to be in Russia!

The situation on the ground became worse as the Russians pressed forward and secured most of the bridgeheads, cutting off an escape route for our troops. As things became critical for the men on the ground, so, too, was it for us in the air. Night missions were now called for to resupply our desperate soldiers on the ground.

On January 11, 1943, I flew in one of three He 111s on a special night drop. Five hundred liters of gasoline in two parachute containers were loaded into the bomb bays of each aircraft. Heavily loaded with fuel and stripped of ammo, the three of us took off in heavy snow that darkened the Russian sky. By all accounts, this would be a one-way trip.

Our target drop zone was a series of flares arranged in the form of a swastika positioned in the center of the Citadel. We were told that in order for the parachutes to work, we had to be below three hundred meters, an easy target for Russian gunners. The target area was easy to find—I just flew toward the glowing horizon that appeared to be the gates of hell!

We dropped down to fifty meters as we approached, and the Russians opened up with every gun they had. Big, white-hot fireballs streaked in my direction, and it looked like every one was going to hit me. From all directions, the firestorm surrounded me, and I did not think I would make it through alive. At least it would have been a quick death had I taken a direct hit in the belly.

If I pulled up now, they would get me for sure. I pushed the throttles to the stops and streaked over the fires below. If I had any hope of survival, I would have to do it at a higher level. I climbed to one thousand meters and circled over the glowing swastika. What happened next was almost surreal: as I pushed the nose over into a steep dive, up came the fireballs from the antiaircraft guns. "Three hundred and twenty meters!" screamed my navigator over the intercom. I pushed the bomb release button and gave her full throttle as I pulled back on the control lever with all my strength and darted through the fiery sky while our packages floated downward.

We landed back at our base, and our commander praised us for a job well done—the gasoline had reached the target! On January 17, I flew my seventy-fourth and final mission over Welikije-Luki: the Russians had taken the city. Our crew and what was left of the squadron were sent back to Germany for some much-deserved rest. Alive, but mentally beaten, we had survived, unlike so many who were killed or captured; for this I received the Iron Cross, first class.

Over four months passed after the bloodbath at Welikije-Luki, during which I was not allowed to fly because of night blindness. I don't know where or how I got it, but my crew recognized it right away during a night bombing run over Russia. On my approach to landing, I misjudged my height and almost ended the careers of five souls and an He 111. I was now only allowed to bomb during daylight hours, but soon I would be back in the thick of things.

OPERATION CITADEL

On July 4, 1943, eighteen He 111 crews stood at attention and listened to our commander as Hitler's special order was read to us. Tomorrow morning, Operation Citadel would begin. The advanced front of the Russians was to be destroyed by attacking from two sides—north from Kursk and south from the Orel curve. The front was to be separated and the enemy destroyed, leading to a new German advance toward the east. Large Russian tank and artillery gatherings were reported throughout the area. Our job as He 111 crews was to continuously bomb Russian artillery positions strung out along the front. The largest tank battle the world had ever known was about to begin.

The entire Luftwaffe seemed to be gathered in the area: Fw 190s, Bf 109s, Ju 88s, destroyer Me 110s, He 111s, and the most feared weapons a Russian tank would encounter, Ju 87D Stuka "tank busters" armed with thirty-seven-millimeter cannons. These flying tanks tore apart Russian T-34 and KV-1 heavy tanks like a hot knife through butter. We had over 1,800 tactical aircraft, three thousand tanks, and nine hundred thousand men assembled in the greatest concentration the German war machine had ever pulled together. We were doomed from the start; Hitler waited too long to attack.

The Russians could see the writing on the wall as Hitler delayed and delayed the offensive, waiting for bigger and better tanks: Tigers and Panzers. The Russians built up their fortifications and poured men and material into the bulge. Hidden and waiting for us to attack were four hundred thousand land mines, twenty thousand artillery pieces, 2,400 aircraft, 3,600 tanks, and 1.3 million men. At least there would be plenty of targets to pick from!

I was the lead plane of the lead squadron, and my He 111 was fully loaded with six 250-kilogram fragmentation bombs. A light rain began to fall while I made short work of the preflight and cranked up the engines on the 111. At 2:50 a.m. on July 5, 1943, I raced down the runway at our advanced airfield—Oslufjewo—west of Orel. My He 111 lifted into the dark morning sky as I led *Kampfgeschwader* 53 on the first wave of an unbelievable air armada. From 2,700 meters, all I could see was fog and smoke below—no antiaircraft and no fighters—as we dropped our bombs on the artillery positions. Uneventful and unbelievable that not even one Russian plane rose to attack us. Maybe this would be over soon? On my second mission, however, reality struck me right between the eyes with a deadly blow.

That second mission began at 6:40 a.m., and we had no fighter escorts as we made our way to Kursk. Everywhere I looked, the sky was full of He 111s with their bellies full of bombs. It reminded me of the *Parteitag* flights we used to make when the army marched and the Luftwaffe flew in review to impress the German people and political groups during rallies.

I had an He 111 tucked in close on either side of me as we climbed to 3,200 meters. The two 111s were like chained dogs and stayed with me as our gunners searched for Yaks and MiGs. As we approached the target area, I could see the fires and smoke from the raging battlefield below. Burning tanks and black smoke obscured our target area as we began our bomb run, and antiaircraft fire streaked toward us as we maintained our track to the target. So far, so good—no Russian fighters spotted. I quickly looked left and right and saw the bombs fall from my wingmen's 111s. No bombs fell from my plane, and before I could ask why not, my bombardier shouted over the intercom, "New course—make another approach!" I curved away and assumed the two chained dogs would stay with me on my next run. However, they disappeared below and I circled around for a new approach. I was all alone and seconds away from my drop; that's when the gunners called out the four Yaks coming in from above.

Our bombs fell on the artillery pieces as the Yak fires opened up on us and tore apart my left engine. At first I thought I was only losing fuel and coolant because when I looked out, all I saw was white streams of vapor. But my gunners in the back yelled over the intercom, "There's flames coming out, the engine's on fire!" I then heard more shooting from them as the Yaks made another firing pass at us. My left engine was engulfed in blue-and-black flame and the navigator yelled for the crew to jump.

"No!" I yelled back. "We are still over Russian lines. Stay in your positions!" I pushed the 111 over in a very steep angle and made some abrupt control movements to confuse the Yaks, making them think I was out of control and going to crash. Playing possum seemed to work, as the Yaks broke off their attack. Now I had to find our lines and a place to land.

The fire was spreading over my wing as I began to set up for a crash-landing. Just ahead was a huge golden field of wheat. The wheat was overgrown and quite tall; who has time to harvest with a war going on? I bellied the burning He 111 in, and it was like landing on a featherbed, since the wheat cushioned the crash. The five of us jumped

Willi, in dark glasses, sits with one of his injured crewmen after crash-landing his He 111.

through the flames and disappeared into the wheat field. I drew my pistol when I heard a tank approach.

After all I had gone through, I was not going down without a fight! The rumbling and clattering noise of the tank drew closer, and I peered through the thick wheat. A large German cross was painted on its side. What a great sight! My crew and I enjoyed vodka and a cigarette as we sat on the tank and watched a group of our 111s circle and wag their wings at us. Even more good luck for us: we had landed near the command post of Field Marshal Kluge and were invited to join him for breakfast.

Three days later, I picked up a new He 111 near Orel and rejoined the battle. On July 14, I flew my ninety-third combat mission against Russian troops near Staritza. At this point, it was clear that Operation Citadel had failed miserably. Our group, KG 53, was decimated to just a few 111s, and we were ordered to pull back. It was my last enemy engagement of the war.

For the rest of the war, I was assigned to various factories as a test pilot or ferry pilot, and in the closing months of World War II, I became an Arado 234 jet pilot. I ferried these twin-engine jets from factory to factory in German airspace that was controlled by P-51 Mustangs and P-38 Lightnings. Most of my flights were high and fast to avoid the Americans that were everywhere!

Almost noiseless, the Arado had a completely different feeling from the prop planes I was used to. The higher you flew, the faster you went, and in the air it was just beautiful. It was very maneuverable with great aerodynamic features and could climb like a homesick angel! I often wonder what I could have done with one of these over the Russian front.

Willi Kriessman made two separate flights in Ar 234 Bureau Number (BuNo) 140312 during March 1945. In June 1990, he was reunited with his old mount at a Silver Hill facility in Sweetwater, Maryland, where his old Arado resides as part of the Smithsonian collection. Willi passed away on December 18, 2012.

1943

THE TRAINING BEGINS TO PAY OFF

Although the war in Europe had been dragging on for almost four years now, there seemed to be a stalemate as the Allies and Axis forced continued to slug it out with one another. For the Germans, what had seemed like an easy victory over the Russians was now becoming the continual slaughter of the Luftwaffe and retreat of the German army. Unlike their American Allied counterparts, who were required to fly a certain amount of combat missions before returning home, the Luftwaffe's rule with respect to the Russian front was a simple one: fly until you die!

IVANS AND INDIANS

FIGHTING THE ALLIES WITH "PITCHFORKS"

LIEUTENANT COLONEL NORBERT HANNIG, LUFTWAFFE (RET.) BF 109 AND FW 190

Like most young German pilots before him, Norbert Hannig learned how to fly in a glider at an early age. On December 1, 1941, he joined the Luftwaffe.

It was during my initial flight training in early 1942, after performing loops, rolls, and Immelmann turns, that I knew I wanted to fly fighters for the Luftwaffe. I was granted my wish in December of 1942 when I was sent to No.1 Fighter School at Werneuchen near Berlin. My instructors were all high-time fighter pilots, many of them gaining their experience on the Russian front.

One instructor, Maj. Hannes Trautloft, stood out from the rest. He had seen action on the Russian front with *Jagdegeschwader* 54, also known as the "Green Hearts." What struck me the most, though, was his concern for his fellow men and the camaraderie they developed as they relied on each other day in and day out. From that day forward, I was determined and focused to someday fly with JG 54 on the Russian front. But first I had to master the squirrely Bf 109.

The 109 was a very tricky aircraft, and you had to fly it with smoothness and great finesse, mostly because of its narrow landing gear. We were told time and time again to advance the throttle slowly and to always keep the nose pointed straight down the runway, using mostly right rudder. I must confess there were times in training that I thought I was going to push the right rudder pedal through the cabin floor as I tried to keep the front of the 109 from swapping ends with the tail section! Flying the 109 was very emotional and demanded complete concentration—especially when we learned how to fly formation.

We flew in a standard line-abreast formation of four 109s, with the leader slightly out in front. The British called this the "finger-four" and we called it the *Schwarm*. At first we would be bouncing around chasing our leader, but as soon as we settled down and got the hang of it, our four planes seemed to fly as one.

After successfully completing this phase of training, we had one more step to go before either washing out of fighter

Lutwaffe pilots pose in front of a Bf 109 with a snow camouflage paint scheme, which helped it blend in with the harsh Russian winter.

school or earning our keep on the front lines. I was sent to a base in southern France, where we were introduced to our instructors. These pilots were all highly experienced front-line fighter pilots who were on temporary duty for the sole purpose of teaching us the latest tactics learned at the front. For the next three weeks, seven days a week and up to four flights a day, all I did was eat, breathe, and sleep how to fight the "Ivans" with the 109. In late March of 1943, all my training was complete. Although there was action on the western front, I volunteered for duty on the Russian front. When I received my posting, I was all smiles—JG 54, the Green Hearts, currently based south of Leningrad. I would soon be up to my eyeballs in Ivans.

PITCHFORKS: THE FOCKE-WULF 190

For me, the 190 was everything the 109 wasn't. The Fw 190s, or "Pitchforks" as we called them, were easy to taxi around in and even easier to take off with because of their wide undercarriage. I could now push the throttle all the way forward on take-off, and the 190 stayed true with very little rudder input, even with a more powerful BMW 1,700-horsepower engine out front. In the air, I could yank my stick backward, forward, and sideways and shake it all around as the fighter reacted to all of my commands. But the real advantage the 190 had over the 109 was the amount of firepower it carried. The 109 had two machine guns and one cannon. In contrast, the 190 had four cannons, two in each wing, and a pair of 12.7-millimeter machine guns on top of the motor housing. If an enemy aircraft flew into this stream of fire, it would be torn to shreds in an instant. That is, of course, if you could count on the fact that none of your rounds had been sabotaged.

On May 27, 1943, I was assigned to fly along with another 190 as we escorted an Me 110 acting as an artillery spotter to take out a Russian bridge using some big railway guns that were behind the German lines. We joined up with the Me 110, and as we got close to the Russian lines, we heard them over the radio begin to scramble some of their fighters. Off in the distance, we observed plumes of dust swirling around on the ground as the LaGG-3 fighters clawed their way to the sky—the Ivans were on their way! As we counted the growing swarm, we realized that we were outnumbered eight to one—but for us, these were odds we could handle, especially in the 190. As the artillery rounds erupted on the target below, the Me 110 was satisfied, wagged his wings at us, and turned for home. We could now concentrate on the Ivans.

At that time, the Russians were very disorganized and did not fly in any sort of tactical order like we did in the Luftwaffe. Over here there were two, then down below there might be three or four of them; some flew toward the right while others flew left, and some even did loops and rolls. It was

Luftwaffe ace Norbert Hannig strikes a pose in the cockpit of his Fw 190.

controlled chaos to say the least. All we did was climb above them like a couple of wolfs and wait until one would break ranks and make a run for it. Soon a brave one turned toward me in a climb and started to fire his guns. All of his rounds went wide, and he turned toward the protection of the flock—that's when I pounced on him.

His pale-blue undersurface and red five-point star filled my gun sight as I hammered away at him.

Green Hearts on patrol: Fw 190s headed out looking for enemy fighters over the Russian Front.

Pieces of the LaGG began to shred away, and he began to trail black smoke. My first victory! But my celebration was short lived. My leader flying next to me said, "He's still flying—have another go at him." I couldn't believe the amount of black smoke pouring out of him, and yet he was still flying straight and level as if he were on some sort of training mission. Once again I rolled over, lined him up in my Revi gun sight, and fired. The LaGG suddenly blew up in front of me, and my 190 turned into a fireball as I began to spin—had I been hit as well?

I knew I was still over the Russian side, so for me, bailing out was not an option at this point. I was able to stop the spin, but I could not see out of my windscreen because it was covered in oil. I was able to pump some fuel onto the armored glass, which cleaned some of the oil off, giving me a clearer picture of my damage. There was a one-square-meter section in my right wing that had been ripped open from the leading edge all the way back to the main spar. One of the barrels of the cannon had been split open like the petals of a flower, and my right wheel was dangling in the breeze. To make matters worse, I was trailing black smoke and had no idea where I was. My wingman instructed me to turn right; he steered me back toward our lines and then warned me of the Ivans that were on their way. Smelling blood, they tried to finish me off.

Four of them dived toward me and I had but one option: turn into them and fight. I fired my remaining guns as they flashed underneath me. My wingman gave chase as well, as my would-be pursuers scattered and made a run for their own lines. We continued toward ours and found a front-line emergency landing strip carved out of a heavily wooded forest—not a good place to land a stricken fighter, but I had no other alternative. I tried to slow the 190 down as best I could, but the linkage to my engine had been damaged, and the engine was stuck on almost full power. I turned my ignition off; this cut my power, and I attempted to dead-stick my fighter. I was coming in way too fast and saw the trunks of some trees out in front of me getting bigger every second—I would have to go around.

I flicked the ignition back on, but all that did was make the engine sputter. I grabbed for the primer pump as fuel streamed into the engine. It growled back to life, and I cleared the trees by mere feet. I came back around to try it again, and this time I sideslipped the 190 down onto the field. The first thing to go was my left gear, which sheared off, and then the dangling right gear leg was the next to go. As I slid straight ahead, both my wings came off and my fuselage broke in two. When I finally came to a stop, all that remained of my Fw 190 was my cockpit section and motor—I hoped that every aerial victory wasn't going to be like this!

After some investigation, it was learned that a cannon round had exploded prematurely in my barrel, and this caused the extensive damage to my fighter. Unfortunately, the people that were forced to manufacture the rounds were anti-German sympathizers, and they sabotaged the fusing system. Thankfully, they were never loaded in my 190 again, as I turned my attention to the American "Indians" on the Western Front.

FW 190S VS. P-51 INDIANS

By late 1943, having slugged it out with LaGGs, La-5s, La-7s, Il-2s, and Pe-2s, my victories were in the double digits. The number of Russian airplanes fighting on the front always seemed to increase, no matter how many we shot down. The Ivans quickly became superior in numbers to ours, both in the air and on the ground, as our troops were in a constant state of "advancing to the rear." As we rapidly lost ground on the Russian front, I was sent back to Germany to become a flight instructor and impart my knowledge and wisdom to those who would eventually replace me. But that all changed when the American bombers began to bring fighter escorts with them all the way to the target area—including our training grounds.

By June of 1944, it had been decided that the Luftwaffe could no longer afford to let seasoned fighter pilots simply fly along with pupils on training flights. Instead, it would now be on-the-job training for most of these fledgling students, as we were assigned to lead them in intercepting the American bomber streams. We didn't have to wait very long—the order to scramble was given when our radar picked up a large formation of bombers and escorts crossing the Baltic island of Rügen. The "Indians" (Americans) were on their way. We climbed to the same altitude as the bombers, with hopes of making a head-on pass at them; unfortunately, it didn't work out that way.

Because we arrived too late, we found ourselves below the B-17s. I had a 190 on either side of me as we climbed into the vertical and began to fire at the bellies of the bombers. As soon as the shooting began, I looked up and saw contrails arching down toward us. At first I saw four sets of lines, then eight, and finally twelve, and I knew what was dragging

those condensation trails down—Mustangs. All at once I had twelve shiny P-51s parked on my tail. They held their fire for fear of hitting one of their own bombers and waited for me to clear the stream. When I did, I threw the 190 into some Russian aerobatics as I began to yo-yo it around the sky. The Mustangs tried to hang on to my evasive maneuvers, but their shots went either high or low with every move of my stick.

I spotted some cumulus clouds up ahead and I made a dash for them. I began to fly a tight circle around the

The last view many Allied tail gunners saw was the front end of an Fw 190 roaring in from behind with machine guns blazing away.

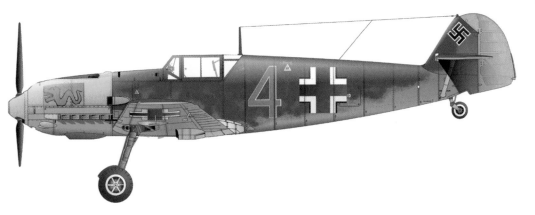

A Bf 109E-3 of JG 3 "Udet." *Björn Huber/Creative Commons*

cloud bank as the Mustangs gave chase. As I flew over the top of a large cloud, I pulled my stick back hard, tromped down on my rudder, threw the 190 into a spin, and quickly spun down into the center of the cloud. When I felt safe, I let go of the stick. The 190 righted itself, and I shot through the bottom of the cloud deck. I looked up, and all I saw were those Mustangs buzzing around like a bunch of angry bees on the outside of the cloud, waiting for me to emerge. As I raced out of there, I listened on the radio to reports of other dogfights around me. Suddenly I recognized one of the voices—that of a fellow 190 pilot who had been part of my initial flight, reporting that he was on the deck with a Mustang on his tail. I knew he couldn't be far away, so I pushed the 190 over and raced for the deck.

It was easy to spot my wingman—not only did he have one Mustang on his tail, but he had three others right behind the first, ready to jump in at a minute's notice. The 190 was fishtailing wildly as the Mustang's shots missed their mark—most of the time. By the time I finally caught up to the group, I let go with a burst of cannon and machine-gun rounds at the three trailing Mustangs, and they scattered when they saw the cannon rounds exploding right under them. As I drew closer to the lone pursuing Mustang, I yelled for my wingman to stomp down on his left rudder. By the time the Mustang pilot figured out what had happened, all he had in front of him was empty sky. My rounds tore into the P-51, and with no altitude to evade, he nosed over and cartwheeled into the ground. My wingman's 190 was riddled with bullet holes, but I fared much better— only seventeen holes. We learned later that the twelve of us in our 190s had gone up against 250 bombers and dozens of P-51 Mustangs. Suffice it to say, only one Luftwaffe fighter landed undamaged that day, with the majority of the others shot down. It was the beginning of the end for us, even with the introduction of "wonder weapons."

ME 262 FOLLIES

On April 6, 1945, having returned back to the Russian front with JG 54 in November of 1944, I shot down two Russian Il-2s that had been making a bombing run on our base. These were my last victories of the war, and my final score would stand at forty-two. On April 7, I was ordered to return to Germany to convert to the Me 262 jet.

It was like being inside a car! I could see forward with no restrictions, and when I pushed the lever forward, the 262 started moving forward slowly until the power came up. It felt like I was airborne in a matter of seconds when I pointed the nose up, raised the undercarriage and flaps, and watched in amazement as the green-and-brown landscape flashed by underneath me. I began to study the cockpit instruments, since many were new to me and not part of the Fw 190 setup. By the time I looked back outside, the landscape had changed dramatically to a stark white, with jagged mountains all around—I was over the Alps, heading straight for Switzerland! I quickly reversed course and returned back to the airfield. After I shut down the engine and climbed out, I was considered checked out in the 262!

I only had completed about twenty 262 missions, most of them in a ground-attack role against advancing Russian troops, before the war came to an end in early May of 1945. Although I had flown the front-line German fighters throughout my combat tour, I was forced to "steal" a Fieseler Storch in order to flee the advancing Russians. For a fighter pilot like me, it was a hard thing to swallow when I had two olive drab–colored liaison aircraft, both with big white stars, pull up next to me and order me to land. But better to surrender to a white star than a red one!

Norbert Hannig served on the Eastern Front from 1943 to 1945 and scored forty-two kills.

WORLD AT WAR: Before America's entry into the war, the Army Air Corps and US Navy of the 1920s and 1930s were just hollow shells. Some of the main American military planners believed the next war, like the last one, would be fought primarily in the trenches. As other countries in Asia and Europe seemed to be producing new radically designed fighters and bombers at an alarming rate, the United States was quite content with its current inventory of outdated equipment and lack of pilots to fly them. Unfortunately, it took a world war to change that thinking, but the outcomes were impressive. In a relatively short time frame, while aircraft manufacturers were rolling out new airplanes seven days a week, the military Training Command was literally transforming hundreds of thousands of "farm boys" into fighter and bomber pilots and ended up producing the largest air armada the world would ever know.

KINGS OF THE COCKPIT

PAUL H. POBEREZNY, PRIMARY FLIGHT INSTRUCTOR, HELENA AERO TECH, THOMPSON-ROBBINS FIELD
FAIRCHILD PT-19 AND PT-23 AND STEARMAN PT-17

Paul Poberezny was born on September 14, 1921. In 1936, while living in Milwaukee, Wisconsin, Paul's high school shop teacher, knowing that Paul's head was always in the clouds, gave him a wrecked Waco glider. Paul rebuilt it and taught himself how to fly. Even before the war began, Paul co-owned an American Eagle biplane that he flew at the age of seventeen.

"Although they may never actually fire a gun against the enemy, the instructors at a primary flying school are dealing a more damaging blow to the Axis than a squadron of B-17 Flying Fortresses. Nearly every man at the controls of a combat plane owes a great part of his ability to fly to his primary flight instructor. The average primary flight instructor has been carefully selected by the United States Army Air Forces to teach the fundamentals of flying to cadets." —44-G and 44-H Aviation cadets class book, March 1944

I was still in my early twenties back in 1943 when I began teaching cadets how to fly at Helena Aero Tech in Helena, Arkansas. By the time I arrived at Helena, I had about 145 hours of civilian flight time, and most of that was in a 1928 American Eagle I owned back in my hometown of Milwaukee, Wisconsin, before the war, which was powered by a World War I Curtiss OX-5 engine. I received additional hours of military flight time after I joined the service in 1942. When I arrived in Helena, I went through a short eight- to nine-hour instructor course and considered myself an amateur.

Flying these primary trainers—the PT-19 and PT-23, along with the Stearman PT-17 — was not a challenge for me because of all the time I had in a 220-horsepower Waco, the American Eagle, and a Waco glider I used to fly. For whatever reason, flying came natural for me, but it wasn't for everybody. I can still remember my last check ride: I was in the rear cockpit of a PT-23 and we were approaching to land; I looked to my right and saw another cadet in a PT-23 land right on top of a third, and the propeller went through the rear cockpit. Needless to say, I already knew the outcome for the occupant before we landed.

Eventually I was given five cadets to teach how to fly, and one of the most challenging aspects for me was using the long rubber Gosport tube to communicate with the students. Some instructors taught from the rear seat, but I chose to sit in the front. It was great visibility for me and limited for the student, but it was the best way to prepare them for the much bigger trainers and fighters that lay ahead in their training—they

A World War II Ranger engine ad depicting Fairchild PT-19 trainers of the Brazilian Air Force.

had to learn to judge their heights from the ground. I would watch them in the rearview mirror as they came in to land and caught more than one of them looking at the back of my head. A couple of times I reached down and took out the fire extinguisher, turned around, and held it in front of them like I was going to clunk them on the head with it while we were still high enough in the air. They quickly learned to look out of both sides of the PT-23 when they came into land!

When I became a flight instructor, I was forewarned that some of the cadets might have prior civilian flight experience and I should make sure that we taught them the "army way" of flying an airplane. Well I, for one, could not tell the difference between flying an army PT-23 or flying my own American Eagle back in high school, because it was all the same to me. I have to say that the only difference was that the army had specific procedures we had to instill in each cadet; back in civilian life, the only procedures I followed were that I tried to make sure I took off and landed into the wind!

Most of my students soloed at between eight and ten hours, and I thought the PT-23 was a great airplane to use to teach these men how to fly. It had the same 220-horsepower engine as a PT-17 did, but the PT-23 had much wider gear, and it didn't have the tendency to ground loop like the Stearman did. The PT-23 was also a good aerobatic platform, and I showed my students how to do an "English bunt": I would take the plane up into the verge of a stall and then pull forward on the stick, doing a half outside loop. Another maneuver I used to perform in the PT-23, especially if I knew a cadet had stayed up a little too late the night before, was to climb to nine thousand feet and spin down, making eight to ten turns on the way down. Just to make sure he was awake, we would climb back up and do it all over again!

I had my own share of misadventures while flying the PT-23, and at least two of them were my own doing. One time I was out with a student, and I told him to land at one of the outlying stage fields. I hopped out of the plane and told him to shoot a couple of landings, then climb up to two thousand feet and do some aerobatics. I stood on the ground with a fellow instructor, watching my student climb up to altitude, and a sudden horror dawned on me as he began to do his first roll. I looked at the guy next to me and said, "I think I'm in big trouble now!" He looked at me kinda funny and said, "What do you mean?" All I could do was yell, "My parachute's still in the front seat!" Soon afterwards, I watched it tumble out of the cockpit and fall to

Already a seasoned aviator at an early age, Paul Poberezny stands tall awaiting his next student atop the wing of a PT-23. Note the seat-pack parachute.

earth in a field. I got chewed out for that. Another time I was out by myself and couldn't resist the temptation of all those levees that were built up next to the Mississippi River. I eased the power back on the PT-23 and rolled my wheels along the levee tops, having a grand old time. I was really enjoying myself and failed to realize that one of the

THIS UNIQUE WING...

mathematically developed by Fairchild engineers, for the first time gives a full cantilever, low-wing monoplane the desirable stall and lateral control characteristics of the biplane. In the Army's PT-19 it makes possible the first safe primary training in ships of combat type.

Fairchild's position in the aircraft industry, as one of the smaller companies with the most advanced engineering organization and equipment, makes possible the successful pioneering of which this wing is but one example.

FAIRCHILD ENGINE & AIRPLANE CORP.

30 Rockefeller Plaza, New York
Hagerstown, Md. • Farmingdale, L. I.

A wartime ad showing PT-19s in a stacked formation. Note that the "red meatball" insignia was removed soon after the war began to avoid confusion with Japanese markings.

army check pilots saw me having "non–army regulation fun." Needless to say, I really got chewed out for that one, too!

I learned how to fly by watching the mistakes made by others, and as a flight instructor I would pass that information on to my students. It was a wonderful feeling for

Paul Poberezny, standing center, is surrounded by some of his fledgling students. Note that both students and instructor are of similar age. *EAA collection*

A Fairchild PT-23 similar in markings to the one Paul flew as an instructor during World War II. *EAA*

me to see my students become qualified in the PT-23, pass their check ride, and progress to the next level. To me, the PT-23 was a real nice airplane, and I find myself missing it from time to time. It would be nice to roll those big smooth wheels along those Arkansas levees one last time—and not get grief for it!

Paul Poberezny continued to fly well after the war and amassed over thirty thousand hours in over five hundred different airplanes. Whether it was a military fighter, a transport, or a tube-and-fabric homebuilt, Paul always said his favorite airplane was the one he was flying in. In 1953, Paul founded the Experimental Aircraft Association (EAA), which is now located in Oshkosh, Wisconsin. Paul passed away on August 22, 2013.

WORLD AT WAR: With the advancing, superior Japanese military machine literally halted in its tracks at Australia's doorstep, the Allies began to fight back with what they had. Although the Japanese possessed the deadly Zero fighter, new tactics were devised to either beat it or outrun it until new, more advanced fighters began to pour into the Pacific theater.

RUFF STUFF

MEMORIES OF AN EARLY-WAR SOUTH PACIFIC FIGHTER PILOT

MAJOR NORBERT C. RUFF, USAF (RET.)
LOCKHEED P-38 LIGHTNING

Norbert Ruff was born June 4, 1919. He enlisted in the Army Air Corps on December 23, 1940, and earned his wings on December 6, 1941.

By the time newly minted United States fighter pilots entered World War II in late 1941, they faced a Japanese adversary that had been flying combat since 1937. Not only were these "flying samurai" pilots old hats; they also flew a trump card in the form of the Zero. As the rays of the rising sun extended over the vastness of the South Pacific, the two things that stood in their way of reaching the Australian shores were a jumping-off point near the southern tip of New Guinea and the untested, untrained, and outgunned fighter pilots of the Army Air Corps.

The pilots of the 80th Fighter Group, known as the "Headhunters," gather in front of their scoreboard.

As far as I am concerned, the P-38 Lightning did more to win the air war in the South Pacific than any other airplane, including what the navy had. Although the P-38 was big and heavy, it could whip a Zero in a dogfight as long as you kept your speed up. But best of all, you could still make it home if you lost one of your engines. No other fighter in the theater could make that same claim.

ROUGH, TOUGH, AND READY?

December 6, 1941, was a day that I would never forget. After months and months of enduring the various rants and complaints of my Army Air Corps instructors, most of whom had shouted at me from the back seats of PT-17s, BT-14s, and AT-6s, I finally turned the tables on them when silver wings were pinned to my chest. As a brand-new second lieutenant, I carried a set of papers that proclaimed I was to be sent to Selfridge Field in Michigan to learn how to fly fighters. Less than a day later, my whole world, along with everyone else's, was turned upside down.

We received word that the Japanese had bombed a place called Pearl Harbor. Naturally, I thought it was up near Alaska—what did I know? I was just a farm kid from Wisconsin. I realized it was serious when they told us to report back to base, and I knew these were desperate times when they sent me on to Florida to learn how to fly P-40s with the 49th Fighter Group. But by Christmas of 1941—having yet to sit in a P-40, let alone fly one—our airplanes were crated, and we were told we were being sent to California for deployment to a combat area. The military could not afford to wait to train us while the Japanese were ravaging the Pacific.

On February 1, 1942, after twenty-one days at sea, our convoy landed at Melbourne, Australia. Most of us were overzealous and cocky. Some in the group thought that Japanese were all inferior pilots, wearing thick glasses and flying airplanes that couldn't handle the simplest turning maneuvers. It didn't take us very long to realize that we were the inferior ones—in both pilots and aircraft. After a blindfold checkout and a few prayers, I finally got to fly a real fighter—a P-40N Warhawk. But by April, after a whopping twenty-four hours total time in the P-40, never firing its guns or learning air-to-air combat maneuvers, I was reassigned to a newly formed fighter squadron—the 80th.

The 80th FS was part of the 8th Fighter Group, which also included the 35th and 36th FS. Instead of P-40s, we were assigned P-39 Airacobras and their British counterparts, P-400s. Built by the Bell Aircraft Corporation, the Airacobra was the first tricycle-geared fighter ever produced. It had a door on each side that opened like a car door and windows that rolled up and down. Once inside the roomy cockpit, the forward visibility was excellent. The 'Cobra had plenty of guns, too: a thirty-seven-millimeter cannon (twenty-millimeter on the P-400) that fired through the propeller shaft, a pair of nose-mounted .50-caliber machine guns synchronized to fire through the propeller arc, and four .30-caliber machine guns, two on each wing. On paper, the P-39 appeared to carry quite a punch, but in the air, it wasn't worth the paper it was written on. We struggled to get it up to eighteen thousand feet. Needless to say, the Japanese fighters and bombers operated well above us, and they held the upper hand on when and where they wanted to fight.

AIRACOBRA COMBAT

In mid-July of 1942, our squadron was sent up to 12-Mile Aerodrome near Port Moresby, New Guinea. The island of New Guinea lies just to the north of Australia, and it was all that stood in the way of the conquering Japanese. In fact, most of New Guinea

An early wartime air-to-air shot of a P-38 belonging to the 80th FG on a long-range mission. Note the under-wing drop tank.

was already under Japanese control when we arrived, and the only things preventing them from taking Port Moresby were the thirteen-thousand-foot peaks of the Owen Stanley Mountains, which cut the south end of New Guinea in half, and a bunch of determined P-39 Airacobras.

Most of my early combat was "on-the-job training," and I went out on strafing missions in P-400s with our already-seasoned sister squadron. The Japanese were attempting to land troops at a place called Buna, which was only twenty minutes away by air on the other side of New Guinea. We caught them out in the open with six of us in our 'Cobras roaring over the beach, firing our guns, while geysers of water erupted around the dozen landing barges and the Japanese troops on the ground scattered every which way. We were the lucky ones that day because the Zeros failed to show up to protect their troops on the ground—their rain-soaked field was too muddy to take off from.

As a ground strafer, the P-39 was king, especially at treetop level. But as an air-to-air dogfighter, it was absolutely, positively a nonmaneuverable brick compared to the Zero. To make matters worse, there were only a handful of pilots among us that had any combat experience, and those that did had come from England and were teaching us how to fight the "Battle of Britain way." The tactics we were taught might have worked against the heavier Bf 109s or Fw 190s, but not against a tight-turning Zero. Without a supercharger, we couldn't get to their altitudes even if we tried—especially when they escorted their bombers in a perfect V formation over our field on an almost daily basis.

When we weren't dodging falling Japanese bombs, we flew escort missions for B-26 Marauders, B-25 Mitchells, or C-47 Skytrain transports as they dropped bombs, troops, and supplies onto the jungles below. We got in on the bombing campaign ourselves during September of 1942 when we went from mainly strafing to dive-bombing, hitting Japanese positions near Myola Lake with one-hundred-pound belly-mounted bombs. After slogging through month after month of continuous combat, our squadron was redeployed to Milne Bay, which lies on the easternmost tip of New Guinea. Although we had originally been scheduled to be in combat only six weeks, we were now approaching five months, and our biggest enemies—malaria and dengue fever—were taking their toll on our squadron. Half the men, including our CO, "Coon Dog" Connor, were sent back to Australia to recuperate. Those of us left did what little we could to fend off the daily Japanese bomber attacks. Times were tough, the mosquitoes and sweltering heat were tougher, and with no fresh food of any kind, we became desperate.

In January of 1943, the Japanese bomber campaign intensified, and our base took a real beating on the 17th, as Type 97 "Sally" bombers escorted by Zeros roared over our field and just about decimated us. A couple of our P-39s were able to get airborne and clobbered a few of the Sallys before they got out of range. When the smoke cleared, two B-17s, one B-24, two Lockheed Hudsons, and a P-39 lay in ruins, while over ten thousand gallons of aviation fuel burned nearby. Over 150 bombs had rained down on our field, tearing up our runway and entire camp. When we didn't think it could get any worse, a shot-up B-26 Marauder, appropriately christened *ShittenGitten*, came limping in and belly-landed in between the bomb craters. A few days later, with seventy-five Airacobra missions under my belt and with only a third of our original squadron left, we were finally withdrawn and sent back to Australia. Not just to rest, though, but to get checked out in a new fighter—the P-38 Lightning.

P-38 CHECKOUT

The Lightning was a helluva lot bigger of an airplane than the P-39, especially in wing area, overall height, length, and weight, but it could fly circles around the 'Cobra in combat. What a difference a pair of twin engines makes, and with superchargers to boot! We could now climb up into the forty-thousand-foot range with enough power left over to tangle with the Japanese fighters. Instead of the Zeros knocking on our front door, we smashed theirs open on our terms. The front nose contained four .50-caliber machine guns and one twenty-millimeter cannon. It was an awesome, powerful gun platform with lots of ammo—just point the "fire hose" at the target and let the stream of lead find its mark.

The P-38 had self-sealing tanks, and even if we lost an engine, we could still make it back to base. That was a comforting fact, especially during those long over-water flights. The Lightning was quick and agile, and even though the Zero was lighter and more maneuverable and could turn tighter at slower speeds, we were faster, tougher, and better armed. The Zeros always wanted to sucker us into a slow-turning duel. But if you kept your speed up, you could turn with them, as long as you did it on your terms—not theirs.

Our checkout in the Lightning was quite simple. You flew it automatically with the throttles, and you flew it just like you would drive a Caterpillar tractor. If you wanted to make a hard left turn, you simply pulled the throttle on the inside engine and, at the same time, pushed the throttle of the outside engine to the stops—it would roll on over. You never took your left hand off the throttle knobs. As long as you performed all of your combat maneuvering at high speeds, the P-38 held the advantage. Woe unto the pilot who cut his speed to turn with a Zero—the advantage was lost and, in some instances, so too was the pilot. The airplane was very true in all of the inputs it received from the pilot, as long as you remembered the golden rule: always check your six o'clock. Ninety

Ron Fagen's P-38, painted in the markings of *Ruff Stuff*, cruises over a Wisconsin lake. *EAA/ Jim Koepnick*

A rare wartime color photograph of Norbert Ruff.

percent of the pilots shot down, no matter what side they were on, never saw their adversaries—a fact I exploited a handful of times during my P-38 combat tour.

TURNING THE TIDE: REVENGE OF THE HEADHUNTERS

In early April of 1943, not only did we have a new fighter to fly but we also had a new CO—Capt. Edward "Porky" Cragg. I never saw Captain Cragg turn away from a fight, no matter the odds. He was tough and aggressive and flew the P-38 to its limits and beyond, especially during combat. Captain Cragg also gave our 80th Fighter Squadron the infamous name of "the Headhunters," after the local tribes that rescued downed Allied pilots and killed Japanese ones. We returned to the front lines and were based at a very familiar place—Three Mile Aerodrome in Port Moresby. Although on the ground we were in familiar surroundings, things in the air would be totally different. I was assigned an olive-drab P-38 that I christened *Ruff Stuff* on the nose. It was more or less a play on words in the world of aerial combat—most of which I would soon encounter.

On May 21, our squadron was sent out to fly top cover for a bunch of C-47 transports on their way to Wau. As soon as we started climbing after takeoff, we were sent to intercept bogies over Salamaua. There were eleven of us in our P-38s, and we made a quick climb to twenty-three thousand feet. Someone called out two dozen Zeroes, Oscars, and Hamps above us. As the order to drop tanks came across the radio, we pushed our throttles forward and our noses upward. We split up into sections and tore into the Japanese fighter formation. All around the sky, there were burning airplanes falling and spinning downward. When all was said and done, there were six fewer Japanese airplanes in the sky that day, and all eleven P-38s returned to base. Although I didn't get any that day, my turn would soon come.

In late July, we were sent out again on another bomber escort mission near Madang. As we were stooging around, focusing on our escort duties, we were jumped by Zeros and Oscars. I tacked onto the tail of one Oscar as he tried to shake me with his wild maneuvering. I held on for the ride and finally was able to get some good hits on him. I saw him start to burn, and watched as his canopy slid backward. He bailed out of his stricken fighter, and as his chute opened and began to blossom, I became completely awestruck by this sight. I had been flying combat for over a year and had seen a lot in that time, but now I was in shock—I was amazed to be reminded that there had been a man attached to that airplane! To me, combat had always been airplane against airplane—nothing more, nothing less.

On September 13, 1943, our mission consisted of fifteen P-38s sent out on a fighter sweep ahead of a formation of incoming B-24 Liberators. Near Dagua, New Guinea, I was leading a flight of three other Lightnings at around twenty thousand feet when we spotted an equal number of Japanese fighters nearby. I ordered our flight to "strip tanks," and we dove into the Oscars. I quickly maneuvered behind a fleeing Oscar and gave him a quick squirt. He started to burn and bailed out almost immediately. However, I almost became a victim of my own golden rule— I became so engaged in that Oscar that I failed to see two more behind me trying to revenge their buddy whom I had just shot down. Thankfully, my wingman did his job, letting loose on the pair of fighters and scoring hits on one as it rolled over and headed downward.

The other guy must have figured there was someone behind him, and he, too, rolled his Oscar over and headed for the deck. I followed after him and we swirled around slugging it out, each of us trying to get on the other's tail. I finally gained the advantage at five thousand feet; my rounds tore into him and he crashed into the jungle below.

On September 15, sixteen of us were sent out to cover B-24s near Wewak. The bombers stayed at fifteen thousand feet while we cruised back and forth above them at eighteen thousand feet. About twenty miles from the target area, someone called out a lone Oscar below us just above the undercast. Suddenly other Oscars and Hamps began to appear, and their numbers grew to over twenty-five. We stripped our tanks and dived down on them. I tacked onto a Hamp about 250 yards away, giving him a long burst and closing on him rapidly; at sixty yards, the plane disintegrated in front of me and exploded. That was my last victory during a very long war.

In October of 1943, after 125 combat missions in eighteen months, I was sent back home and wound up teaching brand-new fighter pilots the finer points of P-38 combat. I was the last 80th FS pilot left in the group from the original cadre that had landed on New Guinea in 1942. I guess I never got over playing with Bell-built, tricycle-geared airplanes, because in April of 1945, I became one of the first five pilots selected to fly the P-59 Airacomet jet. Although it gulped fuel by the truckload and flew about as fast as a P-38, it nevertheless ushered in the jet age for the United States—boy what we could have done with them back in early 1942!

Norbert Ruff achieved four aerial victories during his combat tour. He passed away on November 28, 2007. A P-38 Lightning owned by Ron Fagen of Granite Falls, Minnesota, is painted in the markings of Norbert's Ruff Stuff P-38.

FIRST BLOOD

COLONEL JAMES E. "ZEKE" SWETT,
MEDAL OF HONOR RECIPIENT, USMC (RET.)
GRUMMAN F4F WILDCAT

James Swett was born on June 15, 1920, and earned a private pilot's license before enlisting in the naval reserve in August 1941.

In November of 1942, I was assigned to VMF-221, not as an original member of the squadron, but as a replacement pilot for all the men who had gone through holy hell at Midway. The group had lost a tremendous number of pilots and planes on the tiny Pacific Island as they stood and fought the Japanese onslaught.

After my advanced fighter training in Hawaii, I was sent to a place in the South Pacific called Guadalcanal and became a member of the "Cactus Air Force"—the code name for Guadalcanal. Our living conditions were very basic, and we slept in tents next to slit trenches. When the Zeros strafed us, which was on a daily basis, we simply rolled out of our tents into the trench and waited for them to leave. Sometimes our parked airplanes took the brunt of the damage from the strafers.

Our group was assigned the little barrel-chested, stubby fighter called the F4F Wildcat. I liked the Wildcat because it was a good old airplane; it wasn't very maneuverable, but it was an excellent, hard-hitting, almost fortress-like fighter plane. The Wildcat could absorb a tremendous amount of punishment and, at the same time, return the favor with its six .50-caliber Browning machine guns. It was very sluggish in a turn compared to the Japanese Zeros we went up against—the Zeros were much lighter than we were and could fly rings around our Wildcats—but if we got behind them and gave them a burst, they lit up and burned easily.

Medal of Honor recipient Jim Swett poses in front of a USMC fighter.

When I joined the squadron, where everyone was given a nickname, I was given the name Zeke from the Al Capp cartoons and was forever stuck with it. Zeke was also another name for the Zero, so it took some getting used to!

My first combat mission was on April Fools' Day, 1943, protecting the air over Henderson Field. I certainly felt like a fool, a big air battle raging off in the distance while I droned around, boring a big circle in the sky with my Wildcat. Although I hadn't fired my guns in anger yet, I would more than make up for it on my next mission.

It was still pitch-dark when I took off and led an early-morning flight of seven other Wildcats from our strip, known as Fighter-2, on April 7. The runway was totally blacked out, and our only reference was a couple of beams of light at the other end; as long as you flew toward the lights and took off before you hit them, you would be just fine. As we made our way toward the Russell Islands, we made contact with the fighter director, code name Knucklehead. We flew around the Russells for a while, never spotting a Japanese airplane. When our fuel gauges began to creep toward empty, Knucklehead told us that there were some Japanese planes stirring around near Bougainville, possibly headed our way. I didn't give that piece of news much thought, because if they were on their way to Guadalcanal, they were still hours away.

Our flight returned to Fighter-2 and refueled. After we were topped off, we went back up and circled around near Guadalcanal for a few hours. I thought it had the makings of my earlier uneventful mission—just boring holes in the sky. I took my flight back to Fighter-2 and landed a second time, but soon I would find myself busier than a one-armed paperhanger! We began to get reports from the coast watchers up north that the Japanese were on their way down in force. Unbeknownst to me, there was a big storm brewing just beyond the horizon, and it contained almost two hundred Japanese fighters and dive-bombers, all of them heading our way.

Our ground crews topped off our gas tanks once again, and just for good measure, my ordnance man shoehorned an additional fifteen rounds of ammo into each gun bay. I would soon find out that every little bit helped! We took off again and were still climbing when I was told to take my flight to the Florida Islands near Tulagi, circle, and wait for further instructions. Tulagi was only forty miles away, with a group of Allied ships anchored offshore that included some tankers, minesweepers, corvettes, and destroyers. Our job was to protect the fleet from the Japanese dive-bombers.

I was still climbing and leading my flight through fifteen thousand feet when all of a sudden we ran right into the middle of a large formation of Japanese Aichi D3A "Val" dive-bombers and their Zero escorts. My God, there were airplanes all over the sky, and most of them had red meatballs on their wings! I estimated over one hundred fighters and seventy-five dive-bombers. There were just eight of us, and all I could think was, "Holy smoke! We're in deep doo-doo!" I brought my flight around, turned toward them at full throttle, and dived headlong into the middle of the hornet's nest. Brother, it hit the fan like right now!

Because I was the lead F4F, I was way out in front of the rest of my flight and didn't realize that they were getting mauled by the Zeros. I concentrated on the Vals that were filling my windscreen. They were painted in a dirty olive drab and were strung out in multiple V formations, never looking back as they made their dives toward the ships in the harbor. I guess they thought that the Zeros would take care of all the Wildcats behind them. They thought wrong.

The Grumman F4F Wildcat was a very tough fighter. Though unable to turn with a Zero, it nevertheless could dive and absorb all kinds of punishment.

I nailed one Val right away, just before he went into his dive, and flamed him before he knew what hit him. I stayed with the rest of the pack and had to throttle back because I was traveling so much faster than they were; I'm sure those bombs slung below their bellies didn't help their speed any. I burned my second Val halfway down into his dive. My tactic was to get in close to a bomber, hit it hard, and duck away quickly while I looked for the next one. My plan seemed to be working pretty well, and I tacked on to another Val just as he was pulling out at the bottom of his dive-bomb run. I gave him a couple of short squirts and he began to burn like the other two, splashing him in an instant. Although the Vals had rear gunners, I didn't give them much thought as they shot at me because I was concentrating my aim on the wing root near the pilot. I had been taught

early on to squeeze the trigger in short, two- to three-round bursts. That way my barrels would stay cool and not burn out.

The Vals were getting some hits on the ships below; a tanker began to burn and a destroyer took a hit in the stern. Every gun on those ships turned in my direction, because I was right in the middle of those Vals, and the sky filled with antiaircraft fire. The flak from the Allied ships was coming up so hot and so fast that there was no way to avoid getting hit as I pulled out of my dive around five hundred feet. I was trying hard to get the hell out of there when all of a sudden I took a tremendous hit in my right wing, dead center into my outboard gun. That scared the living bejeezus out of me! I looked over and saw my gun barrel sticking straight up through a fresh foot-and-a-half jagged hole in my wing. My right flap was damaged, too, but at least my other five guns were still working. I scanned my instruments, and everything else seemed to be working fine

An F4F Wildcat showing the survival gear that was stowed in the aft fuselage in case of a water ditching. *Jack Cook collection*

on the Wildcat. It was a good time to leave the flak, so I pointed my Wildcat toward the opposite side of the Florida Islands.

I guess the Japanese were trying to do the same, because as I was skirting some low clouds in the area, I ran into another batch of Vals scattered across the sky trying to form back up for the long flight home. I was still down low, below eight hundred feet, when I crept up behind the Vals. I picked the first one out as he made a left turn and was only one hundred feet behind him when I gave him a burst of my machine guns; he burned quickly and that was number four. I slid over to the next Val, and he saw me coming, but there was nothing he could do because he was too low—he quickly joined his friends in the sea below. It was like shooting fish in a barrel, the slow-moving Vals seemingly helpless against my Wildcat. I picked out number six and moved in right behind his tail, raking him with my .50' right along the side of his fuselage, and he began to burn like the rest.

My flight suit was wringing wet with sweat as I closed in on the next Val. The rear gunner, try as he might, could not keep me in his sights as I went for the pilot and walked my short bursts into the Val until he began to burn. As I turned into the number-eight Val, I became overconfident and cocky. I got way too close to him; my propeller swirled behind his tail only twenty-five feet away. The rear gunner let me have it right between the eyes, and his rounds tore into my windscreen, my engine, and everything else hanging out in the open. I gave him everything I had and killed the rear gunner quickly. I was able to get the Val smoking before every gun on the Wildcat stopped firing at once as I ran out of ammunition. I knew I had to get the hell out of there before every Zero in the sky swarmed over me, especially after seeing that long trail of smoke from the damaged Val.

I was only six hundred feet above the Island when I turned for Guadalcanal and began to wonder where my buddies were. The entire aerial combat against the Vals had lasted no more than fifteen minutes. All of a sudden, I noticed my oil pressure gauge racing for the zero mark—moment later, my propeller stopped dead. One of the blades was sticking straight up, just like the middle finger of my right hand! I tried to put my flaps down to slow my descent, but with the right one damaged, the left began to throw me off, so I yanked it back up. I was probably doing over one hundred miles per hour when I hit the

Wildcats on patrol. As the war progressed and more and more of these fighter squadrons arrived in the South Pacific theater, the tables were turned on the Japanese.

An F4F prepares to launch from the deck of a US Navy carrier. Note the small bomb on the wing pylon. Although its primary role was that of a fighter, the Wildcat could perform many other missions as well.

water with one large splash. I bounced once, and that coincided with my face bouncing off the gun sight, breaking my nose. I continued my dive in the Wildcat, this time plunging below the surface as the plane and I sank almost thirty feet together; the F4F had the tendency to float like a lead brick. The water became darker.

I was tangled up in my raft, my Mae West, and my right shoulder harness as I fought to free myself. I was finally able to get out of my parachute and scrambled to the surface with a belly full of saltwater. I was only in the water for about ten minutes when I spotted a Picket Boat heading my way. I fired a couple of rounds into the air from my water-soaked .45-caliber pistol and that got their attention. As the boat came alongside me, someone up above shouted out, "Are you an American?" I yelled back in a not-so-pleasant voice, "Damn well right I am!" I was picked up and brought ashore on Tulagi. I later found out that everybody in my flight was shot up and shot down that day, but thankfully, we all survived to fight another day.

I was full of saltwater and morphine when I was met by a marine colonel. He asked me what had happened, and I said, "I got seven airplanes!" The colonel was ecstatic and poured me some scotch—a drink I despise, but I didn't want to seem like an ungrateful guest. I threw it down and promptly threw it back up in front of the colonel! The next day, I was transferred to a naval hospital, where I recovered from my injuries. While I rested, all my victories were confirmed, and this fact brought about a lot of attention from Admiral Mitscher. The admiral recommended me for the Medal of Honor for my actions on April 7.

I was only a twenty-two-year-old first lieutenant and Marine Corps aviator when I was presented the Medal of Honor by Maj. Gen. Ralph Mitchell on October 10, 1943. At the time I received the medal, I couldn't comprehend what it meant, but I knew it was absolutely awesome, and it forever changed my life. I was asked if I wanted to go back home to the United States and meet President Roosevelt; I was grateful, but asked if we could do that a little later. I was only out of flight training a little over a year, and besides, there was a war on and the navy had invested a lot of money and time in me. I wanted to stay and finish the job of winning this war with my squadron.

MEDAL OF HONOR CITATION

For conspicuous gallantry and intrepidity at the risk of his own life above and beyond the call of duty, as a Division Leader in Marine Fighter Squadron 221 in action against enemy Japanese aerial forces in the Solomon Islands area, April 7, 1943. In a daring flight to intercept a wave of 150 Japanese planes, First Lieutenant Swett unhesitatingly hurled his four-plane division into action against a formation of fifteen enemy bombers and during his dive personally exploded three hostile planes in midair with accurate and deadly fire. Although separated from his division while clearing the heavy concentration of anti-aircraft fire, he boldly attacked six enemy bombers, engaged the first four in turn, and unaided, shot them down in flames. Exhausting his ammunition as he closed the fifth Japanese bomber, he relentlessly drove his attack against terrific opposition which partially disabled his engine, shattered the windscreen and slashed his face. In spite of this, he brought his battered plane down with skillful precision in the water off Tulagi without further injury. The superb airmanship and tenacious fighting spirit which enabled First Lieutenant Swett to destroy seven enemy bombers in a single flight were in keeping with the highest traditions of the United States Naval Service.

James Swett continued to fly combat missions in F4F Wildcats with his squadron, VMF-221. In May 1943, he, along with the rest of his squadron, switched over to the F4U Corsair. "Zeke" more than doubled his earlier score and ended the war with 15.5 victories, all in the Pacific theater. He passed away on January 18, 2009.

LUCK OF THE IRISH

FIRST LIEUTENANT PETER A. MCDERMOTT, USAAC (RET.)
BELL P-39 AIRACOBRA

Peter McDermott was born in 1922 and grew up in Brooklyn, New York. He considered himself a "wise guy" before he enlisted in the service and lost count on how many times he was almost thrown out!

Most Allied pilots considered themselves quite fortunate to be at the controls of Mustangs, Thunderbolts, Corsairs, and Hellcats. These planes all had firepower, speed, range, and an inherent stability built into them. Unfortunately, none of these attributes were found in the P-39 Airacobra. Except for the Russians, who successfully used the Airacobra in vast numbers, most Allied pilots who flew the P-39 did not consider themselves very lucky at all. Most called the P-39 an "iron dog," and that was one of the nicer names!

A proud Peter McDermott points to his namesake on his P-39 Airacobra.

After I earned my wings in early 1943, I was sent to a crummy field in Pennsylvania that had a bunch of Piper L-4s and other low and slow observation planes on it. I was young, I had my wings, and I wanted fighters. There was a war on, dammit, and I wanted to be in the middle of it!

I was known as a wise guy, and I'm sure being from Brooklyn with an accent and an Irish name didn't help me much. After a couple of months, I was thrown off the base in Pennsylvania and transferred to an L-4/L-5 outfit in Charlotte, North Carolina, as its operations officer. They didn't like my attitude either, so I didn't last long there and got transferred again. This is when I really started flying!

I was sent to Georgia for P-39 Airacobra fighter school! This was fantastic flying. We wrung those P-39s out until they could take no more. The instructors, some whom were combat vets, would take eight planes up in trail and then go balls to the wall while we tried to stay with them—straight up, straight down, and through every combat maneuver they could think of, trying to shake us.

I enjoyed flying almost every airplane I had been in, but the P-39 was a real lousy airplane; simply put, it was a dog. But this dog could take a beating and still bring me home, minus some important pieces! I had been listening to all these hotshot instructors telling me how low they had flown the P-39. Not to be outdone, I went out to see if I could go lower. During one of my cross-country flights, I proved I could go lower than the rest; I flew right through a damn tree! Both my wingtips were sheared off, I had holes in between the twenty-millimeter guns, and there was a large hole inboard on the right wing—but I was still flying. I climbed to ten thousand feet, cut the throttle, and pulled the nose back to see where she would stall out. I got a hell of a shudder around 170 miles per hour and returned to the field to try to land.

I made a straight-in approach and never let the airspeed drop below 185 knots. I made one three-point landing followed by three skipping and skidding landings before I finally wrestled the P-39 to the ground. I was in deep trouble now! For my punishment, I had to give a lecture on a Saturday night to the assembled pilots—all of whom just wanted to go into town, get drunk, and catch the clap—on how not to fly through a tree while on a military cross-country.

A new group was being formed while I was in Georgia, and it was called Tactical Reconnaissance. Our class would be the first one to go through it, and our training consisted of aerial photography, strafing, and skip-bombing. The principle tactics used were those learned from the British in North Africa: high-speed, low-level attacks followed by low-level damage assessment utilizing the K-20 camera embedded in the Airacobra's belly were practiced on a daily basis. After months of training, I, along with the rest of the survivors from our class, was given a blessing by the brass, and we became TAC-RECON pilots.

In November of 1943, I was sent to a far-off place in the world called New Guinea. I thought I had finally made it to where the action was and that now, hopefully, I would be given a real fighter plane to help win this war. I reported into my new squadron, the 82nd TAC-RECON, which was part of the 71st tactical reconnaissance group.

When I saw the P-39s on the flight line at Port Moresby, I could have killed myself. I wanted to be in fighters, not in the dopey P-39. Adding insult to injury, New Guinea was covered by jungle and foliage. This wasn't the barren wasteland of North Africa that we were trained to take pictures of. Needless to say, we didn't use our cameras very much. We did use our guns and cannons a lot, however, as we went looking for the Japanese hiding in the jungle. The P-39 carried two .50-caliber machine guns in the nose and four twenty-millimeters in the wings. It also carried a large cannon that fired through the propeller spinner. In theory, the cannon appeared to be a good idea, and it sure looked menacing sticking out of the nose. But in operation, it was a joke; we were lucky if it would fire one out of every ten rounds. During a gun run, I would locate my target in the gun sight, fire the cannon, wait for the "blop," then take my eye off the sight as I waited and watched the round hit somewhere close to the target. It was just a big old popgun with a lot of problems. War is hell, especially in the cockpit of a P-39.

Primarily, our squadron went after Japanese barge traffic, airstrips, and troops hidden in the jungle and wherever else a short-range, low-altitude, lightweight fighter was needed. Eventually I got my own P-39, probably because no one else wanted one, so I named it *Brooklyn Bum 2nd* in honor of my mother and father back home, who were faithful Brooklyn "Bum" Dodger fans. I also had the squadron painter add a yellow horseshoe straddling a green shamrock and the words "Erin Go Bragh" ("Ireland Forever") to the door. Being Irish and flying P-39s over the jungles of the South Pacific, I figured I needed all the luck I could get, especially when my tentmate and I got called into the CO's office!

The CO of our squadron, a Major Gordon, was a real nice guy, but as far as a combat pilot, he hardly ever flew missions and wasn't that good behind the stick. One day, he called Lt. Joe Grenda and me into his tent and started chewing our butts off; he had caught the two of us doing low-level aerobatics and buzz jobs over some high-ranking enlisted SOB. Lieutenant Grenda and I both flew together back in the states, and we could fly circles around most of the guys in the squadron. Since we were the new guys on the base, the major thought he needed to teach us the proper way to operate US military aircraft. He said to us, in a very stern voice, "I'm going to take you two up and show

RIGHT: A white-tailed P-39 makes a diving turn while pulling contrails from its wingtips. About the only maneuver a P-39 could do to shake a Japanese fighter was to point its nose down and dive away from danger.

OPPOSITE PAGE: P-39s were tasked with holding the line in the South Pacific until other, more advanced fighters such as the P-38 Lightning arrived on the scene.

Pied Piper of the Pacific

Getting rid of rats takes on a new distinction as the rest of the world moves to overpower Axis treachery. And nowhere is a better job being done of it than by the gallant members of the U. S. Army Air Forces. For heroism in the southwest Pacific this announcement of the award of the Silver Star to Lt. Clifton H. Troxell comes from General MacArthur's Headquarters, Australia, October 16th:

...alia. ...attended ...School and Case School o... ...ied Science, was cited for gallantry over New Guinea.

Piloting an Airacobra fighter, he downed one Jap Zero and scattered others which attacked transports he was escorting. After breaking up the numerically superior enemy formation he continued his patrol.

With the devastating fire power of his cannon bearing P-39 Airacobra, this modern Pied Piper of the air destroys the rats which threatened to overrun civilization.

When the rats are gone, he'll come back to a world in which the technical advances that war has brought to Aviation will be put to even greater use. We, at Bell

Aircraft, will have the engineering ability, the means of production and —most important—the tradition of Aviation pioneering to play our part in that coming era. © Bell Aircraft Corporation, Buffalo, New York.

Airacobras for victory—

FUTURE PLANES FOR PEACE

BELL *Aircraft*

PACEMAKER OF AVIATION PROGRESS

you fighter tactics." Holy smokes! I stood there trying not to laugh, and Joe and I looked at each other thinking the same thing: "*He's* going to show us fighter tactics?!" Both Joe and I were laughing hysterically inside.

We were based at Dobodura, New Guinea, which had a wide, steel-plank runway. The three of us cranked our P-39s up as we prepared to go on our mini training flight. Little did the major know that he was the one about to be trained! I was number two and Joe was number three as we taxied behind the good major on our way to the run-up area. Major Gordon cocked his Airacobra forty-five degrees to the runway and began to do his run-up. He never looked at us and had his head so far up his butt he never saw me next to him. He opened his throttle and his P-39 lurched forward, beginning its takeoff roll. I don't know why I did it, but I followed him right down the runway and practically stuck my wingtip right in his ear.

I was just waiting for him to look my way and see that we were now on a formation takeoff, but he had no idea I was even there. As soon as I saw his wheels getting light, I

A group photo of the 82nd Tactical Reconnaissance Squadron taken on New Guinea in late May 1944.

sucked my gear up and moved closer to the major. He looked over at me with these big wide eyes and his big open mouth; he damn near spun in!

Joe took off behind us, fighting our prop wash the whole way, and cut the turn to catch us. Joe stuck his wing into the major's other ear, and we looked like one perfect airplane as we flew alongside the major. Major Gordon began looking side to side at us as the sweat began pouring down his face. Finally, he hit his rudder pedals very gingerly as a sign for Joe and me to go into trail. The major did some half-assed tight turns and that was it. We returned to base, he never said a word to us, and he never flew with us again.

Because our P-39s had such limited range, we never ventured out more than two hours' flying time from our base. I never saw any Japanese airplanes in the sky—only crashed ones in the jungles below. Our missions became so routine, shooting up the same targets and using the same tactics, that at times it became boring for me. On one mission I decided to have a little fun with my wingman.

Another tentmate and I were out shooting up an enemy village we had been to many times before. My wingman pulled into a Lufbery circle, and I was right behind him as he set himself up for his gun run. When he made his turn in, I cut right under him, and my

P-39 *Brooklyn Bum 2nd* high over New Guinea with Peter McDermott at the controls.

prop was mere feet away from the belly of his P-39. I waited for him to fire, and when I saw his tracers going off, I fired all my guns at once. My bullets whizzed underneath and out in front of him. He pulled straight up and began screaming over the RT, "Ack-ack! Ack-ack!" I couldn't stop laughing at the shrillness in his voice. When we landed, he damn near punched me out!

In the course of a year, our squadron moved eight different times, and each time we were told that we would be getting replacement fighters. They just never told us when, and I damn near missed the chance to upgrade. On one of my last flights in the P-39, I was sent out over the Pacific to escort the PT boats coming back in from their night raids on the Japanese navy.

I was at five thousand feet, sitting pretty and looking real nice with the PT boats somewhere down below. Suddenly, my prop began to overspeed, and I had a runaway. I was waiting for the engine to freeze up at any time, and the longer I flew, the more I worried about jumping. I just couldn't get myself to bail out because I knew I had a better chance surviving a shark-infested-water landing than jumping from a P-39. In order to bail out from the Airacobra, you had to pull the door off, roll out onto the wing with your chute and survival pack strapped to your rear end, and hope and pray that when you rolled off the trailing edge of the wing, you didn't get hit by the horizontal stabilizer. We pilots talked about this frequently, and we all agreed we were too scared to jump.

Thankfully, the P-39's Allison engine kept on ticking, and I made it back to an emergency strip in one piece. Shortly thereafter, we finally got new fighter planes. Because we were such a bastard unit, we got a bunch of war-weary P-40s — just like us, a bunch of castoffs! The P-39s were given to the Australians, and that was the last time in over fifty years I saw *Brooklyn Bum 2nd*.

I had flown over 134 missions and survived, sometimes barely. Each time, though, the P-39 brought me back home. On my last P-40 flight of the war, I couldn't resist buzzing the group HQ building. Unfortunately for me, my Irish luck ran out, because a full-bird colonel was there watching the whole thing, and when I landed he arrested me and had me for lunch. Obviously, he didn't have a sense of humor!

P-39 Brooklyn Bum 2nd *was literally pushed into the weeds and left to rot, as it was considered "war weary," in the fall of 1944. Well after the war, it was rescued and restored and now flies with owner Rod Lewis in Texas.*

FEBRUARY 1943-DECEMBER 1943

BURMA BANSHEE BRAWL

COLONEL PHILIP R. ADAIR, USAF (RET.)
CURTISS P-40 WARHAWK

Philip Adair was only seventeen years old when he saw the war clouds rising in Europe and Asia. He tried to enlist but was turned away by the Army Air Corps because they required a college degree. That all changed on December 7, 1941.

I had survived the Great Depression as a farm boy growing up in the dust fields of Oklahoma and later earned my wings in the Civilian Pilot Training Program on the windswept fields of Casper, Wyoming, flying a fifty-horsepower Piper J-3 Cub with a tail skid and no brakes. By September of 1942, I was a newly minted second lieutenant hauling a behemoth of an airplane called the P-47 Thunderbolt around the skies of

P-40s of the "Burma Banshees" of the 89th Fighter Group await their next mission. The Japanese were said to fear anything with a skull on it, so the group made sure their skulls were painted white and very large! *Phil Adair*

115

New York. I was a member of the 80th Fighter Group, 89th Fighter Squadron, stationed at Mitchell Field to train in our "Jugs" for the war in Europe. In the air, the P-47 was stable and solid and an all-around efficient gun platform. But once you've pulled the power back, it was more like a homesick brick and came down fast.

In February of 1943, I had flown for the last time in stateside training and watched the Jug I was to fly in combat be loaded aboard a ship that would cross the Atlantic bound for England. I looked forward to flying and slugging it out with the Luftwaffe with the rest of the 80th Fighter Group preparing to join the fight in Europe. Unfortunately, the military brass had other plans for the 80th, and I would not see my beloved P-47 until much later in the war, as our Jugs were pulled out from under us in the middle of the night by Gen. Hap Arnold.

General Arnold gathered us together and informed our group that we would be embarking on a very important mission. He couldn't disclose our final destination but assured us that where we were going we would be vital to the war effort. The bad news just kept flowing from the general's mouth, and he told us that we would no longer be flying P-47s. Our "new" plane would be the Curtiss P-40 Warhawk—lighter, slower, and with a lot less firepower than we were used to in the Thunderbolt. In less than a week's time, we hurriedly trained a total of twenty-five hours each in the air on our new fighters before we abandoned our cold-weather gear and left for parts unknown.

Although I had some misgivings about the Warhawk, I found it to be a good, honest airplane. It was slow and short on range, but it was a reliable, hard-charging workhorse. The P-40 was "fairly" maneuverable; that is, you had a better-than-fair chance of get- ting shot down by a Japanese Zero if you tried to turn with one! There were two ways to outmaneuver a Zero: one was to duck into the nearest cloud and stay put, and the other was to push your nose down, build up speed, and dive away from them. This latter was a maneuver I became very proficient at when I entered the combat arena in late 1943.

Instead of turning east with the rest of the convoy that was headed for England, our ship zigzagged its way south. New York to England by boat took less than two weeks, but for those of us in the 80th Fighter Group, it seemed that General Arnold had trans- ferred us to the navy—we sailed for fifty-three days on three different boats before we arrived at our final destination, Calcutta, India. It didn't take us long to figure out why we had left our cold-weather gear behind. Hot, sticky, humid conditions and constant rain welcomed us as we made our way to our fighter base in the Assam Valley.

By the time we arrived in 1943, the Japanese had been fighting, conquering, and expanding their empire southward since 1937. They had set their sights on Northern India and were already in control of the Burma Railway by the time we had arrived. It was tough going for the US, British, and Chinese composite forces on the ground trying to halt the advancing Japanese. Most, if not all, of their supplies, including ammo, fuel, and food, were sent up north by air over the "Hump"—the Himalayan Mountains—in C-46s and C-47s. Our main job was to protect the Hump route from Japanese fighters that prowled over the thick green Burma jungles, looking for an overloaded, unarmed transport to shoot down.

I was assigned to "D" flight as its commander, with three other P-40s assigned to me. To signify the 89th Fighter Squadron, we painted our spinners blood red and had a large white skull painted on both sides of the nose. We knew the Japanese were superstitious

Original artwork created by Phil to decorate the cowling of his P-47 Thunderbolt while stationed at Mitchell Field, New York. It was later used as wheel art on his *Lulu Belle.*

and somewhat afraid of anything that resembled death, so we added an extra surprise for them: because we flew a lot of dive-bombing missions in support of the ground troops, we installed eighteen-inch air-raid sirens on our bellies and turned them on when we went into our dive-bombing attacks. We called this the Banshee wail, and it scared the hell out of the Japanese!

I personalized my P-40 with the name *Lulu Belle*, after a girl I had known back in the States. I was also an old-car nut and loved the cars from the early 1930s, so as a tribute to my passion, I painted my main gear and tail-wheel tires with a can of white paint I had brought along. I now had something no other fighter pilot had—a customized P-40 Warhawk! Unfortunately, my artwork attracted more than I bargained for in December of 1943.

NAGAGHULI AIRFIELD, ASSAM VALLEY

On December 13, I had just completed my forty-third combat mission of the war—a three-and-a-half-hour patrol over the Hump route with no Japanese aircraft encountered. Our four-plane flight had just landed at Nagaghuli, and the place looked desolate with all other serviceable P-40s off on other missions. I had no sooner shut down *Lulu Belle* than my crew chief, Carol Peake, began servicing "his" airplane. Carol was very proud of that P-40, especially the electric starter I had scrounged up and installed to replace the hand-cranked one some eager Curtiss-Wright engineer had bolted on to save weight. I walked to the alert tent one hundred feet away and waited for the rest of my flight to come in.

I had just laid my head back on the couch and started to relax when all of a sudden the red alert sounded and I took off running for the flight line. Sergeant Peake had already hit the electric start, and the Allison engine was running by the time I climbed up on the wing. Sergeant Peake climbed out the right side and I jumped in from the left. I hit the throttle, not even bothering to buckle up, and I was airborne in less than a minute, hauling the P-40 skyward.

Our standard operating procedure was to climb to twenty thousand feet, rendezvous over the field, stay off the radio, and keep our mouths shut. By the time I reached twelve thousand feet, I had buckled myself in and searched for the other P-40s in my flight. I began to circle the field, spiraling upward, and saw that none of the others in my flight had taken off yet. As I was circling, I saw a flight of four aircraft off to the east, just above the haze. By the time I made my next circle, I was completely shocked at what I saw. This was no longer a flight of four aircraft; it was four flights of twin-engine Japanese bombers! They were in their typical finger-three flight, with three in front and three in back. I counted twenty-four of them heading north and stopped counting when I saw their escort fighters suddenly appear out of the haze.

I had staggered up to twenty thousand feet all alone and had a front-row seat of what was below me. I must have counted over forty single-engine Japanese fighters flying around in loose formations, with some of the pilots performing aerobatics for the bomber crews. I had never seen so many airplanes in the sky at one time, not even friendly ones. The Japanese planes were all over the sky, with the "Charlie" bombers staying down low at 12,500 feet. The fighters, on the other hand, seemed to be all over the place and ranged from right above the bomber formation upwards to twenty thousand feet. Because of the thick brown haze that hung in the air, they had not detected me as I neared the pack.

I contacted control and reported the Japanese formation to them. They responded back that what I was seeing was forty miles to the east, not the fifteen miles I was reporting. I tried to tell them they were wrong and felt that the formation was going to make a 180-degree turn and overfly the Tenth Air Force headquarters and bomb it. Control assured me that wasn't going to happen because they had reliable reports from ground stations that the unknowns were farther east. That's when the Japanese formation began a coordinated turn.

When they rolled out of their turn and took up a new course, it was clear that I had guessed right about their intentions. I called control and gave them the bad news and the ETA of the bomber formation over the Air Depot Group HQ. I called control one last time and said, "I'm not going to let them get by for free!" I decided that I had to do something to mess up their attack, but I didn't hold out much hope for my success.

I positioned myself above the fighters and the bomber formation so I could hit the bombers just before they reached their bomb-release point. I flew out in front of them, off to their left, as I dived down into them. I started to fire at a long range out because I knew that the sight of my tracers would shake things up a bit. I hit the first flight and then swung around into the second with my finger on the trigger and took some shots at them, too. Before I knew it, I was behind the fourth flight of bombers, looking for a target.

As soon as the shooting started, the bombers began to bounce around, moving up and down out of formation. I tacked onto the tail-end Charlie in the last flight and zeroed in on his left engine. I could see flashes on the fuselage and engine area as my bullets tore into him, but I couldn't stick around to watch anymore and dived underneath him. I started to break and saw several Zeros heading for me. I had figured this was going to happen, so I pushed the stick full forward into the left-hand corner, pulling negative g-forces as I dived away doing outside rolls. I stayed in my dive with the throttle at war-emergency power until I figured I'd shaken the Zeros. When I looked back, I saw empty skies with nobody chasing me. I climbed back up for another go at the bombers as they began to reform.

Maybe the Japanese couldn't see me in the haze, because no one made a move to cut me off. I started to make another pass on the bombers, but before I could get near them, it looked like every Zero in the sky was turning into me and wanted a piece of my P-40. I knew I couldn't get close to the bombers—because it would have been like reaching into a hornet's nest—so I settled for picking off a fighter or two.

I climbed back up on top and figured if I stayed out of range of the bombers, which had already dropped their bombs, I could work the edges against the Zeros. I picked out one of them and tried to get a shot off at him, but he was quick and knew I was gunning for him. He made a sharp turn and disappeared, so I picked out another one. This guy was a little more stupid as he waited too long to turn. I started to fire and he turned right into my bullets. His landing gear began to drop, and his engine was on fire as he went into a spiral and crashed in the jungle near Naga Hills.

I climbed back up toward the formation as they neared their lines and went for broke. I thought, "What the hell, might as well take another whack at those bombers." Stupid jerk! I managed to get into position for another attack, but before I could get in range, I had Zeros on my right, Zeros on my left, and Zeros above me. I was outnumbered almost forty to one and didn't think those odds were in my favor, so I went into my escape maneuver once again. I rolled the P-40 over, and all I could see was a Zero, mad as hell, coming straight up at me with his cannons and guns blazing away.

I couldn't get out of his way fast enough, and it sounded like a shovel full of gravel hitting my fuselage. I heard a wham, wham, wham, followed by an explosion with a ball of fire coming out from behind the armor plate in back of my headrest. I grabbed the trim tab and turned it all the way forward to assist my escaping dive. As I pushed the P-40's nose downhill, I kept taking hits and other tracers went whizzing by just over my head. The fire in the rear area went out as the ground raced up toward me.

I tried to pull back on the stick and it wouldn't budge. I remembered the elevator trim crank and I started cranking the nose up. The trim wheel was freewheeling, and the trim cables shot out as I yanked off the power and reefed the stick back with both hands. I was finally able to get my nose out of the jungle and up into the sky where it belonged, but my troubles were far from over since I was 125 miles from my base. I was alone, a long ways from home, and over enemy territory in a P-40 with full nose-down trim—none of which was good!

It was very hard to hold the nose above the horizon, even with both hands, as I turned back toward friendly lines. I tried to latch my seatbelt around the stick, but it wasn't long enough. I kept losing altitude and my luck turned from bad to worse when another aircraft appeared in front of me, headed in my direction. I was able to get a quarter mile away from him and saw that it was a Zero, smoking like the devil and losing altitude faster than I was. I figured he was one of the ones I had hit earlier, and we watched one another

RIGHT: The Curtiss Warhawk served in every theater of operations during World War II.

Veterans of *Every* Battlesky

No other American-built fighters have fought so many battles, have downed so many enemy planes—over mountain, jungle, desert and sea—from the bleak Arctic to the blistering tropics—as have the Curtiss pursuits, veterans of the battleskies of World War II.

CURTISS-WRIGHT
Corporation
AIRPLANE DIVISION
BUFFALO • COLUMBUS • ST. LOUIS • LOUISVILLE

Member: Aircraft War Production Council, East Coast, Inc.

FIRST
Since the Birth of Aviation

CURTISS **WARHAWK**
LATEST OF A LINE OF FIGHTING HAWKS

All of the 89th Fighter Squadron's P-40s lined up at Nagaghuli for a long-range mission into Burma. *Phil Adair*

go by in the opposite direction. The Zero showed no move in my direction, so I thought out loud, "Oh, what the hell!"

I hauled the P-40 around and came screaming up his rear end with a bead on his tail. At one hundred yards out with the sight dead center on his engine, I squeezed the trigger, which only brought a "kerthunk, kerthunk, kerthunk" sound from the pneumatic system recharging my empty guns! With so much forward speed, I of course went screaming by him, and I became the hunted. The Zero simply pulled over and started shooting at me, but I moved out of the way and his tracers zipped over my left wing. Luckily, I wasn't hit, and I turned for home once and for all!

I was about ninety miles away, and my arms were so tired from holding the stick back that I could barely keep the nose above the horizon. As my adrenaline wore off, reality set in and I knew I would never make it back to base, so I decided to bail out. I called control and gave them the grid map location. As I looked down at the dense jungle below, I said to myself, "Man, if I can just fly another hundred yards, it will save me two days of walking." Then it hit me—I came up with the best idea I'd had all day. I flipped *Lulu Belle* over on her back, and, although the jungle was still in plain view below, I was now holding altitude—even gaining some. The P-40 ran pretty well inverted for a couple of minutes before the engine loaded up and wanted to quit. I rolled the P-40 back over, waited for the engine to clear, lost a little altitude, and then flipped back over. I continued doing P-40 flips the rest of the way home until I reached Nagaghuli.

At about a half mile out from the airfield and at one thousand feet, I pointed the P-40 toward the south end of the field. I was still inverted as I pulled back on the power and flipped the gear handle down. I squeezed the pump switch, saw down and locked on the landing gear indicator, and rolled *Lulu Belle* back over as I hit the flap switch and cut the throttle. It wasn't my usual three-pointer, but I couldn't have cared less; we were down in one piece.

When I finally rolled to a stop, I was so tired that I had to be pulled out of my cockpit by some of the ground crew members. At the briefing, I found out that the Japanese bomb pattern had fallen short of the HQ area with little damage done to the base. I had sixteen bullet holes in *Lulu Belle*, including the one that had shattered my trim cable. But the P-40 was a tough old bird, and three days later we had her flying again. There was just no stopping a Burma Banshee!

Philip Adair flew a total of 113 combat missions in P-40s before converting to his beloved P-47 Thunderbolt. He was credited with one Zero destroyed and one Zero and one bomber probably destroyed on December 13. For his actions and bravery on that mission, Lieutenant Adair was awarded the Silver Star.

> Second Lieutenant Philip R. Adair, 0728534, A.C., is hereby recommended for the award of the Silver Star for gallantry in action on 13 December 1943. On this date, Lieutenant Adair, as pilot of a P-40 N-1 type fighter did singly attack a formation of 24 enemy bombers and 40 enemy fighters and did successfully destroy one fighter. His first attack was instrumental in breaking up the enemy formation sufficiently to affect their bombing accuracy and caused some of the formation to release their bombs before they arrived over the target. Lieutenant Adair repeated his attacks until his plane was so damaged that further combat was impossible. The gallantry and courage displayed by Lieutenant Adair in combat and the determination that was required of him to successfully land his damaged plane is worthy of the highest traditions of the Army Air force.

WORLD AT WAR: While the once-fierce German and Italian desert air and ground forces began to advance to the rear, the Allies began to gain a foothold as they attempted to push the Axis into the Mediterranean Sea and then springboard onto the Italian mainland. Like their brothers in the Pacific theater, the pilots operating out of desert bases held the line until more advanced fighters began to trickle in to their theater of operations.

RUTHLESS RUTHIE

FLYING WITH THE CHECKERTAIL CLAN

FIRST LIEUTENANT GEORGE NOVOTNY, USAAF (RET.)
CURTISS P-40 WARHAWK AND REPUBLIC P-47 THUNDERBOLT

George Novotny was born in Toledo, Ohio, in 1922 and earned his wings in January of 1943.

I had always wanted to be a fighter pilot—the "man in charge," if you will. After I earned my wings in 1943, I was given the choice of single-engine fighters or multi-engine bombers. Although multi-engines may have sounded safer, I knew that the only person who would be able to put up with my flying abilities was me! I was sent to the 54th Fighter Group in Baton Rouge, Louisiana, to begin my indoctrination into becoming a fighter pilot. Most of the guys in the group had just returned from combat in the Aleutian Islands, and the whole group was getting ready to go to the Southwest Pacific.

My fighter checkout was in the Curtiss P-40 Warhawk. When I pushed the throttle forward for the very first time, I watched in complete horror as that long, pointy nose swung to the side—there was a lot more torque with the P-40 than what I was used to in the AT-6! I ended up zigzagging down the runway, trying to correct my rudder and stick mistakes. In all honesty, I wasn't impressed with the P-40 at all. Not because it tried to kill me that first time I took off in one, but because about the only thing it

A smiling George Novotny about to step into the cockpit of his P-47 Thunderbolt. *Jack Cook collection* could do well in combat was dive. It took forever for the Allison-powered P-40s to struggle to sixteen thousand feet, and believe me, we weren't able to get much higher than that. By the time I got comfortable in the P-40, with visions of white-sand beaches and tropical Pacific weather, I was told I would be sent to North Africa. Thirty-six hours later, I was half a world away in Casablanca and a new member of the 325th Fighter Group, known as the "Checkertails."

JOINING THE CHECKERTAIL CLAN: EARLY P-40 COMBAT

By May of 1943, I was flying combat with the 317th Fighter Squadron at the controls of a P-40F—now that airplane was a real dog to go into combat with! It had a Rolls-Royce Merlin engine that replaced the Allison, but it still couldn't get us much past eighteen thousand feet. Most of our early missions were escorting B-26, B-25, and A-20 twin-engine bombers. I recall one mission during which we were supposed to rendezvous with some South African A-20 Havocs, and it was darn near impossible to keep up with them. They were faster than we were, and our tongues were hanging out trying to keep up with them. Even at full throttle, the P-40 lagged behind. Like I said, it was a dog, but in a turn chasing tails with an enemy fighter, it was a real scrapper.

My first victory occurred on July 20, 1943, when our group was sent out to bomb an airfield on Sardinia. We came in low over the Mediterranean, about fifty feet above the wave tops, to avoid the radar. Right when we got there, we found some Italian fighters taking off, and they broke into a large circle. Our group formed up and went into a circle as well. The trouble was, we were going in one direction and the Italians were going in another. Each pass was a head-on one, and I spotted multiple machine-gun flashes all in front of me. I answered back with the P-40's six .50-caliber machine guns and got some good hits on a Macchi MC.202. This guy kept on coming, and I thought he was going to ram me. We were down to around five hundred feet, chasing one another, when his smoke turned to flame and he broke off his attack and bellied in.

Ten days later, on July 30, I was back over Sardinia once again on a sweep. I was tooling along with my wingman at ten thousand feet when I spotted a pair of 109s below us at four thousand feet going in the opposite direction. They never saw us as they cruised by below, as if they were on a Sunday drive. I wheeled my P-40 around and over and went diving after them. The P-40 was a good diver and I decided to take the tail-end Charlie. We were using a fixed ring sight, and I led him by one ring as I swallowed out my dive to thirty degrees. When I got within range, I gave him the works with my machine guns.

I saw him begin to smoke and pieces begin to fly off. I wasn't paying attention to what was around me and feared there may have been another set of 109s above me covering the lower two. I hauled the P-40 around hard into a turn and was at first startled by the airplane right next to me—thankfully, it was my wingman, who had stuck to me like glue and was right where he was supposed to be. I got another 109 about a month later, and by early September of 1943, we were taken out of combat operations and sent back to Casablanca. Not for rest and relaxation, but to check out in our new mount: the P-47 Thunderbolt.

JUG JOCKEY

In Casablanca, our P-47Ds were delivered to us on flattops, and about all the mechanics had to do was mount the massive thirteen-foot propellers to them. I was thunderstruck at the enormous size of these behemoths. I remember thinking out loud, over and over, "Boy, is this a damn big airplane!" I mean, for a fighter it was beyond huge.

I could see right away why they called it the Jug. The fuselage looked just like a milk jug—one that was thirty-six feet long—and the engine itself was like a round block of solid steel. There wasn't much that could stop it. I would see them with cylinders completely shot off and yet they kept on ticking. The P-47 was powered by a Pratt & Whitney R-2800 radial engine that could produce a jaw-dropping 2,300 horsepower. Underneath the fuselage, embedded in the P-47's belly, was a turbo supercharger along with water injection to give it that extra kick in the pants when we needed it most. But I figured we needed all the power we could get to pull along the almost seventeen-thousand-pound max weight of the Jug.

The wings were just as huge as the rest of the airplane, at over forty feet in length—I guess they had to be to house the four .50-caliber machine guns in each wing. What impressed me the most, however, was the size of the cockpit. I used to joke that I could get up from my seat and run around inside of it! Compared to the P-40 "doghouse," which we were strapped into without a whole lot of wiggle room, the Jug was more like a spacious living room. We sat under a razorback canopy of glass and framework, and we were protected by armor plating. The Jug looked all business on the ground, and in

A pair of Curtiss P-40F Warhawks launch from a forward airfield on their way to the combat area.

the air it was a hard-hitting killing machine. We were finally on the offensive instead of the defensive.

The first thing I noticed about flying the P-47, compared to the P-40, was that when we hit twelve thousand feet of altitude, the Jug kept on chugging along all the way past thirty thousand feet. I knew then we had more than a fighting chance against the Germans and Italians. The Jug was a lot faster than the P-40; the Warhawk struggled to get above 360 miles per hour, whereas the Jug could tool along at over 435 while at thirty-two thousand feet.

Another big factor besides speed was our range. In the P-40, for example, our missions were between one and two hours in length. Although we could carry a seventy-five-gallon belly tank, we rarely flew with one because of all the problems we had when we tried to release them. They always seemed to hang up, especially when we encountered enemy fighters. With our P-47s, though, we carried a "hybrid" drop tank our mechanics came up with. Instead of the standard 105- or 75-gallon wing tanks, we carried the 165-gallon wing tanks that our sister P-38 fighter groups carried on their Lightnings. Now it seemed we could go on forever—or at least until our butts were numb!

We finally were not only able to climb above the B-17s and B-24s, but we were able to shepherd them all the way to the target and back again. But the big thing we had to watch out for was avoid getting too far away from our base, strip our tanks, rattle around with the Luftwaffe, and hope and pray we had a good tailwind and enough fuel to make it back home. Unfortunately, some guys would learn the hard way about fuel management.

After twenty hours of P-47 checkout, our group was ready to put the Jug to the combat test.

FEARSOME FOURSOME: JANUARY 30, 1944

In late December of 1943, we moved to our new base at Foggia, Italy. I had been assigned my own P-47D, which I named *Ruthless Ruthie* after my fiancée back home in Ohio. On this mission, our group was sent out along with the heavy bombers to bomb and strafe German airfields in and around Udine and Villaorba, in Northern Italy. But instead of our P-47s flying shotgun above the bomber stream, we stayed down low—real low. This was done in an effort to catch the enemy with their pants down. On most bomber missions, the Germans picked up our bomber stream as it formed up over Foggia and headed north. The Luftwaffe was in no hurry and waited us out until we got close enough. They fired up their 109s and 190s, along with what remained of the Italian fighters, and quickly climbed above the bomber stream waiting to pounce on the B-17s and B-24s.

But today was totally different. There were sixty of us that took off from our base—the 317th, 318th, and 319th Fighter Squadrons. We were well ahead of the bombers, and we climbed no higher than fifty feet above the ground to avoid German radar. We flew over three hundred miles over the waves of the Adriatic Sea as we raced north. I was part of "A" flight in the 317th Fighter Squadron, which was led by Capt. Herschel "Herky" Green. I was flying Captain Green's wing as his number two while Flight Officer Cecil Dean and Flight Officer Edsel Paulk were Captain Green's number three and four. The P-47 was a great formation flyer and stayed rock steady as our pilots stayed glued to one another. As we neared our target area, the 319th Fighter Group stayed down low while the 318th zoomed to over thirty thousand feet, and our squadron climbed in between the others to around eighteen thousand feet.

We could see the airfield up ahead, and it was evident our dirty little trick had worked; there were all kinds of Do 217s, Ju 52s, and MC.202s scrambling to get airborne. We rolled our Jugs over and made a dive for the airfield. The Jug really built up speed quickly, so much so that I thought I would tear the wings off! We kept on screaming downward and it looked like we were going to overrun the planes on the ground. We throttled back because the twenty or so Ju 52 trimotors trying to take off in front of us were a lot slower than we were. It would have been very easy to ram them from behind, but not very smart. The Ju 52s were only able to get up to five hundred feet by the time we opened up with our eight .50-caliber machine guns. It was like shooting fish in a barrel, and I hit one right away on my first pass.

We wheeled around in a 180-degree turn, and I got on another one in an instant. The real danger in all of this, however, was not the enemy airplanes but all the other Jugs that were shooting at targets all around me. As I tacked onto the Ju 52, I made short work of

him and he crashed below like the first one I'd gotten. We really had to hurry up because the B-24s and B-17s were inbound ready to annihilate anything else that couldn't make it skyward. There were fires burning all over the place as we tore out of there as fast as we had come in. On my way out of the target area, I spotted a Henschel Hs 126, a small two-seat reconnaissance aircraft that carried some light machine guns. I was really moving and was probably only three hundred feet away when I opened up on him with a snapshot. In an instant, he disintegrated in front of me and I flew right through what was left of him. There wasn't much; those eight .50s could knock a building over!

Captain Green got six that day, I got three more, and so did Dean and Paulk. We became known as the "Fearsome Foursome." All told, that day our group scored thirty-eight victories while the bombers destroyed another seventy enemy aircraft on the ground. Unfortunately, it wasn't all good news, as the Checkertails lost two that day.

LEFT: Famed Checkertail commander Herky Green explains to fellow pilots and ground crew of the 325th Fighter Group how he bagged his latest victory. *Jack Cook collection* **BELOW:** A Curtiss P-40 awaits its next mission.

A black-and-yellow checkerboard adorned the fighters of the 325th FG, including this P-47 Thunderbolt. *Jack Cook collection*

WRONG TURN: MARCH 18, 1944

I was out on a bomber escort mission when I got word that one of my bunkmates was turning for home with fuel issues—he couldn't get his belly tank to transfer fuel. I elected to stay with him as cover to make sure he got back OK. As we droned on near Udine, Italy, on our way home, I noticed a 109 on my right-hand side. I knew I couldn't leave my buddy, so I pretended I was an Fw 190, which resembled a P-47 at a distance, and gave the 109 pilot a wing waggle. He took the bait; he kept on flying and never turned into us. I waited until he was well behind us and then racked the Jug around to go after him.

Normally, when we encountered 109s, they would immediately go into a Lufbery circle with us because they were much better turners than the P-47s were. But the one thing we could compensate with was our speed advantage. Once we pushed the throttle forward, our circles naturally became bigger—outside of the 109s—but we could turn the circle faster and catch them before they could catch us. Once you learned the tricks of flying the Jug, you could coax it into a pretty tight circle. As you pulled and pulled back on the stick, you felt for the vibration telling you it was about to stall and to do something else before it fell out of the sky. Needless to say, the 109 I got that day had made a wrong turn with the wrong guy.

The Fearsome Foursome accounted for fifteen victories on a single mission. Standing left to right are Novotny, Paulk, Dean, and Green.

ITALIAN STALLION: APRIL 6, 1944

Our group was on a fighter sweep in the Yugoslavia area near Trieste when I spotted a Macchi MC.202 above us. The 202 must have seen all the Jugs below, because he did a quick about-face and ran away from us. I immediately pushed the stick forward and pointed the Jug's nose downward to build up energy. When I felt that I had gained enough momentum, I pushed the throttle forward, hauled back on the stick, and kicked the water injection on. The P-47 surged and I could feel it moving quicker. I began to fire at the 202 as the distance between us began to shorten up a bit. As quickly as I felt the speed increase, the water injection only lasted a brief moment, and the Jug began to decelerate. I kept on firing and was on the verge of a stall when the 202 began to smoke. As I regained flying speed, the 202 spun in and crashed below.

In mid-April, I was up again with the group near Budapest. I spotted a Reggiane Re.2001, and I swear this guy was as blind as a bat. I began to approach him from behind and he never flinched, flying straight and level, rock steady—a deadly sin for a fighter pilot. I could have easily sat back behind him all day long and fired at will. I figured at this stage in the war, the Italian pilots we encountered were becoming poorer and poorer with their fighter tactics. I'm sure they didn't have the training opportunities that we had, especially with hundreds of bombers and twice as many fighters overhead on any given day. It was an easy victory, and my last one of the war. By late May of 1944, the Checkertail Clan flew its last P-47 mission and was ordered to turn its Jugs in for P-51 Mustangs.

Although I liked the Mustang, it was no Thunderbolt. The cockpit was tight and the engine was very susceptible to flak, ground fire, or any little nick. By the time we went operational with the Mustangs, my tour was over and I was sent home. I was assigned to the training command and became a P-47 instructor teaching French pilots of the Free French Air Force the finer points of flying and fighting with a Jug. It felt good to be back home—both in the States and in the cockpit of the P-47 Thunderbolt.

George Novotny ended the war with eight aerial victories in Europe. He flew the P-40 Warhawk, the P-47 Thunderbolt, and the P-51 Mustang. He served as an instructor pilot until the end of the war.

1944

THE NOOSE BEGINS TO TIGHTEN

Although the German Luftwaffe was still quite deadly when 1944 rolled around, fighting on multiple fronts was taking its toll on the fighter pilots of the Third Reich, who were tasked with protecting the Fatherland. Waves of Allied bombers targeting military, industrial, and other strategic targets roared overhead both day and night. Desperate times called for desperate measures to try to stop this onslaught.

STEEL FIST OF THE LUFTWAFFE

FELDWEBEL (FLYING SERGEANT) OSCAR BOESCH, LUFTWAFFE
FOCKE-WULF FW 190

Oscar Boesch was born on May 18, 1924, at Höchst in Austria. He was a qualified glider pilot when he joined the Luftwaffe in 1943.

In January of 1944, a small, elite group of Luftwaffe fighter pilots was formed to defend Germany against the escalating Allied bomber assaults. All of these men were volunteers, and most of them had been emotionally touched by the destruction of their homeland. A dedication to their country, along with their own personal convictions, led them to become members of *Sturmstaffel*—the Luftwaffe's volunteer bomber-ramming unit.

Flying specially armored and specially equipped Fw 190s, the men of the Sturmstaffel made a simple yet fearless declaration in defense of the Reich: "I volunteer for the Sturmstaffel of my own free will. I am aware of the basic objective of the *Staffel*. The enemy will be shot down at the closest range. If that becomes impossible, ramming will be the only alternative. If these fundamentals are violated, I will face a court martial or be removed from the unit."

Oscar Boesch prepares to climb into the cockpit of his heavily armored Fw 190.

Luftwaffe ace Oscar Boesch

On April 22, 1944, I had just completed my training in the Bf 109 as a high-altitude fighter/escort-fighter. We were to protect the Fw 190s during their attacks on the Allied bombers. I had spent the last three years of my life training in gliders and became a seasoned Luftwaffe glider pilot. Now in my late teens, I would soon be placed into the cockpit of one of the finest fighters the world had ever seen.

En route from our training base in southern France to my assignment in Germany, I was invited to the home of a fellow 109 pilot for some celebration on becoming new fighter pilots. His home was located in the center of Hamm, and it felt like I was on a holiday as we enjoyed coffee and cake. The party ended abruptly, however, with the shrill of air-raid sirens and the droning of Allied heavy bombers. We just made it into the basement cellar of the house as six hundred B-17s unloaded their bombs onto the city. I had never been so frightened in all of my life! This was not a fortified shelter, and I could feel the walls caving in around me as the shock waves and hammering of high explosives ripping through the city above. At that moment, with bombs raining down and exploding above and dust and smoke covering me, it became clear that I had to help defend my homeland. I was forever changed!

Hamm was flattened, and my own convictions and obligations became stronger. My desire as a fighter pilot to do my best to protect and defend our cities and the innocent civilians led me to volunteer for a special squadron that was dedicated, able, and willing to do just that. Sturmstaffel 1 (assault-fighters) would be my home for the remainder of the war.

After a short interview with Major von Kornatzki, commander of Sturmstaffel 1, he produced a piece of paper signed by all his pilots. In less than a minute's time, I added my name to the declaration, committing myself to attack the bombers at all costs. Shortly after that, I was introduced to the fellow pilots and realized they all had similar reasons to join. Ironically, a slogan on the wall read "Cowards fall first!"

My introduction to the Fw 190 consisted of three training flights. From the first minute I sat in the cockpit, I could see that this was a much better aircraft than the 109. I felt comfortable right away with the cockpit layout and location of the gun switches and gun sight. The only thing I had to get used to was the big BMW 801 engine out ahead of me. All forward visibility was blocked until I became airborne.

I took off in the three-point attitude because the 190's wheels were forward of the center of gravity. There was no way you could do that in the narrow-geared 109, unless you wanted to chase your tail round and round! Our 190s also had some extra weight added to them for protection against the Allied bombers.

Five-millimeter armor plates (*Panzerplatten*) were bolted to the sides of the fuselage, along with thirty-millimeter armored glass panels attached to the canopy area. The twenty-millimeter wing guns were removed and replaced by Mk 108 thirty-millimeter cannons. The internal fuel load allowed us to remain in the fight for one and a half hours, and with the addition of a single belly tank, we added another forty-five minutes to our flight. If a Tiger tank had had wings, this is what it would look like!

One thing I discovered on my arrival was that the losses to the Staffel since its inception in January 1944 had been fifteen pilots—100 percent! I was told these losses were a necessary sacrifice to defend the homeland. It was the belief of the high command that Allied bombers over Germany would soon disappear because they could not sustain the heavy losses we inflicted upon them. If we could shoot down a couple dozen bombers every day, then the Americans would surely stop in the next few weeks. We were never told that, on any given day, one thousand Allied bombers roamed at will over Germany.

Little did I know that my homeland was like a house with no roof: unprotected from the elements. I, for one, never expected this dramatic of an air war to be going on, and we were never briefed on how bad it truly was. Our focus and attention were only drawn to the never-ending "Dickie Autos" (heavy bomber stream). And April 29, 1944, on my first combat mission, it would be no different.

My test of courage came in the early-morning hours of April 29. It had been reported that a heavy bomber formation was over France and that Berlin was a likely target.

Oscar, second from right, poses with fellow Luftwaffe pilots. Many in this photograph did not survive the war.

At 10:00 a.m. I lifted off and flew wing on Lt. Werner Gerth as he led our flight of over a dozen Fw 190s from our base at Salzwedel (120 kilometers west of Berlin) to attack the incoming bombers. An hour later, we found what we had been looking for: over forty B17s still loaded with bombs and without escort fighters.

We spread out and lined up behind the bombers. From one-half mile away, I saw the muzzle flashes and flickering of the B-17s' defensive guns as they tried to bracket me. I couldn't hear them, I couldn't see them, and, so far, I couldn't feel them. I picked out a B-17 and let its wings grow in my gun sight with my finger resting on the trigger. That's when I got hit.

The first bang shocked me. The second bang arrived seconds later, followed by a third one that tore the top glass canopy away from the 190. Tremendous noise and minus-fifty-degree-Celsius air invaded the cockpit. In terror, I flew right behind a B-17, blasting my guns and watching the hits as it fired back at me. I aimed for the tail gunner to knock out his guns; they fell silent as I went in for the kill. All around me there were a series of explosions and tracer rounds as other Staffel pilots tore into the formation; every shot had to count. A combination of cannon and machine-gun rounds raked the B-17s.

I didn't have time to think about living or dying. I just concentrated on shooting the bombers down. Fire began to spread over the inner wing of the B-17 I was following and soon became uncontrollable—the Flying Fortress corkscrewed down and away from the formation. I soon found another one in this target-rich sky. This B-17 was fortunate, for the moment, as even though my cannon rounds tore into his engines and ripped through his metal skin. He would not go down, but he fell back from the safety of his formation and began to trail black smoke. He was a long way from England as he turned for home and the unknown Luftwaffe fighters that lay ahead.

As fast as the battle had begun, it was now over. I dived for the deck as I was low on fuel, freezing cold beyond belief, and without any means to contact the ground controllers: my antenna was attached to the top of my shot-off canopy. My greatest fear was P-51s, and my head jerked from side to side looking for them to come out of nowhere. Fighting a P-51 was hopeless, as our Fw 190s were just too heavy and I was too damn cold!

Luckily for me, I never saw any Mustangs, but my flickering low-fuel light told me I must land soon. More good luck—an airport right under my wings! The field below contained a Junkers factory with a big white cross laid out on the grass. It was a signal for the factory workers that this was a target for incoming bombers and to seek shelter immediately. I only hoped I could make it in before the bombs went off, and I certainly knew what that was like. I came in over a row of trees and my landing was superb. Touching

An Fw 190 owned by Rudy Frasca prowls the skies looking for Allied bombers. *EAA/ Jim Koepnick*

down, I soon noticed that the grass runway canted downhill. I applied the brakes, but my forward speed increased as my tires began to hydroplane over the wet grass. I quickly passed between two bomb craters, through a hedgerow, and into a plowed field. That's when my luck ran out.

The 190 flipped over on its back at a high rate of speed, and I found myself completely embedded in soil. I dug out large clumps of earth from my mouth, choking on the dirt I couldn't remove. My fingers scrambled to find the master cutoff switch as I felt gallons of gasoline begin to run over my body. I thought the damn tanks were empty! There was no way I could get out of my coffin, and I didn't think anyone saw me land because of the alarm. With my dying breath, I cried for help, but no one answered and I began to lose consciousness from the lack of oxygen and high-octane fuel fumes.

And then a miracle happened! I was brought back to life by resuscitation from a nearby rescue team. They had dug under the cockpit and pulled me out. After a few hours of recuperation, lucky to be alive, I traveled back to my unit. So ended my first mission—in the thrill of victory and agony of defeat! According to reports, of the 679 bombers that were dispatched to bomb Berlin, 65 of them were shot down, compared to a loss of 38 Luftwaffe fighters. In a few days, I would get to do it all over again in the skies over Germany.

My right arm was still bandaged from fuel burns, and my neck was strained and sore as I prepared for my second combat hop. At 8:45 a.m. on May 8, 1944, I was one of twelve Sturmstaffel Fw 190s to depart Salzwedel to attack the approaching bombers on a track from Braunschweig and Berlin. Over 750 B-17s and B-24s, escorted by 700-plus fighters, were on their way to destroy my homeland. We flew west and began our climb through a solid layer of clouds.

When we broke out on top, we spotted a large B-24 formation above us. Suddenly, a friendly flak barrage filled the sky in front of us, and shells exploded near my 190. An oil leak appeared, trailing over my wing root, compliments of a German eighty-eight. With my engine damaged, I decided to push on and jammed my throttle forward. If I could keep the engine running until it ceased, I could fulfill my mission. With my oil temperature at maximum and no fighter escort in sight, I raced up toward the formation of B-24s that was at twenty-four thousand feet.

A B-24 burned relatively easy as I began to hammer away at it with my cannons. I looked from side to side and found I was all alone; there were no other Fw 190s to assist me. In front of me was a frightening view of four-engine bombers as far as my eyes could see. With the horrifying memory of Hamm still fresh in my mind, I flew through the wall of fire from the B-24s' guns. I held my finger on the trigger, spraying rounds throughout the formation.

One went down in flames and another was damaged as I flew through the fires of hell. I was so close to the B-24s I could have reached out and touched them. I was shot to pieces by their gunners as I locked another one into my gun sight. With a short pull on the trigger—nothing? I was out of ammo! Now I would have to sacrifice my faithful, crippled fighter by ramming the port wing of a B-24.

I came roaring in on one of the B-24s and hit his prop wash. My Fw 190 became uncontrollable, like a leaf in the wind, and I was thrown up and back. I could not aim the 190 as I tried for the Liberator's outer wing. If I could just ram his aileron, I could then bail out while my victim crashed below. As I flew above the bomber's wing, I went over in a sixty-degree bank dive trying to hit him with my wingtip. About three feet over the B-24, I closed my eyes for the impending crash. But it was not to be, as I was pushed back from his turbulence. I came back in and tried it again. This would be my last pass, as the guns on many B-24s had shredded me to bits. Shrapnel exploded all around my 190, and I began to disintegrate. A jagged piece of metal pierced my head, painfully slicing through my scalp.

My Fw 190 was out of control and raced downward at over eight hundred kilometers per hour. Fighting to free myself from my straps, I bailed out in a near vertical dive. I thought the air stream would tear me into hundreds of pieces as I fell back to earth. I was in a free fall for over two minutes through the bitterly cold sky; we had been warned not to pull the ripcord too early because the Mustangs would tear us up. You could never guarantee a safe landing by parachute or by plane over Germany!

I entered into the safety of the clouds and pulled the cord, floating the rest of the way down under my billowing parachute. I made a soft landing in a farmer's field near the city of Goslar. I was beaten up with frostbite to my nose and ears, my head was bleeding, and I was shaken up by the whole ordeal. I was glad, however, to have survived to fight another day with the Sturmstaffel. I was also on the fast track to becoming an Allied ace: two Fw 190s lost on two missions!

This Fw 190 is painted in the exact markings of the one Oscar Boesch flew as a bomber rammer. *EAA/Jim Koepnick*

Although I had tried to ram that B-24, I was not a kamikaze. I liked to live and celebrate in the evenings, just like my opponents did. We in the Sturmstaffel were far from dead and had a great outlook for our success. The battle may last for only a few minutes, but the flight of over two hours in a state-of-the-art fighter was so beautiful and satisfying that this was always a reason to celebrate on both sides.

> *During Oscar Boesch's combat tour, he was shot down eight times, with four bailouts and four crash landings. In his 120 combat missions, he successfully downed thirteen American, British, and Russian aircraft. On his final combat flight of the war— April 24, 1945—he collided with a Yak-9 Russian fighter near Berlin and was immediately captured and became a prisoner of war. After three days, he escaped and evaded recapture by walking one thousand kilometers back to his home in Austria. The Sturmstaffel unit that Oscar flew with suffered an incredible loss of seventy-six pilots and 120 Fw 190s. After the war, he returned to his first love: glider flying on the air-show circuit. Oscar passed away on June 4, 2012.*

WORLD AT WAR: Unlike in World War I, in which a majority of the air war was fought during daylight hours, the advancements in both technology and aircraft—on both sides—allowed World War II pilots to fly missions literally twenty-four hours a day. But it was the threat of the "Night Stalkers" on both sides that evoked an eerie feeling for those who had to operate at night.

HUNTING THE HUNTERS

MEMORIES OF A NIGHT INTRUDER PILOT

FLYING OFFICER JAMES "LOU" LUMA, RCAF
DE HAVILLAND MOSQUITO

James Forrest "Lou" Luma was born in Montana on August 27, 1922, and joined the Royal Canadian Air Force in July of 1941.

The seemingly constant, endless air war over Europe did not stop when the sun went down. The skies over England came alive almost every night as British Bomber Command sent wave after wave of medium and heavy bombers from its bases in England to selected targets all over the Nazi-controlled continent. Not only did these brave bomber crews have to deal with an onslaught of blinding searchlights and deadly flak from the German positions on the ground, they also had to contend with the ruthless Night Hunters of the Luftwaffe. The Germans had perfected the use of aerial electronic equipment in their single- and twin-engine fighters to assist them in locating the British bomber stream and then knocking the bombers out of the sky. To counter the Luftwaffe's nightly terror reign, twin-engine de Havilland Mosquito fighter-bombers were sent out to seek and destroy the German night fighters.

In the summer of 1941, my mother and father had warned me about the dangers of hitchhiking or taking rides from strangers before I made my way across the United States from my home in Seattle to the school I was attending in Wyoming. Of course I didn't listen to them, because, as an eighteen-year-old kid, I thought I knew more than they did. As I headed east with my thumb hanging out over the road, a fellow American who happened to be a sergeant pilot in the Royal Canadian Air Force (RCAF) picked me up. As we drove across the country, the sergeant, who worked as a flight instructor, filled my head with flying adventures and told me that the RCAF was actively enlisting Americans.

Well, let me tell you, that really enthused me because all I ever wanted to do was learn how to fly. When he finally stopped the car to let me out, I did a 180-degree turn and headed for home to get my parents to sign a letter of permission. Soon afterwards, I found myself in Canada as a new recruit with the RCAF. I was in elementary flight training when Pearl Harbor was bombed and chose to stay with the Canadians because I lacked the educational requirements for the Army Air Forces. After earning my wings, I received a commission as a flying officer. My initial assignment was as a staff pilot, flying gunnery students on training flights. In early 1943, I was reassigned to combat and told I would be flying the Mosquito. Heck, I didn't know what a Mosquito was, let alone had ever seen one in Canada. I was just content to be able to fly something.

I knew the Mosquito was at least a two-seat airplane because I was paired up with a navigator. His name was Colin Finlayson, and we would be crewmates for the duration of my tour. We did our initial training in the Cessna "Bamboo Bombers" while still in Canada. When we arrived in England in the summer of 1943, we were told that we would be flying the Mosquito and assigned to 418 Squadron as night intruders. I couldn't wait to begin my role as a fighter pilot, and the only thing left for me to do was to get checked out in the Mosquito. By today's standards, I had very little flying experience; after all, I had just earned my wings and still had a lot to learn. But our commanders knew better than to leave us on the ground for too long; they thought we might run the risk of losing our edge. That's when I met one of the most beautiful aircraft I had ever seen.

The Mosquito at that time was considered one of the fastest airplanes in the world—if not the fastest—pre-jet. My checkout in the Mosquito reflected its speed: very, very fast! The one I trained in had only one set of controls, so I rode in the navigator's seat and tried to absorb every word the instructor shouted to me over the noise of the powerful twin Rolls-Royce Merlin engines. The instructor taught us how to take off, bring it back around, and then land it. The checkout was very minimal; that was the one and only time I flew with him. After that, I was all on my own.

There were a couple of things about flying the Mosquito that took some getting used to. In order to get to the cockpit, you had to squeeze through a small door on the right side of the nose. Because the pilot sat higher in the left seat, the navigator sat lower in the

Glass-nosed Mosquito *The Spook*. *Jack Cook collection*

right seat, with all his navigational equipment right in front of him. If the Mosquito were hit and the debris or flak struck the navigator, killing him or knocking him unconscious, it would be very dicey, if not impossible, for me to get out of the cockpit; it would be pretty tight to try to squeeze past him. Thankfully, I never had to experience that scenario.

Once I got into the cockpit and sat at my seat, I found the layout of the instruments and flight controls to be quite pleasant. The control stick was a combination of a yoke with a single short stick mounted on top of it. On the stick itself, I had a series of buttons that controlled the four 20-millimeter Hispano cannons and four .303 machine guns that were embedded in the nose under my feet. The one great benefit I liked about this gun arrangement was there was no need to worry about the point of convergence, like you had to if you flew a fighter with the guns spread out in the wings. In the Mosquito, all you had to do was point your nose at your target and squeeze the trigger. When I flew the plane at night, I was careful not to squeeze the trigger for more than one and a half seconds, as I didn't want to risk burning out the barrels from the hot lead racing out of them. But then again, there was really no need to squeeze it any longer than that because the combination of the two types of guns was very lethal—everything they hit would blow up instantly.

Another issue I had to deal with was the awesome power of the two Merlin engines turning two big three-bladed propellers in the same direction. Because the Mosquito had such a relatively small rudder, there was always a big swing of the nose on takeoff if you didn't catch it right away. You had to stay on top of it by adjusting your throttles and working the rudder. But once I got the knack of it, it became second nature for me. The same could be said about flying the Mosquito at night as I prepared for my first combat mission of the war.

In July of 1943, I was reassigned to the US Army Air Forces as a first lieutenant. I ended up staying with the RCAF, though, because I had already gone through operational training with Colin and they didn't want to split us up after we had trained so hard and so long together. Besides, we had become a very close team as we prepared to make our first combat flight together.

I made my first operational flight in the Mosquito on September 20, 1943. Typically, my navigator and I would go up and fly our standard gray-and-green camouflage-colored Mosquito for half an hour to make sure all our equipment was working and that the airplane itself was in good working order for the long mission ahead. The Mosquito Colin and I usually flew in had the nose art of a character from the comic strip Li'l Abner, adorned with the lovely pipe-smoking, shotgun-toting hillbilly girl named Moonbeam McSwine. Because the plane was made out of wood, some of the chaps in 418 Squadron referred to them as "flying furniture." But there was nothing fragile about this twin-engine fighter-bomber, which could fly low and fast in all kinds of weather and carry a hefty bomb load, both internally and externally, along with extra fuel in wing-mounted slipper tanks. All in all, I was delighted to fly the twin-engine wooden wonder.

The difference between the intruders that we flew and the British night fighters was that they had Airborne Interception radar—AI—on board and we didn't. The night fighters also had a line in the sand they couldn't cross, usually just before the continent, for fear that the AI would fall into German hands. We, on the other hand, flew all our missions over the continent looking for targets of opportunity, German airfields, and, of course, our counterparts: the Luftwaffe night fighters. However, before I mixed it up with the Luftwaffe, I had started out looking for German trains, and I soon found that these were some of the most dangerous missions I had ever flown.

When we took off from our base at Ford, the night was as black as coal as we climbed to our initial altitude of one hundred feet and proceeded toward the channel. The Mosquito had an ultraviolet light that shined down on the instrument panel, and the instruments would glow just enough for me to see them. Thankfully, they weren't bright enough for the eyes of a prowling German night fighter pilot. We also had a radar altimeter in the Mosquito to assist us as we neared the French coast, and Colin would call out the altitude to me. We stayed at five hundred feet or below until we passed over the German guns on the coast and hoped they would remain quiet until we passed by. When we thought we were out of German gun range, we climbed to one thousand feet and went looking for trains or anything else that moved in the shadows below.

The German trains were easy to spot at first; you just looked for the open firebox as the engineer shoveled coal into it. But hunting trains at night was very risky. When we saw the glow of the coal fire, I would push the Mosquito over and aim for the flickering flames. Usually a short burst from the cannon and machine guns was all it took, and Colin would yell for

American Mosquito pilots Lieutenant Tunnel and Lieutenant McCarthy of the 654th Bomb Squadron, 25th Bomb Group, are all smiles after returning back to base safety with only a "little nick." *Jack Cook collection*

me to pull up. I remember one time after we hit a train and it blew up, the ensuing explosion lit up the area as we went racing overhead with our wings below the hills and tree line. After a while, the Germans figured out our tactics and would park a decoy train near a bend in the tracks. As the unsuspecting Mosquito came down to attack the dummy train, the crew couldn't judge the rise in terrain fast enough and would slam into the side of the hill. There were other times that Mosquitos came back with fir cones from pine trees embedded in their wings. After we began incurring Mosquito crew losses more frequently, we were ordered not to attack the trains anymore. In reality, it wasn't a very profitable operation. What was profitable, however, was hunting the Luftwaffe.

FIRST VICTORY: ME 410

On January 21, 1944, we took off from Ford at 10:15 p.m. on a night-intruder mission to the Lake Steinhude area in Germany near Hannover. Because of the haze from low clouds, it was difficult for Colin to pick out our pinpoints on the way to the target. As we drew closer, we found an airfield with two sets of lights burning near the perimeter of the field. We orbited for a little while as we obtained our fix and found we were overlying Wunstorf. Nothing seemed to be moving as we headed south over the lake. Suddenly, we spotted two small white lights behind us on the far side of the airfield as we turned

Lou Luma, with pipe, stands with fellow RAF Mosquito crewmembers in front of one of his mounts.

around to investigate. The lights were moving upward, and I knew it was a German air-craft taking off—but why had he left his lights on?

Unfortunately for him, that was his worry, not mine, and I began to stalk him from five miles away. As he began his climb out to reengage the bomber stream, I stayed five hundred feet below his altitude and began to match his speed so I would not overshoot him. I could see that he had one light on under his nose and one under his tail. I must have followed him for fifteen to twenty miles as I began to close in. For whatever reason, I misjudged his speed from below and did overshoot him, doing a quick figure eight to port and another one to starboard to put myself back on his tail. By this time, I could see the flame from his exhaust as I eased the nose of the Mosquito into him. Colin was along for the ride at this point and was busy keeping his fingers crossed as I brought my nose up from five hundred feet below; at 250 yards away, I opened fire with both cannon and machine guns. In less than three seconds, the once-dark silhouette I was chasing turned into an Me 410 engulfed in flame. Large pieces tore away from him as the fireball I had just flown through grew larger.

Colin observed him dive down and explode below. After finding no other night fight-ers, we turned for home and landed back at Ford around 3:00 a.m. The ground crew found some pieces of Me 410 plywood embedded in the leading edge of my starboard wing; I guess I had been closer than I thought! I learned later that the 410 pilot had shot down a handful of British bombers that night and had returned to refuel. What he forgot to do, however, was turn his lights back off when he took off, committing the ultimate sin of a night fighter. His mistake was my fortune, and the Luftwaffe lost one more night fighter. This same scenario would be repeated again and again.

SECOND VICTORY: HE 177

On February 13, Colin and I were scrambled to intercept a twin-engine, long-range He 177 maritime bomber that was returning from an Atlantic submarine patrol. British intel-ligence had found out where he was heading and the exact ETA of his intended landing back on occupied French soil; he never made it. Near Bordeaux, France, we found him as predicted and set him on fire easily—he crashed below. Relatively speaking, that was an easy mission compared to our next aerial victory.

THIRD VICTORY: FW 190

On March 6, we were sent to Toulouse and Mont-de-Marsan in southern France on an anti-Luftwaffe training patrol. The Germans were using the cover of darkness to train their pilots and thought the skies around these bases would be safe. They thought wrong.

As we flew near a place called Pau near the Spanish border, Colin and I spotted an aircraft with a red light on his port wing. Colin identified it as an Fw 190, and we maneuvered in behind the single-engine fighter and shot him down as if it were routine. However, in the ensuing explosion, we picked up a large piece of debris from the 190 that tore into our starboard radiator. Five minutes later, while cruising in the darkness at eight hundred feet, we lost our starboard engine due to overheating.

I feathered the propeller and shut the engine down to let it cool. A little while later, I unfeathered the prop, restarted the engine, and climbed to two thousand feet, when the engine quit for good. It would be a long trip on one engine over occupied

An RAF Mosquito displays its capabilities with one engine turning and the other stopped.

territory, but Colin plotted a course for home. Lucky for us, the German night fighters were flying elsewhere as we neared the French coast at Saint-Brieuc. I pushed the nose of the Mosquito over and dropped to five hundred feet, flying at our normal channel-crossing altitude. The worst was yet to come: we had to overfly one of the most heavily fortified areas on the coast. It reminded me of an earlier mission when we had been returning to Ford and our compass went out as we overflew another heavily defended town, Dieppe.

The pitch-black night sky was soon filled with searchlights and flak as every gun in the port city opened up on us while night turned to day. To protect my vision, I ducked my head under the instrument panel, and Colin held the map over my head so I wouldn't be blinded by the searchlights. Colin would then guide me into the searchlights and away from the flak. I was twisting and turning the Mosquito, and, at the same time I was climbing and diving five hundred feet at a time. All we could do was corkscrew through the barrage, and we made it out of there by the skin of our teeth.

Thankfully, this mission was less troublesome, even though I had one of my fans standing still. As we tried to communicate with British control, we soon found out we had lost our radio, too. British radar had spotted us leaving the coast, however, and followed us back towards Ford. Because of our uncertain condition, an air-sea-rescue Beaufighter was waiting in the blast bay with a crew onboard and engines running, awaiting the word to scramble. We were grateful for the offer of assistance, but thankfully it was not necessary. We landed back at Ford minus one engine but with another victory under our belt.

FOURTH AND FIFTH VICTORIES: JU 34 AND JU 52
My Mosquito missions were not limited to flying just at night. On our days off, we could volunteer for daylight "Ranger Missions," which consisted of a pair of Mosquitos flying as a freelance team looking for trouble. These did not count toward our total number of missions, but we could pick our own targets, and we tried to go out on days with low overcast but good visibility underneath the cloud layer. There was no way we wanted to

be over a target in clear skies with a bunch of German fighters buzzing around above us.

We picked a good target on March 21—better than we both expected, it would turn out—and we took off in the afternoon and raced low-level over the channel crossing into France. Our primary target was the German air base near Strasbourg in eastern France; we had intelligence that the airfield there would contain a variety of aircraft, and we weren't disappointed when we arrived. There were Luftwaffe fighters, bombers, transports, and gliders strung out all over the field as we came roaring over the fence. It was hard to miss that day. I destroyed a Do 217 and an He 111 on the ground, along with damaging two Go 242 gliders and two Bf 109s parked nearby. The other Mosquito I was flying with also racked up an impressive score by damaging or destroying a Bü 131, a Do 217, and six more Go 242s.

We didn't leave the airfield unscratched, however—I slightly damaged my Mosquito. I was making my gun run in on one of the big Gotha gliders when Colin called out an He 111 parked off to the side near another group of gliders. When I turned toward the He 111, my slipper tank struck one of the Gotha's twin tails and tore the drop tank from my wing. It's kind of ironic because in order to survive an attack on an airfield, you had to stay low to avoid the German flak and perimeter guns but be watchful that you didn't fly too low and risk striking a parked aircraft. And to think this is what I did on my days off!

As we were heading back toward home, I spotted a Junkers W 34 single-engine transport and gave it a quick squirt. It went down in flames crashing below. It wasn't long after that, however, that I encountered one of my toughest opponents of the war—a Junkers Ju 52 trimotor, big and slow and made of corrugated metal. I had a very difficult time of trying to get behind him, not because he was fast but because he was so slow!

Because I had to slow the Mosquito way down, I worried about stalling it out as I began to fire at the Ju 52. What I saw next shocked me: I was hitting him, but he wouldn't go down! I was so used to firing my guns at night and seeing the airplanes I hit explode in front of me, but the Junkers was one tough old bird and kept on flying while taking my hits. It took a lot of cannon shells to finally put him down, but at last he started on fire and went straight in. Even though I was an ace by this point in the war, it was by far my hardest victory.

Lou Luma finished his tour with 418 Squadron in April 1944 after flying thirty missions and was awarded both the British and the American Distinguished Flying Cross. He had hoped to join an Army Air Forces P-51 Mustang squadron but was instead assigned to a weather-recon squadron that flew unarmed Mosquitos. Late in the war, Lou received tragic news when he was informed that his good friend and navigator Colin Finlayson had been shot down and killed with another Mosquito pilot. They, along with so many others, had paid the ultimate sacrifice in defense of our freedoms.

WORLD AT WAR: Unfortunately for the Japanese, in 1944 it was almost impossible for them to replace a seasoned fighter pilot with one of equal quality. Many of Japan's elite had been bested by superior Allied pilots and airplanes, and it became tougher and tougher for the Rising Sun's dwindling numbers to stand and fight against a seemingly numberless armada of Allied fighters.

MEMORIES OF A HELLCAT ACE

LESSONS LEARNED

COMMANDER ALEX VRACIU, USN (RET.)
GRUMMAN F6F HELLCAT

Alex Vraciu was born on November 2, 1918, in East Chicago, Indiana. From the day he saw his first airplane, he dreamed of one day becoming a fighter pilot.

Sensing a war looming in 1940, I had obtained a pilot's license under the Civilian Pilot Training Program during the summer of my senior year at DePaul University. Graduating in 1941, I declared myself for the US Navy and entered flight training just prior to Pearl Harbor. While at flight training in Corpus Christi, Texas, a fellow by the name of "Butch" O'Hare spoke to us after he had been awarded the Medal of Honor.

My first combat assignment was with the 6th Fighter Squadron, VF-6, onboard *Independence* (CVL-22) with Butch as squadron commander, and he selected me as his wingman. I learned my trade from one of the best! Butch was a natural-born leader who instilled confidence in his pilots. He had a quiet demeanor—never said much, but then, he never had to. We listened to him because of his reputation and experience and absorbed what he said.

In war, one often learns to do things from people who may have learned early on the hard way. For example, I learned to ditch a plane in the water in an emergency—to "feel" the wave, landing on the backside of it. From Butch, I learned how to conserve fuel and ammunition, to get in a little closer when firing, aim at the wing roots, and, lastly, to look back over your shoulder for possible enemy planes before starting a dive.

I had my first enemy action at Marcus Island on August 31, 1943. It was relatively tame—just strafing. Our next action was at Wake Island on October 5. My radio wasn't operative that morning, but I sensed by Butch's actions that something was up. We were on a CAP and intercepted a group of Zeros in a V formation trying to land at Wake Island. We were in a perfect position several thousand feet above them. Butch burned his Zero, but it took him down below the broken cloud level. I got the Zero wingman on my right. It was the first plane I fired on, and it felt good; I practically flew through the pieces as he blew up in front of me.

With Butch nowhere in sight, I took my wingman down and destroyed an abandoned Zero on the ground. While doing evasive maneuvers across the field, I noticed a parked Betty bomber, so I brought our section back around and burned it, too. After returning to the carrier, Butch told me he and his wingman had tangled with another Betty and Zero that apparently were also arriving from another area.

When we returned to Hawaii after the raid, Butch was moved up to air group commander, CAG, and moved to another carrier, *Enterprise*, with the rest of the air group. Butch's VF-6 fighters remained split up on three different carriers, and the squadron received a new commanding officer. We never saw Butch again after that.

On November 20, 1943, flying one of the CAPs over Tarawa, I shot down a reconnaissance Betty snooper low on the water. That was my first Betty aerial victory, and I splashed it on my first pass. At dusk on the same day, *Independence* was torpedoed when attacked by a large group of Betty torpedo-bombers. We were streaming oil, so the carrier was ordered to head for the friendly base of Funafuti, seven hundred miles distant.

We made it safely on November 23, and our VF-6 detachment was ordered to fly to Tarawa to await assignment to one of the other carriers, *Essex*. It was during our time on *Essex* that we learned about the loss of Butch O'Hare on November 26 while flying his Hellcat during a night mission, pioneering night-fighter usage on a carrier.

What happened to Butch that night in the rendezvous of three planes following the breakup of the enemy attack has never been fully determined. The turret gunner on the TBF Avenger in the group asserted that when a fourth enemy plane tried to join up on their formation, he fired at it and the turret gunner on the enemy Betty shot down Butch in the crossfire. It was a bitter loss to us all, and I made a vow to get ten of those damn Bettys!

This staged navy publicity photo shows Hellcat ace Alex Vraciu stepping out of the Hellcat's cockpit, his nineteen victories on display.

On the Kwajalein raid, January 29, 1944, our division was not scheduled on the first two flights that day so I wasn't too hopeful of any action. There didn't seem to be any enemy planes airborne, so we prepared to strafe targets of opportunity. Tom Hall and I were at the tail end of our group of planes as we started down; out of the corner of my eye, I spotted a string of Bettys flying low over the field. I positioned my section for a high-side run on the tail ender who was flying straight and level. I was taught to wait and get in close before firing, but today I couldn't wait. That was probably the best deflection shot I ever made—I barely touched the trigger before the Betty caught fire and crashed into the water.

Alex poses in the cockpit of one of the F6Fs he flew, White 19.

Looking ahead, I saw another Betty flying at about three hundred feet. On my first burst, his port engine and wing exploded and he crashed into the lagoon as well. There were two more Bettys in line up ahead, and I headed after the nearest one while Tom Hall pursued the farthest one. I pulled up a beam out of range, and I could see the tail gunner already firing at me with his twenty-millimeter cannon. I made flat-side, high-deflection runs with the Betty jinxing and turning into me. Only one of my guns was operative for the rest of the attack—the firing would stop after one or two rounds—and I made seven or eight passes on the Betty before it nosed into the sea.

The next morning, we prepared for another predawn launch in support of the Kwajalein landings as *Intrepid* swung her nose into the wind. I watched as Tom made his deck launch; suddenly, his left wheel hit a stanchion off the port bow of the ship and his belly tank exploded—his plane ended up in a huge fireball and fell off the port side into the water. The war for Tom Hall ended that day, but for me the vivid and horrific memories of what I saw would be forever etched in my mind.

On February 16, 1944, we made our first Truk raid. The two-day operation began at dawn with a seventy-two-plane fighter sweep. It was a new experience for us—all fighters with no bombers to protect. We came in low over the water, then climbed up to thirteen thousand feet as we neared the atoll. Our main objective was to take control of the air and destroy all enemy aircraft in the area. Lou Litte, my wingman, and I were the last two Hellcats of the twelve-plane group from *Intrepid* assigned to this fighter sweep. The flight leader started to spiral our group down to strafe, but just before Lou and I pushed over into our dives, I remembered to look back over my shoulder. There, I saw a group of enemy fighters, Zeros, above and on the port side. I tallyhoed the bogies, but our first ten planes had already proceeded too far down toward the airfield. I could see the enemy leader firing, so I turned my section into the attack, causing him to break off and head downward. There were Zeros all around our two Hellcats. Finally, by scissoring with other friendly planes, we were able to work all the enemy planes down to our level and below. We began to follow them down, and I was able to follow three in this manner and set them all afire. All of them hit the water inside the Truk Atoll.

While I was at a lower altitude on the last kill, I saw a fourth Zero below me dodging in and out of clouds. Every time I got into position on him, he would go back into a cloud. After a bit of cat and mouse, I climbed into the sun to make him think I had gone, then came back down on him. I don't believe he ever knew what hit him as his wing tank and cockpit exploded. Scoring on those four Zeros—one of them a Zero on floats, a "Rufe"—raised my personal score to nine in what I consider the wildest air-to-air action I ever participated in.

Later that night, *Intrepid* was torpedoed in the stern by a low-flying "Kate" torpedo bomber. The ship was forced to withdraw, and Air Group 6 was ordered to return stateside. Not wanting to go, I requested continued combat duty, and the navy obliged by assigning me to Fighting Squadron 16 aboard *Lexington*. I reported to VF-16 on February 27, 1944. We hit Truk again on April 29, and while returning as escort on a morning bombing strike, our flight was attacked by a small group of Zeros. We pounced on them quickly and destroyed them at their best performance altitude—down low. I was fortunate enough to down two Zeros, and this brought my tally to eleven victories.

VF-16's next big engagement came during the first battle of the Philippine Sea in June 1944. Both sides sensed a clash of the carriers was coming, and we had not had a fleet engagement since the crucial battle at Midway in June 1942. On June 12, I sank a large enemy merchant ship in Tanapag Harbor at Saipan. I came in low and lobbed a five-hundred-pound bomb into the ship's stern at the water line, and it went down pretty fast.

On June 14, on the way back from escorting a group of our bombers, I spotted a Betty reconnaissance bomber at about seventeen thousand feet. I requested permission from the bomber leader to go after it, and he said, "Go get him." I dropped my belly tank and went to full power, racing my division up to his altitude and climbing up in the Betty's blind spot at a sharp angle of attack directly underneath it. All of a sudden, the Betty's left wing cocked up steeply—we were spotted! The Betty lowered its nose and started building up speed, putting itself in a perfect position for me. One short burst was all I needed, as the Betty became my number twelve.

As part of the American task force protecting the Saipan landings, we were expecting an attack by over four hundred Japanese carrier planes on the morning of June 19. I was leader of the second division of a stand by a group of twelve Hellcats launched from *Lexington* to supplement the CAP already aloft. The full-power climb was too much for my tired old engine, so I radioed my predicament to the fighter director, FDO, who ordered my group to orbit at twenty thousand feet. A short while later, I received a new vector of 265 degrees as the radar screens began to show another large force of enemy planes approaching. When we took that heading, it led us directly to a rambling mass of over fifty enemy planes. In the eight-minute tail chase that followed, I was able to splash six "Judy" dive-bombers, chasing the last two right into the task-force antiaircraft fire. Looking around at that point, only Hellcats seemed to be remaining in the sky, and there was great satisfaction with the day's events, as I felt that I had contributed my personal payback for Pearl Harbor. I was later told that I only used 360 rounds of ammunition that morning to shoot down the six planes—an average of 10 rounds per gun per enemy plane. As Butch had recommended, conserve your ammunition.

The next day, June 20, was the "mission beyond darkness," and it turned out to be one of the most hectic days of my life. Early in the morning, search teams were sent out to locate the withdrawing Japanese fleet, but it was not until 3:38 p.m. that one of the teams located the enemy fleet. Even though it was going to be extremely tight distance-wise, Admiral Mitscher decided to launch our strike of 226 aircraft at 4:24 p.m. We figured that our Hellcats would have enough fuel for the mission but realized that the bombers would be running on fumes at best on their return. We also knew that by the time we got there and back, it would be pitch dark.

Lexington launched nine fighters, fifteen dive-bombers, and six torpedo bombers. En route to the target, engines leaned to the max; we fighters had to weave over the bombers because of their slow cruise speed. Our group leader took us alongside a high thirty-five-thousand-foot cumulus-cloud buildup that separated our fighter top cover from those of us below. All of a sudden, we were surrounded by Zeros—good pilots who knew what they were doing. Glancing down, I saw that one of the TBM Avengers had just been hit by a Zero and its crew was bailing out. My wingman, Brockmeyer, and I were the only Hellcats remaining with the bombers, and we appeared badly outnumbered. One of the

Overhead view of an F6F with wings folded as the flight crew readies it for another mission.

US Navy Grumman F6F Hellcats head out to tangle with Japanese fighters.

Zeros managed to get on Brock's tail, and he must have been hit because he didn't turn back. I got the Zero behind him, but the Zero got him first and I had the sad experience of seeing my wingman going down.

At this point, I had to use my last-ditch maneuver and dive down toward our rendezvous area, where I joined up on a battle-damaged TBF from another carrier. His bomb-bay doors were dragging, and I pulled up alongside him since I figured he would feel better having another plane with him. He soon gestured toward me, asking me if I had enough fuel, and I nodded my head yes. He signaled that he didn't have enough fuel to get back. The sun was already disappearing on the horizon while my newfound wingman and I stayed down low. With the TBF's wing lights flickering on and off, I believed that he had electrical problems as well. He then headed toward a group of seven of our planes that were circling low over the water. I could hear voices on the radio and one pilot saying,

"I've only got twenty-five gallons of fuel left; I've got to ditch." Another pilot said, "I only have about thirty-five left myself, so I might was well go down with you!" It was dark by that time, and I gave them all a heartfelt salute.

I soon found myself all alone, and I still had almost three hundred miles to go, but I was not worried about fuel. I had learned long ago that it paid to conserve one's fuel whenever possible. After a while, I started to see searchlights on the horizon. I was so amazed that I thought, "My God, I am heading for Yap!"—a Japanese-held island. Thankfully, that wasn't the case.

I could hear a voice on our radio frequency saying, "Land at nearest base! Land at nearest base!" I wanted to get back to *Lexington* and my own sack that night. Arriving overhead, I circled a few thousand feet above the wild melee below to let the planes short on fuel land first. When my fuel gauge told me I had better land aboard also, I let down into the *Lexington* landing pattern but was given a constant wave-off. A plane from another carrier had made a crash landing, fouling the deck, so I slid over to *Enterprise* next door and landed aboard on my first pass. I taxied forward of the barrier and then heard the crash horn, which told me that somebody had crash-landed behind me. The SBD behind me had taken a wave-off earlier, and the pilot forgot to put his wheels back down on his next pass. Thoughtfully, after I took several long drinks of water to quench my thirst, the ship provided us with medicinal brandy to relax us.

Over the next few days, all but thirty-four missing fliers were rescued in one of the finest search-and-rescue efforts in the history of the US Navy. Conversely, Japanese naval aviation had virtually ceased to exist. When their remaining carriers sailed again four months later in the second battle of the Philippine Sea, also known as the Battle of Leyte Gulf, they merely served as sacrificial decoys—no naval pilots or planes were left. VF-16 was then given a thirty-day leave, but personally, I received my promotion to full lieutenant on arrival at San Diego and was labeled the top navy ace. With the kamikaze threat escalating, the timing was right, and I was able to obtain a set of orders to return back out to the Pacific.

My luck ran out early on December 14, 1944, when I was shot down by antiaircraft fire on my second mission while strafing near Clark Field, Luzon, Philippines. After parachuting to safety, I spent the next five weeks with USAFFE guerillas and was given the honorary rank of brevet major while with them. For the final week of this episode, I found myself in command of 180 men dodging Japanese to meet General MacArthur's advancing Americans. I marched into an American camp sporting a Luger and carrying a Japanese sword.

> *After surviving service on six carriers (two of which were torpedoed), two ditchings, and with two parachute jumps, Alex was to be known as Grumman's best customer. Alex was the US Navy's leading ace for four months in 1944 (June to October) and ended World War II as the fourth-ranking naval ace, having shot down nineteen enemy planes and destroyed twenty-one more on the ground.*

KILLER CORSAIRS

MAJOR THOMAS HARDY, USMCR (RET.)
CHANCE VOUGHT F4U CORSAIR

Thomas Hardy was born in November of 1918. He received his first airplane ride in the 1930s, when a grateful line boy took him up as a thank you for cleaning his Aeronca C-3. From then on, Tom wanted to fly.

CHECKERBOARD CORSAIRS

After graduating college in 1939, I was hired by Pratt & Whitney as an experimental test engineer working on the new R-2800 radial engines. When the war broke out, I ended up joining the navy because the army wouldn't take me—they thought I should serve my country at Wright Field as an engineer. I tried to tell them I wanted to be a fighter pilot, but they still refused. The navy, on the other hand, accepted me with open arms. After surviving primary and basic flight training, I really knew I wanted to fly fighters when we got to do gunnery in SNJs, otherwise known to the air force as AT-6s and the RCAF as the Harvard.

After earning my wings, I ended up joining the marines and did some early fighter training down in Florida in a Brewster Buffalo, which I thought was a real smooth-flying airplane. It had an electric-controlled prop, which to me was very quiet. I liked the Buffalo but only got fifteen hours in it before I was sent on to join Marine Fighter Squadron 312 at Page Field, Parris Island, South Carolina, in June of 1943. It was with VMF-312 that I met the bent-wing, long-nose Corsair for the very first time.

Pilots of VMF-312 pose in front of their squadron emblem and an F4U Corsair.

I was a little nervous flying Corsairs for the first time because so many guys there had told all of us what a dangerous airplane it was to fly. But after I had my blindfold cockpit checkout and flew it five or six hours, I thought the F4U was a great airplane. One of the things we had to get used to was flying it blind on landing because of that long nose, only looking out the windows on either side. The trick was to look out of the corners of your eyes when you came in to land. A lot of guys didn't like flying it and made out that the Corsair was tricky, but I never felt that way about it.

They were pushing us to fly a lot because they needed fighter pilots on the front lines, so every day we learned something new. We went up one day with a five-hundred-foot ceiling and driving rain, and we were practicing takeoffs and landings from an airfield with its runways that extended toward the ocean. After one takeoff, I found myself in a rain squall, so thick you couldn't see through it, when all of a sudden some guy in another Corsair was coming at me head-on. I banked hard to go over him on the right-hand side, and suddenly another Corsair was on the right side! I racked that sucker into a ninety-degree bank at two hundred feet off the deck, said a quick prayer, and went into the rain squall, unable to even see my own wingtips. By the time I got my head out of the clouds and back on the gauges, I saw that I was in a forty-five-degree nose-down turn. I quickly righted the Corsair back to level, and I could feel my wheels hitting the water! I pulled back hard and climbed for any altitude I could get to try to get some air under my wings—I kept going straight up and came out at eight thousand feet. I flew east for fifteen minutes to make sure I was clear of everyone else and then dropped my nose and went back into the soup, breaking out at five hundred feet. By the time I hit land again, I was over a P-51 base that was fifty miles to the north of ours, so I knew where I was. When I got back and called the tower for permission to land, the tower responded, "My God, we thought you were dead." I replied, "So did I!" and came in and made the best landing of the day!

In February of 1944, VMF-312 boarded the USS *Hornet* and set sail for Hawaii, where we continued to train hard until June of 1944. We arrived in the South Pacific in late 1944, but it wasn't until early April of 1945 that we were moved to the front lines—Kadena airstrip on Okinawa. Our squadron had the distinction of being the first marines to land F4U Corsairs on that airfield. Most of our missions were combat air patrols and air strikes. Life was far from dull being so close to the front lines, and the Japanese made sure that we knew they were still a force to be reckoned with. If they weren't shelling us, they were either strafing our airstrip or sending a high-flying photoreconnaissance aircraft over our base to see what we were up to.

CUISINART CORSAIR: MAY 10, 1944

We had been having an almost daily visit from a high-flying, twin-engine Japanese "Nick" that we believed was taking photos of the fleet anchored around Okinawa to pick out kamikaze targets. For almost a week, this guy stayed at the same twenty-thousand-foot altitude and on the same course, and every time we went up to try to get him he just climbed higher and scooted back to Japan. But his luck ran out on May 10.

There was a flight of four Corsairs already up at twenty thousand feet on patrol when word came down from the radar people that a bogie was inbound. Immediately, the Corsairs stripped their belly tanks and pointed their noses skyward to try to reach the Nick's altitude of twenty-five thousand feet. Two of the Corsairs had a hard time climbing, so they were ordered to turn back, while the remaining two F4Us, flown by Capt. Ken Reusser in the lead and Lt. Bob Klingman on his wing, kept on going. The Nick must have spotted the pursuers, as it started its own climb to a higher altitude. By the time the Corsairs reached the thirty-five-thousand-foot mark, they were both struggling to stay in the thin air. The rear gunner of the Nick was able to get some rounds off at his pursuers before his gun jammed. Lieutenant Klingman tried to return fire but his guns froze up as well. He told me later that he believed the Cosmoline on his guns had not been cleaned off completely, and because of the extreme cold temperatures at this altitude, the actions on the guns became so still as to prevent them from firing. The Nick was having problems of its own and managed to reach thirty-eight thousand feet before leveling off.

Lieutenant Klingman had the newer, less war weary of the Corsairs and was able to match altitude with the Nick as he closed the distance. He later told me that he could see the Nick's rear gunner beating on his machine gun trying to get it to fire, but to no avail. Lieutenant Klingman did not want this Nick to escape, so he thought he could just use his propellers to cut enough of its elevators to make it lose control. He began to slowly close in on the Nick, but at a point of about twenty feet behind the Japanese twin, the blast from its propellers prevented the Corsair from getting any closer. Not to be outdone, Lieutenant Klingman simply moved his Corsair over to one side and was able to reach a point slightly ahead of the rear of the elevator. Nosing over, he was only able to chew a little bit of the rudder and elevator before being blown back again by the Nick's prop wash.

Lieutenant Klingman describes the moment he chopped the tail off a Japanese aircraft to a group of marine pilots and ground crew. Tom Hardy, shirtless with arms crossed, smiles as he listens.

The lieutenant tried a third time, and this time he changed tactics and climbed slightly above the Nick, easing his plane ahead. Because of the long nose of the Corsair, the forward visibility was blocked, and instead of chewing on the elevator, Lieutenant Klingman's propellers dropped down into the fuselage and through the right-side elevator. The impact tore six inches off each of the prop blades of the Corsair, but the damage to the Nick was far worse. Both aircraft went into a spin. Lieutenant Klingman was able to recover about one thousand feet later, but the Nick kept on spinning, losing both its wings at around fifteen thousand feet before crashing into the sea below.

Lieutenant Klingman said that all hell broke loose after he cut up the Nick, and it felt like the big R-2800 engine was going to jump its mount before he could retard the throttle. With his rpm set as low as he could, he knew it was doubtful he would be able to return back to Okinawa, which was now three hundred miles away. Nursing his engine the best he could, he tried to estimate just how much altitude he could afford to lose and still reach Okinawa without wrecking his engine. By the time he descended to ten thousand feet, he was out of fuel but had the field in sight. With a dead engine and the chewed-up propeller blades windmilling, his Corsair hit the ground hard just a bit short of the runway, and it bounced him back into the air as he set it back down on the very end of the strip. End of story? Not quite.

Our airfield was only five or six miles from the front lines, and we were continually shelled by a large Japanese gun hidden on Shuri Mountain. We had lost so many airplanes that we were constantly short of Corsairs and didn't have individual F4Us assigned to us. On May 11, I had been out on a CAP over a picket-boat destroyer with three other Corsairs about fifty miles off Okinawa. I was stationed in the number-four position, where normally it was a little difficult to maintain my position with the other Corsairs. Each time the flight is reversed, it is frequently necessary for the number-four man to add a little throttle. But on today's mission, I thought that it seemed to be easier to get back into position after each turn. It seemed that I had just a little more power than the other Corsairs.

When the mission was finished and I returned back to base, the Corsairs' crew chief jumped up onto the wing to help me out of my parachute. I asked him if this Corsair had a new engine installed because it flew so nicely. He looked at me, smiled, and said, "Oh no, this was the airplane that Lieutenant Klingman was flying yesterday when he chewed that Nick up! We just put a new propeller on it, patched some holes in the wings and cowling, and ran the engine up." I looked at the mechanic in shock and said, "I'm sure glad you didn't tell me that before I took off today!"

When I left Okinawa two months later, the Corsair was still on the line, giving good service! Quite a tribute to the Pratt & Whitney R-2800 engine I fondly remember working on.

COMBAT ESCAPADES: THE TROUBLE WITH TONYS

During my almost sixty combat missions while in the Pacific theater, I only encountered Japanese airplanes seven or eight times. By that point, most of the Japanese fighters and the "old hands" who flew them had been ravaged in earlier battles with Hellcats, Lightnings, and Corsairs. Most of our work was close air support for the mud marines on the ground—they had to fight for literally every inch of the islands they invaded. But when we weren't strafing or dropping napalm on the well dug-in Japanese, we protected the navy ships the best we could from the tenacious kamikaze attacks.

My first aerial encounter was while flying twenty miles southwest of Okinawa near a group of islands called the Kerama Retto. There was a destroyer nearby on patrol, and just around sundown, we were scrambled to intercept some incoming bogies. I was initially flying wing on Captain Reusser, but Reusser was practically deaf, and on past patrol duties he would pass the lead on to those of us that could hear better. In typical fashion, he passed the lead on to me and dropped on my wing as we swapped places. We were flying in the second section of two planes when we received word from the destroyer that it was under attack. At that point, Captain Reusser called out that he saw two planes ahead against the darkness. As I looked around to turn my head to one side, I saw his tracers zip forward and set one of the airplanes on fire, sending it cartwheeling into the sea.

I could clearly see the remaining enemy plane below me—a "Tony." I peeled away and headed for him, and I could see his outline against the water. I was looking west and he was moving from the north to the south. I could see his long inline engine nose, and I didn't doubt for a second that it was a Japanese Tony. He was moving right to left,

and it looked like he was going to get into the darkness, so I aimed about twenty feet ahead of him and squeezed off twenty-five to thirty rounds. As I was turning left, he passed underneath me so I rolled around, never losing sight of him as he went into a left turn. I thought I had missed him but was shocked to see his left wing hit the water; he cartwheeled in. I never knew whether I hit him or just plain scared him to death—either way, it was one less Tony we had to contend with.

KAMIKAZE SCUD RUNNER

I was flying a CAP over the fleet and was the leader of a four-plane flight of Corsairs. The ceiling was very low, maybe four hundred or five hundred feet above the sea. Around noon I spotted a lone fixed-landing-gear Oscar below me that had tried to sneak around us from the backside of a cloud. I racked my Corsair up into a left bank, and I could see that he was going to pass out of my line of sight. I couldn't turn any sharper, so in desperation I just touched the trigger and saw two tracers from each of my six guns—three on each side. I tried to pull in front of the Oscar and tried to hit him like I was shooting doves. I saw my rounds arching toward his plane, but I released the trigger pull just as quickly because there wasn't any point of filling the sky with lead. As he cut

Marine Corps Corsairs form up over Okinawa as they look for Japanese targets below.
Jack Cook collection

off my turn, I drifted behind him and found myself in a stall, but I was elated when I saw two of my tracers tear right into his cockpit. The rounds seemed to track right behind the engine, and that was like throwing a match on a can of gasoline. The Oscar blew up.

When I got behind him again, he was heading downward, and I racked the Corsair over and looked down at him through my canopy no more than fifty feet above him. I saw the pilot slumped over on his stick and knew he was a goner. When I landed back at our base, the gunnery staff sergeant counted my rounds and told me I had fired a total of only nineteen—roughly three out of each gun. I have to chalk that kill to all the dove hunting I had done as a boy. Snap shooting really helped me on that one!

JUST IN THE NICK OF TIME

During my last combat encounter, I was leading a flight of Corsairs in low visibility under a solid overcast. Out ahead in the muck I could see another Corsair chasing a twin-engine Nick. The Corsair was from another flight, and this guy was not only shooting wildly at the Nick, he was also going way too fast and ended up overrunning him. I pulled

Lieutenant Robert Klingman checks out the large chunk he took out of his Corsair's propeller when he used it to chop the tail off a high-flying twin-engine Japanese fighter.

Marine Corsairs on patrol over Okinawa. *Jack Cook collection*

in behind the Nick and found that I was moving pretty fast myself and was a lot closer than I wanted to be. When I finally put him in my sight, I had to use the Nick's cockpit as the aiming point. With three .50-caliber machine guns on either side of me, my tracers converged out in front of him by about fifty or sixty yards. I kicked the rudder over, and as my Corsair responded, three of my guns found their mark and my rounds tore into his cockpit—the Nick flipped over and dove right into the water below.

Thomas Hardy ended the war with three confirmed victories. He passed away in May of 2012.

WORLD AT WAR: Air superiority over Europe was well within reach of the Allied Air Force commanders. New tactics to deal with the Luftwaffe included releasing the fighters from bomber escort and allowing them to drop down to the deck and strafe targets of opportunity, such as heavily defended Luftwaffe airfields. There was no rest for a Luftwaffe fighter pilot, but in mid-1944 they still managed to put up impressive numbers of fighters. Unfortunately for them, their experience level was becoming lopsided to that of their Allied counterparts.

RUNT OF THE LITTER

MEMORIES OF A WOLF PACK ACE

COLONEL ROBERT "SHORTY" RANKIN, USAF (RET.)
REPUBLIC P-47 THUNDERBOLT

Robert James Rankin was born on October 23, 1918, in Washington, DC, and joined the Army Air Corps on March 6, 1941. He graduated from pilot training at Luke Field, Arizona, on April 11, 1943, and he checked out in the P-47 Thunderbolt at Tallahassee, Florida.

Don't ever let anyone tell you that size matters, because once I strapped on my P-47, there was nothing that stood in my way. I was only five feet four inches tall when I graduated from flight training in 1943, but my instructors saw something gigantic inside of me. I was one of sixty second lieutenants selected out of four hundred to go into fighters—P-47 Thunderbolts, to be exact. When I first saw the airplane I would fly in combat, my only thought was, "Why in the heck did I ever ask for this behemoth?!" But after I flew the Jug for a while, I really liked it and thought it was a piece of cake to fly—easy to handle, reliable, and stable. There was nothing out there that could beat it in a dive, not even a rock! What I admired most about it, though, were those eight .50-caliber machine guns that stuck out of the wings like great big broom handles.

By the time I arrived in England in 1943, I had 130 hours of P-47 time under my belt, just barely enough to keep me out of trouble. I had great confidence in the airplane and in my abilities as a fighter pilot—you had to have these traits because anything less and you were dead! I also had 20/10 vision, so I

Hubert "Hub" Zemeke, one of the great leaders and main reasons the 56th Fighter Group was so successful, checks his .50-caliber machine guns before his next mission.

could usually spot the Luftwaffe before they spotted me. I was posted with the 61st Fighter Squadron of the 56th Fighter Group, the premier P-47 unit of the entire war. I flew with all of the great leaders, including Hub Zemke, Gabby Gabreski, David Schilling, and the rest. But the person I was most impressed with was Bob Johnson, the first pilot of the European war to break World War I ace Eddie Rickenbacker's record.

Bob was the best of the whole outfit in my mind. He was gutsy and aggressive, and he would mix it up with the Germans as if he didn't have a care in the world. I flew my first combat mission on his wing, and when he spotted the enemy, he turned into me so hard as he went after a Bf 109 that I lost track of him for a few minutes as I was pushed into a cloud; but I was thrilled to death when I found him again. He increased his score and with each victory decreased the Luftwaffe's numbers by one Bf 109. I learned a lot from these guys, and eventually I, too, became a flight leader.

I was what you call "conservative-aggressive"—I didn't stick my neck out when I thought it would endanger my wingman. The thing I learned very quickly in combat was that regardless of how many airplanes you attack, the leader can usually get through, get a kill or two, and be out of harm's way in a flash. It was the guys following behind that would get shot down. I flew seventy-five missions as flight leader, and I am proud to say that everybody in my flight came home. But it was on a mission in May of 1944 that my streak almost came to a crashing halt.

Famous 56th FG ace and squadron commander Gabby Gabreski chats with his ground crew about another successful mission. *Jack Cook collection*

MAY 12, 1944: ZEMKE FAN

Sound and Furious

Rugged bodies and wrathful determination—powerful aircraft willing and able . . . to win the freedom to live in the American tradition—these are the tools fiercely used over all the world's battlefronts.

Our own job is to supply rugged structural, and sensitive control parts for the planes that are driving back the forces of inhuman aggression.

The men and women of General Aviation and its associate companies work round the clock in this service of supply—so that the war will end soon, and that free Americans will again pursue their self-determined ways.

General Aviation Equipment Co., Inc., Ashley and Wilkes-Barre, Pennsylvania, U. S. A.

General Aviation Equipment

AND SUBSIDIARIES: SLATINGTON MACHINE TOOL CO., INC., SLATINGTON, PENNA.
BLOOMSBURG FOUNDRY CO., INC., BLOOMSBURG, PENNA.

OFFICES IN: NEW YORK, MANHASSET, N. Y., DETROIT, CHICAGO, ST. LOUIS, FORT WORTH

Aircraft Structural and Control Parts

A wartime ad depicting P-47 Thunderbolts, the pilots who flew them, and the equipment it took to keep 'em flying.

We knew through our intelligence people that the Luftwaffe was using very prominent landmarks inside of Germany as rendezvous points for their scrambled fighters sent up to attack inbound Allied bombers. The Germans also used an airborne commander in either a Bf 109 or an Fw 190 to direct the various assembled fighters on which group of bombers to hit. Colonel Hub Zemke, knowing this German tactic, decided that we would do something to outfox the Germans. He called it the "Zemke Fan."

Colonel Zemke arranged for our group to fly in three very tight formations on a specific track, the same one to be used by the inbound bombers that day—and to fly forty-five minutes ahead of the actual bomber stream. The plan was for our group to get there just as the Germans were arriving at their rendezvous point, ready to hit the bombers, which, in reality, were us. The plan worked so well that day that the Germans were completely fooled, thinking we were easy prey.

I was leading "Whipper White Flight" in my olive-drab P-47, which I had named *Wicked Wacker Weegie* after my wife. I was leading the westernmost flight of P-47s as we fanned out near Frankfurt when all of a sudden the RT went crazy with people calling out bogies all over the sky. We were at twenty-five thousand feet when I looked out in front of me and saw a great big gaggle of twenty-five to thirty Bf 109s in tight formation, all of them with drop tanks still attached. I ordered my flight to make a beeline for them and press on the attack. They must have seen us coming, because all of a sudden there were drop tanks fluttering and tumbling downward as the 109s split-S'd into every direction imaginable. I was kind of mesmerized by the floating drop tanks and the 109s scattering about like chickens; that is, until a little voice in my head woke me up.

"Hey, what do you think you're doing?" I asked myself. "Wake up, stupid—let's get on up there and press on the attack!" I quickly latched on to two of the 109s that were heading downhill fast. As I chased after them, the one on my left scooted away from my line of sight, so I concentrated on the right one as our speed increased. I had been told long ago that if a 109 pushed over and went straight down, it would not be able to pull out of its dive when it got below five thousand feet; knowing that saved my life. I pulled the nose of the Jug through the 109 and gave it a quick squirt. Given my attitude I couldn't see whether I'd hit him or not, but I knew we were building up speed as his wings began to vibrate violently and flutter.

I glanced at my airspeed indicator and saw the needle passing through 575 miles per hour—just on the verge of compressibility. I knew it was time to pull out of my dive, but when I pulled back on the stick with both hands, it felt like it was buried in concrete. The 109 went straight in and disintegrated before burying its remains deep underground. I looked at my altimeter and saw that it had hung up at 1,500 feet as I pulled out of my dive, just barely brushing the treetops. I glanced over my shoulder and saw that my wingman, Lt. Cleon Thornton, who happened to be on his first mission, was still with me.

Cleon and I started climbing for altitude, and when we got to two thousand feet, there was a 109 all by itself flying straight and level, like it was out on a training flight. I pulled right behind him and gave him a hard burst, my rounds tearing into his cockpit and engine. The 109 did two violent snap rolls and went straight in. I turned to climb once again, and as I reached five thousand feet I heard a call from Colonel Zemke: "Fairbanks leader, I'm ten miles north of Koblenz and I'm over the whole Luftwaffe! There's enough here for everybody!" I was fifteen miles away and raced to help out Colonel Zemke.

By the time I got to ten thousand feet, I could see up ahead the biggest mass of airplanes I had ever laid eyes on. There were German fighters with big black crosses on their wings going around in a circle like flies over a piece of meat. I looked up above and saw a lone P-47, flown by Colonel Zemke, hovering over the cloud of German airplanes. Zemke, for whatever reason, was all alone. I knew that earlier in the flight, one of his wingmen had aborted, so his flight had become a flight of three, but where were the other two? It was not until a long time after the war had ended that I found out the answer.

I received this information directly from my friend Günther Rall, the high-scoring German ace, who was also on that mission that day and had his left thumb shot off before he, too, was shot down by P-47s of the 56th Fighter Group. Günther told me that there were almost ninety German fighters orbiting the rendezvous point when the German airborne commander lost his radio. Günther, who was up on top in his 109, was providing cover for the Fw 190s that were going to hit the bombers when he was ordered to go down and take control and command of the assembled fighters. On his way down, he encountered a flight of three P-47s—Zemke's flight—and shot down both wingmen. Zemke pushed his Jug over and dived for the deck. Günther thought he got Zemke too that day, but he didn't. In fact, after the war, Zemke was able to confirm the two P-47 kills for Günther, increasing his incredible score to 275 victories.

Colonel Zemke was able to get away from that mess and sneaked back up above the swirling German fighters. When I arrived on Zemke's wing, he said to me, "OK, you cover me when I go down through them. I'll climb back up and then you can have a go at them." As Zemke dove down, he immediately found a 109 that was climbing toward

BELOW: A rare World War II color photograph of 56th FG P-47 *Pat* getting ready to taxi out for a bomber escort. *Jack Cook collection* **INSET:** Pilots of the 56th FG stand in front of one of their P-47 Thunderbolts with numerous victory markings displayed on the fuselage.

my altitude and tore it apart. That was the first time in combat that I had actually seen a German aircraft engulfed in flame, and I mean a huge ball of fire. I had seen plenty of black-and-white combat film, but this time it was in living color.

Now it was my turn to go down, so with Cleon still on my wing, I pushed my Jug over and went looking for something to latch onto without being seen. I made a great big wide orbit that was measured in miles as I descended looking for my next prey. It didn't take long; I spotted two 109s flying line abreast, fifty feet apart. I looked around and saw that Cleon was still with me, and I felt as though I could get behind these two without getting my own tail shot off. I slithered in behind the one on the left and gave him a quick burst. The 109 began to smoke right away, his right landing gear flopped down, and he rolled over into a slow spiral. I eased over behind the other 109 by using some right rudder, and the guy didn't move!

There was no evasive action whatsoever from this guy. Maybe he was in shock seeing his leader shot down, or maybe he never saw me. Whatever the case, I gave him a short burst and the same thing happened. His right gear flopped down, his engine was pouring out smoke, and he, too, went over into a spiral. Both 109s stayed together, not too far apart, as they headed down in their death spiral. That was number three and four for the day, but I was far from finished. I was turning and climbing and, at the same time, getting myself cleared again, when I saw a 109 climbing right underneath Colonel Zemke's tail.

I called to Zemke, "Fairbanks, break hard left!"

"Where is it?" Zemke called back.

"He's climbing right up under your ass!"

Oh boy, I thought. *He's going to get me for poor RT procedure when I get back from this one!* At the same time, I maneuvered in behind the 109 and gave him a quick squirt from my guns. I saw some hits in the wing root and canopy area, and I went to squeeze the trigger again. Nothing— just some clicking noise. I was out of ammo! I didn't think I'd hit him enough to do any damage, but I was tickled to death when the guy eased off to the right, popped his canopy, and bailed out.

Although I had shot down five aircraft, I was not about to start celebrating yet. I was a long way from home, out of ammo, and without any of my buddies to speak of flying nearby. Cleon, thankfully, was still there with me as we turned for England. Trouble was, two 109s blocked our way and came in for an attack. All four of us went into a Lufbery circle and went round and round. One of the 109s was gaining on Cleon, so I told him to break down and out of the circle, climb back up, and get behind them. Well, with Cleon's lack of experience, he didn't quite follow directions. He came back down, all right—right in front of a 109.

He got out of there by the skin of his teeth and tried it again. Same thing! On his third attempt, he broke down, and when he came back up, one of the 109s went head to head with him. Cleon let him have it as they went nose to nose. Shooting down an airplane is hard enough, but shooting one down head-on is one tough shot, even for an experienced pilot. Cleon sure experienced a lot on that mission, and he got his first victory—head-on! In the meantime, I was stuck in the circle with the other 109, who I was sure had plenty of ammo. I even got right behind him, dead astern, only forty feet away from chewing his tail off. It was probably a smart move on my part when I told Cleon to break hard and head west, as the 109 was still heading east in his turn.

As we increased our speed and distance from the 109, I pulled my chart out and spread it across my lap, looking for the best place to cross the channel. I was sweating it because I knew that the wingmen were always shorter on fuel than the leader due to all the throttle adjustments they had to make trying to stay with me. I had my head down inside the cockpit and froze for a second when Cleon called and said, "Break!" I quickly answered him and asked, "Fighters or flak?" Luckily it was only flak, but the problem was we were only at ten thousand feet—prime territory for flak guns. I couldn't afford to waste precious fuel by climbing, so we just made some heading changes. I looked back and saw the puffs of flak burst where I would have been had I kept it straight. The antiaircraft gunners couldn't keep up with us as we zigzagged home.

I looked up ahead and saw the North Sea, and I knew we were almost home. At the same time, I saw a huge gaggle of airplanes on a conversion intercept, right on the same course I was on. All I could think was, "Oh God, after all we have been through, what in blazes is going to happen now?" I relaxed when I saw it was a flight of P-47s in close formation; why they flew like that over enemy territory, I will never know, and I didn't care at the time!

As we crossed the channel, we pointed our noses for the long, wide runway at RAF Manston and touched down on British soil. On the rollout, I taxied off the runway, but Cleon was nowhere to be found. He had run out of fuel when he touched down and was stuck on the runway.

I ran into the British Operations building while they towed Cleon back in and called back to the 56th FG headquarters. Zemke was laughing and beside himself when he got on the phone and told me what he had said to the rest of the pilots. "We won't be seeing Rankin and Thomton again—they got themselves bottled up, and there were just too many German airplanes around. There was no way they were going to get out of that big mess." He had written us off! He told me to get back to base and he would hold the rest of the pilots so I could give the debrief.

When Cleon and I arrived back at our base, there was a lot of handshaking and applause as we critiqued the mission. The 56th got nineteen enemy airplanes that day, and I received a big reward from Colonel Zemke for shooting down five 109s: he announced to all my fellow squadron mates, "Make sure Rankin gets a whole chicken at the officer's mess tonight!" I was happy I got five that day, but I was even more delighted to be sharing my chicken with my wingman that night!

Bob Rankin ended the war with ten victories, all of them Bf 109s, and all of them in P-47 Thunderbolts. His last victory was one day after D-Day, June 7, 1944. He passed away on March 14, 2013.

WORLD AT WAR: With the threat of Japanese naval fighters in the Pacific mainly vanquished, the Allied naval forces turned their attention to the mighty Japanese surface fleet, which had inflicted so much damage on the US Navy at Pearl Harbor almost three and half years earlier.

THE BEAST FROM HELL

FLYING THE SB2C HELLDIVER IN COMBAT

LIEUTENANT FOSTER E. LOONEY, USNR (RET.)
CURTISS SB2C HELLDIVER

Foster Looney was born on November 29, 1922, in Fort Worth, Texas. He received his private pilot's license at the controls of a Piper J-3 Cub before enlisting in the navy in 1943.

EARNING MY WINGS OF GOLD

When I joined the navy in 1943 as a nineteen-year-old kid from Texas, I knew I wanted to be a fighter pilot. Heck, every guy who wanted wings in the navy lusted after fighters more than they did a pretty girl. Besides, who in their right mind would want to be strapped to a slow-moving dive-bomber? By the time I was sent to navy boot camp in 1943, I had already earned my pilot's license in a J-3 Cub. I think the time I spent in the Cub gave me a leg up over the other guys, because I wound up finishing first in my class.

My wish to fly fighters came true when I was selected to proceed on to the navy fighter program in Miami, Florida. Unfortunately, that wish turned into a nightmare one week later at morning muster when the base commander advised us that the navy desperately needed dive-bomber pilots. His selection method was quite simple: he walked along in front of us and said, "You, you, and you just volunteered for dive-bombing school at Jacksonville, Florida. Congratulations, gentlemen!"

As if being forced out of fighters into dive-bombers wasn't bad enough, the navy decided to whisk me away from the nice warm Florida tropics to the bitterly cold January temperatures of Chicago, Illinois. And who ever said the navy didn't have a sense of humor? The first order of training for a new dive-bomber pilot was to get us carrier qualified. After getting checked out in the SBD Dauntless, I was sent out over Lake Michigan to practice my landings aboard the short decks of the USS *Wolverine* and USS *Sable*. I actually enjoyed flying the Dauntless—heck, it would pretty much fly itself. It was very stable and easy to fly, kind of like an SNJ. It had two main problems though. One, it couldn't carry any load to speak of, and two, it only had one speed: slow! It didn't matter whether you were horizontal or vertical with it—it flew along at the same constant slow speed.

With my carrier qualifications complete, I was given orders to report to Naval Air Station Alameda, California, where I would meet the SBD's evil stepsister, the SB2C Helldiver.

Foster Looney poses on the wing of his SB2C Helldiver. Many pilots referred to this bomber as the "Big-Tailed Beast."

BEAST OF BURDEN

When I finally laid eyes on the Helldiver for the very first time, all I could mutter was, "Oh my God, it's a monster!" The SB2C was definitely not a Dauntless. The fuselage was longer by over three feet, its wingspan was longer by eight feet, and its max speed of 295 miles per hour made it seem like a jackrabbit compared to the tortoise-like speed of the Dauntless. Although it may have been bigger and faster, the Helldiver, in my mind, won the contest for bad vices. For one thing, it had fully hydraulic brakes—this thing could stop on a dime! That took some getting used to, especially coming off of an SBD, which had more automobile-type brakes that you had to practically push through the floor to get the plane to stop. Not so on the Helldiver; all you had to do was nudge one pedal lightly and you were going to go that way in a hurry whether you wanted to or not. Woe unto the careless Helldiver pilot who didn't have his feet synchronized! Although I thought the ground handling of the Helldiver was bad, I thought the flying characteristics were miserable.

Most airplanes can be flown hands-free with the correct trim settings, but the Helldiver isn't one of them. You had to fly this monster every second it was in the air. If you turned the stick loose for more than a few seconds, it was going to end up wandering somewhere—up, down, or sideways. Even when the later models came out, you still had to wrestle with them to keep them straight and level at all times. The Helldiver just refused to be a normal airplane! Oh sure, it was faster and could now keep up with the fighters and torpedo bombers. And yes, its defenses were better as it carried a higher bomb load, along with twenty-millimeter cannons in its wings and a .50-caliber machine gun in the rear cockpit. On paper it seemed that in all aspects the Helldiver should be a better airplane, but in reality the SB2C was definitely no SBD, and I found out the hard way during combat in mid-1944.

INTRODUCTION OF COMBAT

I had been stationed in Hawaii in 1944, awaiting my orders to report to the Pacific theater. The waiting didn't take long at all, as I received the call to report to the USS

Hornet, CV-12, as a replacement for a dive-bomber pilot lost earlier in a launching accident. When I joined Air Group 2 on May 3, 1944, I was assigned to VB-2 as part of the Squadron Commanders Division. I was assigned a rear-seat gunner named "Frenchy" Chartier, and I thought it was a winning combination—a Texan up front and a Cajun from Louisiana in the back! Because I was the low man on the totem pole, I became the number-six dive-bomber in the diving sequence—also known as the tail-end Charlie. I quickly found out how deadly last place could be.

My first mission occurred on June 12 with strikes against preinvasion targets on Guam. We went after shore batteries and antiaircraft positions on the island and had been briefed on the positions of the targets. The problem was that when we flew over them at twelve thousand feet, all we could see were the tops of trees. It didn't take long for the Japanese gunners to give us a little hint at where they were, however; they opened up on our squadron and tracer rounds filled the air. As the first of our planes pushed on over, I was able to see that the Japanese gunners were well behind the first diving Helldiver. They weren't much better on the second Helldiver as their rounds were well out in front of it. But they were quick learners, and by the time the number-three Helldiver was pointing downward, they pretty much had us zeroed in. I quickly figured out that being the last one to dive would not be the healthiest place to be!

I quickly changed the tactics I had learned in the SBDs and increased my speed, closed my canopy up tight, and increased my angle of approach. I didn't put the speed brakes out very much and I jammed my throttle forward. With that forward speed I wondered if I would have any wings left. But my tactic seemed to work well, as I had the gunners all fouled up. I released my bomb higher than normal and managed to beat them at their own game! The Helldiver turned out to be one tough piece of machinery. It wasn't fun to fly, but it could sure get you there and back.

For the next week, we were sent back to places like Guam, Yap, Iwo Jima, and Chichi Jima as we bombed the heck out of airfields, shore batteries, and antiaircraft guns. On the 19th of June, during the "Great Marianas Turkey Shoot," we returned to Guam, where we beat up Orote Airfield as our F6F Hellcats slugged it out with hundreds of Japanese fighters. Although we had great bombing practice during those first few weeks in June, our real test of strength and endurance would occur the very next day.

MISSION BEYOND DARKNESS

On June 20, 1944, Vice Admiral Mitscher, aboard the USS *Lexington*, began to devise a plan to once and for all destroy the Japanese flattops. He just had to find them first. As we sat in the ready room aboard USS *Hornet*, we got word that a long-range TBM Avenger finally located the armada. The trouble was, it was already late afternoon, and when they told us the coordinates, we did the arithmetic and started shaking our heads in disbelief of the fuel needed and the distance involved—it didn't look very good. Flying 250 miles in a Helldiver was stretching it, and 300 miles was a one-way trip. This would be a maximum-effort raid. My skipper added two more Helldivers to his flight, bringing the total to eight in our division, with another division from VB-2 right behind us adding six more SB2Cs, each of us carrying a thousand-pound bomb.

Our sister carriers and VB squadrons from USS *Yorktown*, *Bunker Hill*, and *Wasp* also launched Helldivers, with a total strike package of fifty-two SB2Cs, twenty-six SBDs, fifty-four TBMs, and ninety-six F6Fs to protect us. Because of our fuel concerns, it was decided that we would launch as soon as possible and not rendezvous around the carrier. Our orders were to go out individually at the most economical fuel consumption we could get, because chances were we wouldn't have enough to make it back. At 4:25 p.m., we began to launch, and twelve minutes later, 240 airplanes were all on their way to the target that lay three hundred miles and almost two hours away. It was a long, slow ride, with our Helldiver flight strung out in almost a straight line as we staggered up to fourteen thousand feet. Funny thing was, I never thought anything would happen to me—you always thought getting shot down or running out of fuel would happen to the other guy. Looking back now, I guess it was foolish thinking, but it was the only way for me to survive.

The scoreboard of Air Group 2 shows a very impressive tally.

HIT THEM HARD!

At about 6:30 p.m., our air group commander, flying above the Japanese fleet in an F6F Hellcat, became more of a band conductor as he called out our targets. Both divisions of our VB-2 Helldiver squadron were called upon to attack the Japanese carrier *Zuikaku*—one of the flattops used in the attack on Pearl Harbor. By the time we arrived, it looked like a super Fourth of July celebration going off all around us. They welcomed us with such a heavy barrage of antiaircraft shells that it actually darkened the already fading light. The *Zuikaku* was in a big, wide turn as we set up our bombing run. Naturally, because I was the tail-end Charlie in my division, I had to wait for the other seven Helldivers in front of me to go before I pushed on over.

A Helldiver over Guam on the way to yet another target.

I decided to go with what had worked for me in the past. I pushed the Helldiver over, kept my speed up, and buttoned my canopy up tight. I was really moving, going hell-bent for everything I could get at full power, as the deck of the carrier grew larger in my sight. I opened the bomb-bay doors and released the half-ton bomb, sending it hurtling for the carrier's deck. I began to pull out and found that my stick wouldn't budge—it was as if it had been set in cement. Try as I might, I couldn't get it to move. I was losing altitude fast, and in desperation I put both my feet up on the dashboard and reefed the stick back with all my might. As I began to level out only one hundred feet off the water, a new problem developed right in front of me—a Japanese cruiser was dead ahead, firing her five-inch guns at me.

I remember thinking, as I zoomed on by with my airspeed indicator bouncing off the stops, that they were a bunch of fools wasting such a big gun on a tiny airplane. By now it was just about dark, with no sign of the setting sun, and I became an even harder target to hit. I asked Frenchy if we had hit the target, and he replied, "Yeah, looks to me like you hit it mid-ship." I felt good about that, especially considering the firestorm from hell we had to fly through. I used the excessive speed from my dive to gain some altitude and zoomed back up to 7,500 feet. The sky was dark, and there wasn't another airplane I could see anywhere around me—it was awful lonesome up there.

BEGGARS CAN'T BE CHOOSERS

As I watched the needle on my fuel gauge slump to one side, I was giving the Helldiver no more rpm than necessary to stay in the air and no more fuel than necessary to keep the prop turning. I was flying toward the location I thought our carriers were supposed to be and had been droning alone in the black sky for what seemed like an eternity. All of a sudden, I saw another aircraft crossing in front of me and thought he must really be lost. I thought, "Oh hell, I might as well be lost with him," as I turned to follow him—and it's good thing I did, because he led me right to a carrier. I could see a small red light on the stern as he made his turn into the groove. As I began to make my own pattern and went past the carrier, the guy in front of me caught the wire and then all hell broke loose. He'd forgotten to safety his guns and tracers were flying all around!

I wasn't about to fly all this way only to get shot down by one of my own, so I stayed clear until the shooting stopped. I made my turn up the groove, and it felt like I was chugging along trying to catch up to the flight deck. When I finally got there, I made the best carrier landing in my career—I had to, since I didn't have enough fuel to make another go around. As the deck hands moved me forward, some kid jumped up on my wing and directed me well past the barrier, and I thought for a second he was going to run me off the bow. As we came to a stop, he looked at me, then looked up and down at the Helldiver and said in a very excited voice, "Hey, you can't land here! This is the USS *Enterprise*, and we can't handle an SB2C!" I smiled at him and said, "Shove it over the side if you like, but I ain't leaving tonight!"

This Helldiver belongs to the Commemorative Air Force (CAF) and is the only example still flying. *Jim Koepnick*

Helldivers also flew with the British Royal Navy.

Frenchy and I had just settled down with a shot of brandy when the world turned upside down—Admiral Mitscher had ordered all the other ships to turn their lights on. Unfortunately, once the lights came on, everybody wanted to get aboard at the same time. It was chaotic in large capital letters. There were airplanes racing to beat one another to the deck, and this caused the decks to be fouled with crash landings as airplanes ran into one another. With no fuel left in their tanks and nowhere else to land, many of the airplanes had to ditch. It was pitiful to watch.

HELLDIVER CIRCUS

For two days, Frenchy and I enjoyed the hospitality aboard the USS *Enterprise* while the crew sorted out the deck, trying to get the airplanes back to their home carriers. When it was our turn to go, they threw in a couple cups of gas for the short flight back to the *Hornet*. As I warmed the engine, I noticed large crowds of sailors gathering up and down the deck and on the catwalks. I had been the first Helldiver to ever land on the *Enterprise*, and now I was about to be the first one to attempt a take-off. I knew the real reason they were watching me: they thought the big beast of a Helldiver would end up in the drink.

With hardly any fuel on board and no bomb load to speak of, however, I knew they would all be disappointed. As I began my deck run, I had the Helldiver flying by the time I got to the forward elevator and had my gear up by the time we passed the bow. I laughed all the way to the *Hornet*!

Unfortunately, when I got back, I found out just how costly this mission had been. Of the fourteen SB2Cs launched from the *Hornet*, only two remained intact, the other twelve ditching or crashing on deck. I was one of the lucky ones, I guess, and had a newfound respect for the Helldiver—it always brought me back in one piece.

For the June 20 mission, Foster Looney was awarded the Navy Cross:

> Action Date: 20-Jun-44
> Service: Naval Reserve
> Rank: Lieutenant Junior Grade
> Company: Bombing Fighting Squadron 2 (VBF-2)
> Regiment: Air Group 2 (AG-2)
> Division: USS Hornet (CV-12)

> The President of the United States of America takes pleasure in presenting the Navy Cross to Lieutenant, Junior Grade [then Ensign] Foster "E" Looney, United States Naval Reserve, for extraordinary heroism in operations against the enemy while serving as Pilot of a carrier-based Navy Dive Bomber in Bombing Squadron TWO (VB-2), attached to the U.S.S. HORNET (CV-12), during action against enemy Japanese forces in the First Battle of the Philippine Sea, on 20 June 1944. Undaunted by hostile anti-aircraft fire, Lieutenant, Junior Grade, Looney carried out a dive bombing attack against major units of the Japanese Fleet and scored a direct hit to assist in the destruction of a large enemy carrier, later returning safe to his base in darkness. By his skill as an airman and devotion to duty, Lieutenant, Junior Grade, Looney upheld the highest traditions of the United States Naval Service.

> General Orders: Commander Fast Carrier
> Task Force: Serial 0438 (August 20, 1944)

Foster spent less than six months in combat and completed over thirty-seven carrier landings in the Helldiver. He passed away on February 6, 2014.

WORLD AT WAR: With Allied bombers and their fighter escorts swarming all over Axis targets from bases in England, Italy and Germany tried valiantly to stem the flow of these bomber streams that stretched for miles and miles. Unable to handle the ever-increasing workload, the Luftwaffe enlisted the assistance of their shrinking Axis cronies.

THE SUMMER OF HELL OVER HUNGARY

LIFE AND DEATH OF THE PUMAS

LIEUTENANT MIHALY (MICHAEL) KARATSONYI, ROYAL HUNGARIAN AIR FORCE
BF 109

Michael was born in 1923, in Nagykőrös, Pest County, Hungary, and joined the Royal Hungarian Air Force while he was still in high school in 1939. Michael had dreamed of becoming a pilot, and his mother thought he had lost his mind!

LEARNING THE ROPES IN THE BF 109

I remember growing up in Hungary and thinking we were stuck between a rock and a hard place when World War II broke out. My father had been a veteran of World War I and was taken prisoner by the Russians, so I grew up listening to his horror stories of being a POW in Siberia. Needless to say, our family despised the communist Russians, but we also wondered if Adolf Hitler was any better. By the time I became involved with the war, the Germans were well entrenched in our country, and, like it or not, we were now a part of the Axis.

Hungary became a vital manufacturer of war materiel for Germany that included tanks, artillery pieces, ammunition, and airplanes. In late 1943, after earning my wings with the Royal Hungarian Air Force, I became very fond of one of those airplanes: the Bf 109. I was taught how to fight and survive in the German-designed fighter by a group of seasoned Luftwaffe Battle of Britain veterans. Because there were no two-seat versions of the 109, they gave us a cockpit checkout and schooled us on what to do and what not to do, especially on takeoff.

Taking off in a 109 demanded your complete attention when you put the throttle forward. The cockpit was cramped and very snug, so much so that I had to fly with my head tilted forward in order for my crew

A mechanic fastens the cowling on a Bf 109 belonging to the Puma Squadron while the pilot waits at the controls.

chief to close the canopy—it felt as if you were an appendage of the airplane. The forward visibility was adequate at best over the nose, and the rearward visibility was even worse; without a wingman along as another set of eyes, you were completely blind. Our Luftwaffe instructors taught us the motto, "Two planes equal one plane, one plane equals none." The wingman's sole responsibility was to watch the flight leader's back while he was busy shooting. Without a wingman next to you, your chances of survival were slim to none.

We were warned that because of the narrow gear and the torque of the 1,500-horsepower Delmar Benz engine pulling us to the left, we had to be quick with the brakes just to keep it rolling straight ahead. I must admit that after I survived my first take-off and began to get the feel of the 109, I became very much at home inside this fighter. It would be a "home" I would occupy until the end of the war.

JOINING THE PUMAS

My early combat was primarily against Soviet MiGs, Yaks, and Lavochkin La-5 fighters. Unfortunately, our air force was not as well organized as that of our Luftwaffe counterparts, and we lacked coordination with other fighter units. Most of these Hungarian units consisted of Me 110s and Me 210s from different fields spread across Hungary. The resistance we put up was sporadic and haphazard, and the enemy fighters mauled the whole lot of them. Because our fighter tactics were deemed unsuitable for defending the skies over our homeland, and because the American Fifteenth Air Force fighters and bombers were now operating from bases in Italy, all of our fighter units were merged into one under Luftwaffe control.

In early May of 1944, the elite 101st Home Defense Fighter Wing was created, and we became known as the Pumas. There were three separate squadrons consisting of twelve Bf 109s in each group along with a handful of spares. Our fighters were all Hungarian-built Bf 109G models, and our paint schemes were similar to the Luftwaffe 109s except that we carried no swastikas, and instead of a German cross we had a black square with a white cross inside—from a distance, no one could tell the difference. I was posted with 101st Fighter Group, 3rd Squadron, and we operated with the rest of the Puma squadrons from our base near Veszprém, just to the north of Lake Balaton. Unfortunately, this large lake situated in the middle of our country was also a landmark for inbound B-24s and B-17s as they made their way from Italy to targets in Hungary, Austria, Romania, Germany, and Poland. Our field was surrounded by trees and hard to see from the air, however, so the bombers left us alone. We, on the other hand, went after them every day.

AERIAL COMBAT: BOMBERS

Our radars could see the Americans forming up over Italy as they made their way toward Hungary. We always had ample warning and didn't take off until they reached the Yugoslavian border, preserving our precious fuel for the impending combat. When we did, we headed for the Austrian border, climbing away from the American flight track. Our hope was that we would join up with fellow Luftwaffe fighters coming down from Austria, allowing us to create a much bigger formation to attack the bomber stream with; we very seldom had a chance to meet up with the Luftwaffe.

By the time we turned back toward Hungary, we would already be over thirty thousand feet. The American bombers, mainly B-17s and B-24s, were relatively close, and

Mihaly Karatsonyi straddles the cowling of his Bf 109 and works on his propeller spinner. Many times, the pilots had to assist in keeping their airplanes in airworthy condition.

most of our combat was either north or south of Lake Balaton. When I saw all those tiny black dots in the distance, my stomach would tighten because I knew something bad was heading my way. The sky was blackened with the massive bomber stream, and unfortunately for us, they always brought fighter escorts with them. Early on, it was the P-38 Lightnings; later, P-51 Mustangs shepherded the bombers. Our orders were not to tangle with the fighters and instead go after the bombers, but inevitably we would end up in a dogfight because there were so many of them and so few of us.

I usually saw the B-17s on the outer sides of the formation with the B-24s in the middle, and I gathered that was because of all the guns on the B-17. We, too, called them Flying Fortresses because of the massive firepower they carried. I never had a desire to attack them from the rear because I figured that would give the gunners more time to aim and shoot at me. Instead, I made my attacks either from the sides or head-on. I preferred the head-on attacks, not only because the closure speeds between the two of us were very high, but also because the gunners would shoot wildly at us as we zoomed on by.

On my very first combat mission, we attacked a formation of B-17s from the side with the sun at our backs. It was surreal because it was dead quiet as I pushed the nose of my 109 closer to the bombers. I figured the gunners must have thought we were P-51s because our silhouettes were very similar. But once I started shooting with my machine guns and cannon, the whole sky erupted in color. Every gunner in that bomber box opened up on me, and the sky reminded me of a Fourth of July fireworks show—except this was not for enjoyment; it was life and death. By the time we finished our attacks on the bombers, the fighters were there waiting for us. Although we tried to go after boxes of bombers that appeared to have no escorts, all they had to do was radio for help and the "cavalry" would be on its way to the rescue.

P-38 LIGHTNINGS

The P-38 was well respected by us because of its tremendous combination of four .50-caliber machine guns and one twenty-millimeter cannon in its nose. We adopted a hit-and-run tactic to deal with the Lightnings, because if you stuck around and tried to fight them, you might end up outmaneuvering two or three of them, but there were always a dozen or more lurking in the shadows, waiting to latch on to your tail. If you hung around too long, you were dead!

On one mission, there were three of us in our 109s at thirty thousand feet. We had just come off an attack from the bombers when we spotted a large formation of Lightnings—over thirty of them—below us. The P-38s spotted us as well, and they suddenly went into this great big defensive circle, with one P-38 behind the other going round and round.

Although there were a lot more of them than us, we held the advantage with our altitude and diving capabilities. Our Luftwaffe teachers who had seen combat over England taught us to exploit the diving capabilities of the 109. We pushed our noses over and dove headlong into the center of the Lightning circle, knowing full well there was no way they could catch us.

I picked out a P-38 and began to fire. I observed strikes on the Lightning and saw that I must have done some serious damage to it because it lurched up and suddenly rolled over onto another P-38. Both P-38s spiraled out of the formation as the three of us in our 109s went through the center of the wagon train without a scratch. I wish I could say the same when I tangled with a group of P-51s a few weeks later.

MUSTANG MAYHEM: AUGUST 7, 1944

As usual, the American bombers were heading our way from Italy. And, as usual, we were outnumbered. For every week that we survived combat, we were granted one day off, but I always traded my day off with someone else because I didn't want anyone else flying my 109!

There were only seventeen of us left in the Puma group to attack the bomber stream, and on today's mission, our job was to escort a group of Luftwaffe Bf 109 heavy fighters carrying additional machine guns in underwing pods. The fighters were out in front of us and three hundred feet below us. I was fortunate in that I had some of the best eyesight in the unit, and I spotted a flight of four Mustangs above and behind us—but my eyes must have been playing tricks on me because the four suddenly turned into twelve and then into thirty-six shiny P-51s. There was no way to warn the Luftwaffe fighters ahead of us, because our groups operated with different radio frequencies. After we radioed our headquarters telling them of our dilemma and asking for instructions, we were simply told to "Keep your formation!" As I looked into some of the faces of the other 109 pilots around me, I could see the looks of despair as we all realized we would probably die on this mission.

The Mustangs pushed over and began their attack on us. I was flying wing on my leader and good friend, Lt. Laszlo Molnar, a proven ace with the Pumas. Our squadron was in the first row of 109s, and Molnar sped ahead to warn the Luftwaffe planes about what was coming—he never made it, however, as a pack of Mustangs latched onto him. I tried to block the Mustangs' shots by pulling up and into them, firing wildly to scare them off, but they just kept hammering away at him. By the time I got turned back around, my leader and good friend was already dead. I dived away, passing through ten thousand feet, and thought I was home free. Suddenly, I saw another 109 being chased by two Mustangs. There was no way I could turn my back on a fellow 109 pilot, so I yanked my aircraft around in a hard turn and watched as the Mustangs began to fill my gun sight.

I picked out the lead Mustang and began to fire, my machine gun and cannon rounds tearing into him. The P-51

A handful of Puma Bf 109s head out to meet the never-ending Allied bomber stream.

began to smoke, but before I could celebrate my success, my 109 was mauled by a vicious pack of Mustangs who had sneaked up behind me. I felt a tremendous jerk as the bullets tore into my 109. I skidded my fighter sideways and looked back—all I saw was Mustangs on my tail. By the time I turned my head forward again, my cockpit was engulfed in smoke and flame; the fuel line on my left side had taken a direct hit. My only thought was, *I've got to get out of here!*

Luckily, I had pulled my oxygen mask off earlier when the Mustangs

Puma pilots take a rare and well-deserved break between missions. By war's end, only a handful of original Puma pilots were still alive.

had attacked my leader. Had I still had it on, the heat from the fire would have eventually melted it onto my face. The Mustangs were relentless and continued to shoot at me. Instinctively, I pushed my 109 over into a steep dive and began to perform a series of evasive turns to try to shake these guys. The fire inside became more intense, so I pulled the canopy lever and it flew off behind me. Suddenly, I was pulled upward as well, but my shoulder harnesses were holding me back—I was literally floating above my cockpit! There was no way I was going to let myself crash in this position, so with all my strength I pushed my arms forward and slammed my hands into my buckle release—I was free from my burning fighter.

I was falling backward with my face to the sky. As I reached for my parachute release, I couldn't find where it was supposed to be; I finally opened my eyes and was amazed to see the release cord bobbing up and down in front of me. I reached out with both hands and pulled as hard as I could—my chute opened, and seconds later I slammed into a tree, plowing through the branches. Thankfully, my chute had snagged on a limb which slowed my descent. I remember becoming very upset because I had wanted to look up and see what a parachute looked like billowing in the wind. With my adrenaline still flowing, I was amazed that I didn't have a scratch on me; that was until I looked down and saw that my pants had been completely burned off of me. The pain from the other parts of my body began to creep in, and, although I was alive, I figured I looked like hell. It would turn out that I had third-degree burns on 40 percent of my body.

I was picked up and placed into a buggy that was pulled by a team of oxen and taken to a hospital. I learned later that out of the seventeen planes that took off that day, only four were in flyable condition for the next day's combat—it was one of the worst days of combat for the Pumas.

THE END IS NEAR

It took me a couple of months to recuperate from my injuries. By the time winter arrived, we had been forced to flee into Austria, since the Russians had overrun our ground troops and were now inside of Hungary. I went back on flying status in February of 1945, after much groveling with my commanders—they were short of pilots, so they took what they could get!

I continued to fly missions in Bf 109s, but this time it was all against Russian fighters. Most of my friends in the Pumas were dead, and I quickly found out that things would never be the same again. After the war ended, and I did my time as a POW, I learned that out of the original forty Puma members, only three of us survived the war. Later, I immigrated to the United States and eventually became good friends with a couple of Fifteenth Air Force P-51 pilots, Bob Gobel and Art Fiedler. Although they had tried to kill me on a daily basis so many years ago, we all became friends. It's funny how war can end up in such irony.

Michael Karatsonyi was credited with five aerial victories while flying with the Royal Hungarian Air Force. He passed away on May 29, 2005.

WORLD AT WAR: The military use of aerial observers in spotting and selecting targets over the battlefield was an old and well-proven tactic long before World War II erupted. Men in flimsy wicker baskets hung below canvas balloons tethered to terra firma. Looking through telescopes, they searched for the enemy, and when they found them, they shouted out their position to the artillerymen on the ground. The use of balloons for spotting seemed to work well until the airplanes showed up in the sky.

The armies of the world soon realized that balloons shot at by enemy aircraft didn't stay inflated very long and burned rather quickly. The survival rate for these observers was extremely low, with no one volunteering to take their place. The emerging use of aircraft for artillery spotting put the balloons out of business and gave the pilot/observer a higher rate of survival. However, flying over the front lines in a lightly armed or unarmed slow-moving aircraft contained its own set of problems. Flak, small-arms fire, and enemy fighters proved to be a daily threat to these aircraft, most of which could not defend themselves.

With the inevitable invasion of occupied Europe still on the horizon, the US Navy began to develop a new type of observation platform. This multitalented airplane could not only observe and report on the battle conditions below but could also spot gunfire, dive-bomb, strafe, and defend itself against the best Axis fighters thrown at it, all while providing close ground support for the troops below. The winning feature of this plan, however, was in the simple fact that the navy didn't have to wait years for a suitable aircraft to be developed. The answer came from a well-proven Pacific fighter: the Grumman F6F Hellcat. Here is a story from one of the original members of Observation Fighter-1 (VOF-1) who flew combat missions during the invasion of southern France.

STRANGERS IN A STRANGE LAND

USN HELLCATS OVER FRANCE

LIEUTENANT COMMANDER ALFRED R. WOOD, USNR (RET.)
GRUMMAN F6F HELLCAT

Alfred Wood was born in 1922 and resided in Yonkers, New York, before joining the US Navy Reserve. After earning his gold wings, he was sent to carrier qualification in 1943.

In 1943, I was part of a navy operational class assigned to carrier-qualify the F4U Corsair. The Corsair was a lot of airplane, especially with its long nose, which housed a two-thousand-horsepower engine. The early Corsairs also had some problems at slow speed that could prove dangerous and even deadly when it came time to land them aboard the carriers.

When our squadron was sent to the Great Lakes to carrier-qualify on the USS *Wolverine*, we had to leave our bent-wing Corsairs behind and use SNJs instead. Our Corsairs were just too much airplane for the *Wolverine*'s short, narrow deck. Flying the slow-moving SNJs seemed surreal compared to the brute-like performance of the Corsairs. In fact, to lower the tail hook on the SNJ, we had to unravel a clothesline that was connected to an armrest inside the cockpit and ran outside down the length of the fuselage to the tail. And these were modern airplanes?!

Just when our squadron was ready to be assigned to a carrier, we were derailed and sidetracked. The navy was having potential problems with landing accidents in the Corsair, so most of our squadron was disbanded and sent to other groups. While they sorted out the F4U's teething problems, I was reassigned to VOF-1 and qualified in the F6F Hellcat.

After successfully slugging it out with the Luftwaffe in his Hellcat, Al Wood receives a well-deserved medal.

Compared to the Hellcat, the Corsair was a lot more airplane and very sensitive to the touch; you just had to rub your hand on the stick a little and it would maneuver any way you wanted it to. It was a faster fighter, but not quite as tight in turns as the F6F. When you flew the Corsair, you had to say to yourself, "Hey, I'm the boss of this thing," and fly it all the way to the deck. The powers that be thought the Hellcat would be a safer plane in low and tight turn conditions and possibly on small carrier decks.

Although we were designated an observation squadron, we still packed a deadly punch. Before we were formed, the navy observation planes we had didn't last very long over the battlefield. They were underpowered and unarmed, and when we lost an airplane, we usually lost the pilot as well. The idea behind using a fighter plane and a pilot trained properly in artillery spotting was twofold.

Our primary mission was to work with our naval ships and army artillery units in spotting targets and directing their shells onto a concentrated area. Once that was completed, we were unleashed to bomb, strafe, and provide close air support to the guys fighting below. The greatest feature of flying a fighter for observation was that if we encountered enemy aircraft, we could turn into them and fight instead of turning away and running. Try that in an army L-4 Cub!

One of the main architects for this new tactic was Rear Adm. Calvin T. Durgin, USN. Admiral Durgin had been flying for over twenty-five years and understood the importance of directing gunfire while maintaining aerial superiority. He was no stranger to battle, either, as he had commanded the aircraft carrier USS *Ranger* during the North African landings. To become proficient in artillery spotting, we were sent to Fort Sill, Oklahoma, where we cross-trained with US Army artillery units and became very good at zeroing in on targets.

In July of 1944, we were deemed ready for combat and loaded aboard the USS *Tulagi*—a Kaiser-built Jeep carrier—setting sail for parts unknown. D-Day and the invasion of Normandy had already occurred a month before we left the United States, and we had no idea where we were headed until we received our briefing in the middle of the Atlantic. Our destination was the Mediterranean, and our mission was to take part in the invasion of southern France.

Our US Navy F6F Hellcats were well known in the skies above the Pacific for tearing the Japanese apart. But in Europe, nobody knew what the hell they were, either Allied or Axis! This was an Army Air Corps theater, not a navy one, and we felt like strangers in a strange land. We were no strangers when it came to fighting a war, though, and were well prepared for what lay ahead: Operation Anvil-Dragoon.

The area and landscape we were tasked with invading was totally different from the Channel Invasion. Instead of Allied air bases only a hop, a skip, and a jump away, like those in England during the Normandy invasion, our closest land base was in Italy, hundreds of miles away. To counter this shortcoming, our task force included another US carrier—USS *Kassan Bay*—with its complement of F6F Hellcats. Our Allied air armada also included a number of British carriers equipped with Supermarine Seafires and Curtiss Helldivers to round out our air strength.

We were further surrounded by destroyers and cruisers that moved into their positions in the morning and swung their big guns toward the beaches and German fortifications that were strung out along the landing zone as zero hour approached. In

Al, standing back row, fourth from the right, along with his fellow squadron mates of VOF-1.

the early-morning hours of August 15, 1944, our navy guns erupted as multiple shells rained down and pounded German forts near the landing zones on French soil. When they let go with those big guns, it must have felt like a small earthquake to the Germans below who survived the first volley.

As we orbited over our predesignated targets, directing the naval shells onto them, the Germans responded with accurate bursts of flak that raked a number of Hellcats in our squadron, creating numerous small holes in the wings and fuselages. Thankfully, the planes were built Grumman tough and never missed a beat! When the navy guns fell silent, it was our turn for a little payback, and I pushed my Hellcat over to make a bombing run on a German fort. The trick was to release your bomb right into the center of the fort; if you did it right, the resulting explosion would spread out from the center and tear the place apart. As we destroyed the German installations one by one, out along and near the beaches, the guys on the ground maintained a foothold and pushed the Germans off the sand. The race inland had begun.

We thought the Germans would stand and fight. We thought the Luftwaffe would be up in force to repel our landing attempts. We thought we would encounter stiff resistance on the ground and in the air. We thought wrong. The Germans were in a full-blown retreat, hightailing it out of southern France. They really slowed themselves up by not wanting to leave their equipment behind, however. With no air cover to protect their run back to Germany, our targets of opportunity were never-ending.

Troop trains, freight trains, convoys of trucks, and motorized vehicles were all heading north. Our Hellcats were loaded with 250-, 500-, and 1,000-pound bombs along with the six .50-caliber machine guns in our wings. We dropped everything we could on them, and when we ran out of bombs—because there were so many targets—we strafed with our machine guns. And if that wasn't enough, we turned back into the stalled traffic and strafed them until we were out of ammo.

Hundreds and hundreds of trains and rail cars, along with countless trucks, tracks, and bridges, were destroyed by our Hellcats as we just about immobilized the fleeing Germans. By the end of the first day, more than 94,000 troops and eleven thousand vehicles had made it to the shore. By the end of the third day, that number climbed to 130,000 men and eighteen thousand vehicles, all hot on the heels of the fleeing Germans. The farther inland we flew, the better the German camouflage became.

Normally we operated at around three thousand feet when we spotted for the navy guns and the army artillery pieces. The big army guns were now firmly in place and pointed toward the runaway Germans. When we began to see "moving forests"—trains covered in foliage—we had to get right on the deck to spot these German goodies. The Germans really knew how to use camouflage to their advantage, but, as we learned in one instance, they didn't know much about farming!

One of our pilots in the squadron was a farm boy from Kansas named Lt. j.g. Dale Dietrich. Out on patrol one day, he spotted a clump of bushes and trees in the middle of a plowed field. What caught his attention was that the plow furrows ran right through the foliage instead of around it. It didn't take long for other Hellcats to show up, and they shot up German cars and trucks hidden beneath the greenery. Smoke and flame quickly engulfed the now-exposed convoy.

We flew from sunup to sundown, and I soon realized that flying in a deep, dark-blue F6F with white numbers and big white stars and bars on the sides and wings didn't stop our own troops from firing on us. On more occasions than I care to remember, we were mistaken for Fw 190s and riddled with friendly gunfire!

On the other hand, our Fw 190 resemblance worked in our favor when we bounced unsuspecting German convoys. When we were about to hit one convoy, they held their fire and waved at us, thinking we were "flat-hatting Focke-Wulfs" buzzing their motorcade. I'm sure they realized who we were when we saluted back with machine guns and

An F6F Hellcat about to catch a wire upon landing.

Hard hitting and relatively easy to fly, with great maneuverability, the Hellcat was a favorite among US Navy pilots.

rockets, and on the next pass they opened up with everything they had. The flak was accurate and deadly, and several of the Hellcats were lost by German flak during our two-week operation. In fact, one of our pilots was shot down and picked up by the Free French, who returned him through France and Spain, and he met us on our return to Quonset Point NAS.

We also managed to put our fighter pilot skills to use against the seldom-seen Luftwaffe. On August 19, 1944, (D+5) I was part of a reconnaissance flight near Lyons when I spotted a Heinkel 111 bomber five hundred feet below me. I was going one way and he was going the other way in a big hurry. In fact, this 111 looked like he was hell-bent for election to get out of France and head north! I called the section leader, Lt. Rene Poucel, and said, "Arm your guns, turn around, and let's go!"

Lieutenant Poucel replied back, "Oh my!" and we both turned into the low-flying bomber.

The 111 was still below us at just over one thousand feet above the ground as he tried to sneak under us. He didn't make it very far before I went for his left engine and walked my hits to the right; my bullets tore into the cockpit and both engines, and the flames began to spread across the bomber. Lieutenant Poucel's hits were a mirror image of mine, and the Heinkel burned and fell apart in midair. Five minutes later, I spotted another He 111.

Our section had split up after we shot the first bomber down, and I found myself alone again, looking for targets on the ground. I saw another 111 below me—he was trying to fly away unnoticed, but it didn't work. I rolled my Hellcat over and went down after him. I had a perfect tail shot as I closed in behind him, not even noticing the rear

An F6F Hellcat is catapult-launched from a lower hanger deck as the ship's sailors watch from above.

gunner shooting at me. His guns fell silent as I opened up with my .50-calibers from one hundred yards out. That's when both engines blew up.

Flame and black smoke poured out of the crippled bomber as it nosed over. The pilot bailed out and went whizzing by me as I followed the bomber down. When the 111 "flying torch" neared the ground, I broke off my pursuit and watched it crash into a railroad station below, blowing that up, too! It was a helluva feeling to knock two Luftwaffe bombers out of the sky—both good and bad, but that was our job and that's what we trained to do.

I still had a lot of ammunition left and a lot of targets on the ground to shoot up, and it didn't take long to find something else to shoot at as we helped push the Germans out of southern France. We had been in combat almost two weeks and destroyed over 487 motor vehicles and two hundred locomotives and train coaches; cut five bridges; and silenced countless gun emplacements. We did a lot better than anybody ever figured we would. It was something new, and no one had ever done it before, since we were the first US Navy spotting squadron, and we proved the theory of using fighters in that role to perfection. Because of our initial success, Admiral Durgin, who treated us like his kids, promised to throw us a party of parties when we got to our new destination. Our squadron was redesignated VOC-1, and with the new name came new planes—FM2 Wildcats. We used the same tactics learned in Europe to defeat the Japanese in the Pacific Island campaign, and, as promised, we had one helluva party on Guam. At the reception, I received a gift from Admiral Durgin that read as follows:

> The President of the United States takes pleasure in presenting the Distinguished Flying Cross to Lieutenant, Junior Grade, Alfred Robie Wood, United States Naval Reserve, for service as set forth in the following Citation: for heroism and extraordinary achievement in aerial flight as pilot of a carrier-based fighter bomber plane during the allied invasion of Southern France of August 1944. Participating in armed reconnaissance flights in the Rhone River area, Lieutenant, Junior Grade (then Ensign) Wood boldly penetrated deep in enemy territory to execute 14 perilous missions in thirteen days. Despite the hazards of intense enemy antiaircraft fire, he personally destroyed a twin-engine bomber and coordinated with his section leader in destroying another. Steadfastly continuing on the same mission, he aided in destroying a locomotive, ten railroad cars and twenty-two motor vehicles. His skill, determination and outstanding devotion to duty were in keeping with the highest traditions of the United States Naval Service.

> Signed, James Forrestal, Secretary of the Navy

My squadron mates and I received many more medals as we spotted, strafed, and rocketed the Japanese back north to their home islands during our tour in the Pacific. We were no longer strangers in aerial observation but pioneers in a new form of warfare that would be carried on in future wars for years to come.

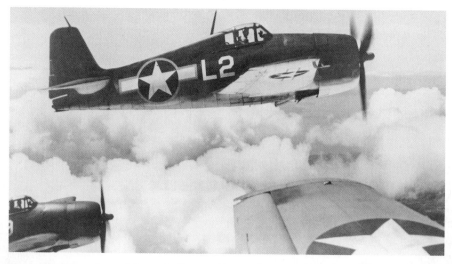

Grumman delivered one of the war's all-around best and most deadly fighters when it produced the F6F.

Hellcats in a hard left turn search for their carrier after another combat mission.

Al Wood was credited with 1.5 victories over the Luftwaffe and passed away on April 26, 2009.

WORLD AT WAR: The telltale battle scars from World War II, both on the ground and in the seas, are still clearly evident today. Concrete bunkers, rusting hulks of ships, and the remnants of machinery and weapons used by a determined Axis and unified Allies still litter the battlefields and waters where men fought and died some seventy years ago. Only one arena remains intact and undisturbed, as if nothing had ever happened, despite the fierce battles between men and machines hammering and clawing away at one another, turning, twisting, and burning with shells exploding all around. Only this domain bears no sign of any combat: the sky above.

Long gone are the thousands of heavy bombers pulling billowing white contrails on their way to targets over occupied Europe. Gone are the black-and-gray bursts of flak that darkened the skies and destroyed countless Allied aircraft, and the thick, oily black smoke and red flame that poured from a crippled bomber as Luftwaffe fighters swarmed over it with their cannon and machine-gun rounds tearing pieces of aluminum and Plexiglas from its deformed wings and fuselage, sending it cartwheeling through the sky. Missing, too, are the airmen covered in blood with broken and missing limbs, struggling to survive as they hurled themselves out of their dying bombers into the freezing atmosphere, praying that their parachutes would open or that death would come quickly.

These battles ended as quickly as they began, and the winds and clouds wiped the aerial battlefield clean, leaving no evidence that death and destruction ever took place. Combat reports and the vivid memories from the survivors are all that remain to tell the tale of what took place high above the war-torn skies.

CALAMITY OVER KASSEL

ANNIHILATION OF THE 445TH BOMB GROUP

CAPTAIN WILLIAM R. DEWEY, USAAC (RET.)
CONSOLIDATED B-24 LIBERATOR

William Dewey was born on October 5, 1922. After earning his wings, he became a B-24 pilot and was sent to England in August 1944 as a replacement. He didn't have much of a chance to get to know the other pilots before being thrust into combat.

Bill Dewey at the controls of the four-engined Consolidated B-24 Liberator.

I flew my first combat mission on August 16, 1944, at the controls of a B-24 Liberator 150 miles south of Berlin. I was twenty-one years old, an airplane commander with the 445th Bomb Group, 701st Squadron, in charge of nine men whose lives depended on me to deliver them safely to the target and back. I was so scared as I prepared for my first mission that I didn't know whether I was supposed to put my flak suit on while we were still on the ground or wait until we got in the air. One of the old-timers on my crew—those with ten or more missions under their belts—just snickered at me and told me to wait until we made landfall over Europe. Flak was everywhere on that first mission, and we took a beating on the bomb run to the target.

Formation flying in the B-24 was tough enough work even without someone shooting at you because of the flight characteristics of that thin Davis wing. You had to work at it continuously, flying the plane every second. It was a harder plane to fly than the B-17, but it had those dependable Pratt & Whitney engines, which really made the difference. Once you mastered formation flying and knew how to regulate your throttles to minimize fuel consumption, you could relax somewhat and concentrate on the guy next to you—but it was difficult to relax too much while flying through a flak-filled sky. Our group flew into a one-hundred-mile per hour headwind as we started our run in on the target.

Our target that day was a railroad yard, and the mission should have been a five-minute bomb run. Instead it took fifteen minutes from the initial point—IP—because of the strong winds. The Germans had 155-millimeter railroad-mounted flak guns strung out along the rails on flat cars, and they all opened up on us at once. Flying at a snail's pace gave the German gunners a slower, easier target, one that was hard to miss. The flak was so heavy that it peppered my crew's B-24, turning it into Swiss cheese. We had holes all over the wings and fuselage, but at least we were still flying. Two other B-24s collided after being hit by flak, and a third was blown out of the sky by a direct hit. It was a bad day for the 445th BG, and the worst was yet to come.

In the early-morning hours of September 27, 1944, our base at Tibenham, like most of the bomber and fighter bases across England, was busy preparing for another strike against Hitler's Fortress Europe. This was my eighth mission, and although I was still scared, I now knew what to expect and when to put my flak suit on! At the morning briefing, when the curtain draped over the large map was pulled back, it showed a red line of thread from our base to our target. Looking at the route, I knew this would be no milk run! Our target for today was the Henschel locomotive works at the rail yards in Kassel, Germany.

The plan of attack was to have the 2nd and 3rd Air Division cross the continent on a southeast course parallel to one another, flying 125 miles apart. The 1st Division was to follow about ninety miles behind and fly between the tracks of the other two divisions as they bombed Cologne. Because the 2nd and 3rd flew to deeper targets in advance of the 1st, they effectively screened the 1st from any enemy attack. After the 2nd Division bombed Kassel, they were to turn south and fall in behind the 3rd Division as the bomber stream headed back to England. Unfortunately for our group, we didn't follow the plan.

The 2nd Bombardment Division put up 315 B-24s, including those of the 700th, 701st, 702nd, and 703rd Bomb Squadrons belonging to the 445th BG. It was a maximum effort for all of us as we flew against the industrial targets of Germany. Over one thousand B-24s and B-17s would be sent out and escorted by half as many P-51s, P-47s, and P-38s to take care of the Luftwaffe. German fighters had been the least of our concerns for quite a while.

In fact, the last time the 445th had encountered the Luftwaffe was on February 13, 1944, when thirteen of our B-24s were shot down. Eventually, because of the long-range fighter escorts and the absence of enemy fighters, the ball turrets were removed from the bellies of the B-24s in the 2nd Combat Wing. We traded the weight of these turrets for a higher bomb load and less wind resistance, which gave us greater range. However, the tradeoff proved to be a deadly mistake on this mission.

The 445th was led by the 700th BS with Maj. Donald McCoy and Capt. John Chilton flying as group lead. Behind them was the 702nd BS, flying high-right position. We were next in the 701st BS, flying the high-high-right position, and bringing up the rear was the 703rd BS in the low-left position. We normally flew a ten-plane formation in each squadron, but on this mission we started out with thirty-nine B-24s, and before long we had four aborts due to mechanical problems. We crossed the channel with thirty-five B-24s and entered the bomber stream.

B-24 Liberators on their way to the target area. Faster than the B-17 Flying Fortress, the B-24 could also fly farther.

I flew the left wing on the lead B-24 in our squadron as we made our way to Germany. Our column in the 2nd Division was sixty miles long overflying the continent. We picked up our "little friends" as Mustangs, Thunderbolts, and Lightnings S'ed back and forth overhead in a protective sweep. Most of the lead B-24s carried the Honeywell C-3 automatic pilot, and with a twist of a knob they could let the machine do the flying. All the rest of us had to rely on good throttle techniques. If you jockeyed your throttles back and forth, wasting fuel, you stood a good chance of going for a swim in the channel on the way home.

The cloud cover began to thicken as we got closer to Kassel. It was a solid undercast with a cloud base around three thousand feet and cloud tops approaching seven thousand feet. There was no way we could drop our bombs visually, so it was planned to drop the bombs on Kassel using the PFF "Mickey" radar in the lead ship. The lead B-24 carried three separate navigators. The "dead-reckoning" navigator was responsible for compositing his figures with those received from the Mickey navigator as he received them from his scope. The pilotage navigator was the third member, whose job was to provide a running double check on the exact position of the formation. Somehow, someone or something in that lead B-24 gave out the wrong information.

As our group neared the IP, there were B-24s in front of us and B-24s behind us with fighter escorts all around. We were supposed to make a turn toward Kassel, but for reasons unknown, Major McCoy in the lead B-24 turned and veered off course to the left, away from the primary target. The other groups ahead of us were now off to our right, dragging the fighter escorts with them. We could see the flak coming up through the clouds, bursting over Kassel as the rest of the bomber stream stayed on track.

The radio chatter came alive as plane after plane in our group called the leader and told him he was off course. Maybe his radar navigator had given him the wrong target; maybe by the time Major McCoy realized he turned the wrong way, it was too late to do anything about it. If he brought the group back around into the bomber stream, he risked the

Staying in tight formation not only allowed B-24 gunners to protect the formation better but also assured a tighter bombing pattern on the targets below.

possibility of running into other B-24s that were coming up from behind. We were now a rogue group, on our own, without fighter escort over northern Germany. What else could go wrong?

Major McCoy came back over the radio and said, "We will bomb as a unit. Keep in tight, and keep it together." We continued east toward our secondary target at Göttingen, which was twenty-five miles northeast of Kassel. We dropped our bombs on the lead plane's salvo and really clobbered it—or so we thought. Actually, the sum and substance of our bombs landed in a farmer's field and probably tore up his potato crop! We also managed to wound an ox that had to be shot because of its injuries.

Our group then began to make a series of turns to get back into the bomber stream and head back to England. One left turn followed by three rights really scattered the group all over the sky; as I flew in the high-high-right squadron at twenty-one thousand feet, we began to overrun the lower squadrons and soon found ourselves out and to the left of the rest of the group. This foul-up probably saved my life.

The first indication that something was wrong was when my tail gunner, Ruben Montanez, called out, "I see flak! I see fighters!" As it turned out, those "flak bursts" were actually twenty-millimeter cannon rounds screaming at us from a group of Fw 190s. They had come up through the undercast in waves of three or four—Fw 190s and Bf 109s flying wing tip to wing tip, thirty to thirty-five planes abreast like a cavalry charge, and all of them were firing at us. Our B-24 began to shake and shiver as our gunners responded, opening up on them with .50-caliber machine guns while the

Late-war B-24 with a natural aluminum finish, similar to the type Bill Dewey flew on that fateful mission.

German cannon and machine-gun rounds tore us apart. The doors to hell had been sprung wide open.

My copilot, Bill Boykin, began calling out the B-24s in the other squadrons falling out of the sky, twisting and burning. The Luftwaffe fighters that strayed too close also exploded as the intercom came alive with our gunners calling the enemy fighters out. Some of them were unseen, the Luftwaffe fighters coming at us from below and hanging on their props to shoot at the unprotected bellies of our B-24s. Our top turret reported five fighters on our tail, and I could feel each round hit the B-24. Within seconds, our intercom was shot out from the waist to the tail.

Those boys in the back paid a very high price, and they were the reason we remained flying. The tail turret exploded in flame as twenty-millimeter rounds tore into it. The tail gunner was covered in blood from the flying glass as he crawled out of the inferno toward the waist. The waist gunners fared no better as the 190s and 109s continued firing. One of them, Walter Bartkow, took a direct hit and was knocked down. He shook it off, got back up, and opened up on an Fw 190 that was parked right next to us. Walt said he could see the guy's oxygen mask and the color of his eyes! The other waist gunner took a twenty-millimeter round to the leg that nearly severed it. We tried to tuck in close to the remaining B-24s, but our numbers were dwindling fast.

Six long minutes had gone by. Then the Mustangs showed up.

The P-51s of the 361st FG, 376th FS, had heard our cries for help, but they had been probably fifty miles away. When they arrived, most of the German fighters had exhausted their ammo and were no match for a fully loaded Mustang. One of the P-51s collided with an Fw 190 in the swirling dogfight as the Mustangs cleaned house. When all was said and done, we counted noses for the flight back home and learned we had only seven B-24s left in our group. Twenty-eight B-24s containing ten airmen apiece would not be with us on the return trip.

Although we were still flying, the odds of us making it back were slim to none. There was a huge hole in the right waist, and the left waist window was shattered. Control cables to the tail were partially damaged, and the twin vertical rudders were frayed and appeared to be disintegrating. Looking out the copilot's window, we could see a three-foot hole in the upper surface of the wing behind the number-three engine, out of which one-hundred-octane gasoline was splashing out. That was the good news, as fighters were seen approaching from twelve o'clock low.

My only thought was, *Oh boy—here we go again!* Thankfully, to our great relief, they were P-38s We were still three hours from home, however, and I had to make a life-or-death decision: I could push on for England and fly over the channel with my B-24 shaking and shuddering, about to implode at any minute; risk ditching; or make a crash-landing in France. I could easily make France, but could not guarantee proper medical attention for my crew, three of whom were critically injured. I made the decision for England and called Colgate air-sea rescue. I gave them a long count and they gave me a steer for England.

I had dropped back from the other survivors because I could only maintain 140 miles per hour without shaking the bomber apart. When I dropped through the clouds, fighting to control the dying bomber, there before me was the most beautiful sight I had ever laid eyes on—the White Cliffs of Dover. Just beyond the cliffs was the huge twelve-thousand-foot runway at Manston. We fired off red flares and headed on final approach, wondering and worrying about the unknown damage to the landing gear.

I got all three gear lights as I slowed for touchdown. In spite of all the damage, the flaps came down, the gear was down and locked with all tires inflated, and the hydraulics worked fine. It was the smoothest landing I had ever made, and it felt like I floated onto a feather bed. When I finally came to a stop, the ambulances came and took the wounded right out of the five-foot-diameter hole that used to be the waist area. There was no indication that it had ever been there—it was completely gone. When I got out and looked at the plane, it looked like someone had taken a huge can opener and torn apart the trailing edges of the rudders. There was hardly anything left of them. The entire plane was riddled with cannon and machine-gun rounds, and as I stood there shaking my head thinking *How did we ever make it through?*, I wondered what had happened to everyone else.

The reports I heard after I returned to Tibenham were unbelievable. Twenty-five B-24s went down in a fifteen-mile radius near the Bad Hersfeld area. Two other B-24s limped to France and bellied into an air base. One more made it to Belgium and crashed there. Two of the Liberators, including mine, made it to Manston. One more crashed in England, and only four B-24s made it back to our base at Tibenham. Out of this entire group, only one B-24 was able to fly the next day's mission. We had been annihilated.

One hundred seventeen bomber crewmen and one Mustang pilot had perished, while twenty-nine German planes had been destroyed and eighteen Luftwaffe fighter pilots killed. It was the highest group loss in Eighth Air Force history, and a day I will never forget.

William Dewey continued to fly B-24s with the newly replenished 445th Bomb Group and finished the war in April 1945 with thirty missions. He passed away on March 25, 2007.

WHEN WORLDS COLLIDE

FIRST LIEUTENANT GRANT A. FULLER, USAAC (RET.)
BOEING B-17 FLYING FORTRESS

She was a sight to behold—a graceful lady on display for all to see. Although I did not fly this particular B-17 Flying Fortress, I did fly one of her many sister ships. I stood and viewed her in the house of Eagles, the USAF museum in Dayton, Ohio. The mere sight of this aircraft opened up my memory gates, and I was flooded with over forty years of sounds, sights, and smells that all came rushing back to me.

I remembered so clearly how, once the last hatch was closed and the order to start engines was given, every man inside a B-17 began to work as one. From pilot to tail gunner, ball turret to bombardier and all the other men in between, the nine of us began our tasks and plugged into the mother ship. The pilot and I would get busy cranking up the four Wright Cyclones and pretty much ignored the dozens of 'Forts (as we called the B-17s) in the other revetments as their crews did the same thing. It must have sounded like thunder outside with so many engines running.

ABOVE: Paul Zak, standing fourth from right, had a front-row seat to the piggyback mission.
RIGHT: Grant Fuller poses in front of a B-17, similar to the one he was flying on the day when two of them collided.

Just as the B-17s in formation depend on the other ships next to them for protection, so was it inside the fuselage for our crew. This was our little world, just the nine of us depending on each other. The same scenario was being played out in the other B-17s next to us as we began our mission.

As I stared up at the museum's B-17, I didn't even notice the man standing near me, looking at the same aircraft I was. Our group, the 100th Bomb Group, was having a reunion in Dayton, and each of us was walking around the B-17, reliving our own memories and not paying much attention to the others nearby. I began to speak to the gentlemen next to me, not realizing his response would answer a question I held for over forty years.

"Were you on the Hamburg mission?" I asked. He said he was, and I asked a follow-up question: "Did you see the piggyback?" He hesitated a minute, looked down, then looked at me and introduced himself as Glen Rojohn, the pilot of the top B-17 involved in the "mating" of two B-17s.

I said, "I had a 'front-row back seat' on that mission, and I saw everything that happened—but what the hell happened inside your B-17?"

Rojohn smiled at me and said, "Do you have time to compare stories?"

So a couple of us old bomber pilots sat down and began to reminisce about an unbelievable, heroic mission.

B-17s converge in a box formation. This offered greater protection from enemy fighters.

A mix of B-17s and one lone B-24 Liberator make their way to the target area. Note the differences in paint schemes and natural metal finish.

It was New Year's Eve 1944 and the "Bloody Hundredth" would lead this mission to the German oil refineries and sub pens of Hamburg. I was in the lead B-17 of the lead squadron. Normally, I would have been up front in my copilot position, but on this mission, a Major Martin took my spot as command pilot, making decisions on what the entire formation did. With no use for two copilots, I flew in the tail gunner's position and became the back set of eyes for the command pilot, overlooking the entire formation.

Our thundering herd of B-17s took off from the base at Thorpe Abbotts, England, and began our steady climb up through the soup. Reaching our assigned altitude of twenty-six thousand feet, I had the best seat in the house. Sitting in the tail-gun position afforded me a spectacular view of the rest of the bomb group, with the high squadron off to my left at twenty-seven thousand feet and the low squadron off to my right below at twenty-five thousand. Lieutenant Glen Rojohn, piloting B-17 *Little Skipper*, flew the tail-end Charlie position of the entire group.

Familiar landmarks came into view through the cloud breaks as we left England and approached the North Sea. Flying over the North Sea was preferable, as there was no flak or German fighters. The German pilots were no more interested in doing battle over freezing water than we were; you had about forty seconds of survival time to get aboard a life raft if you had to bail out. Although Hamburg was not that far away from our base, it felt like we were really moving fast and well ahead of schedule.

During the war we called them tailwinds, but what we really encountered was the jet stream, pushing us along at over 150 miles per hour! Going fast to the target meant a slow crawl back home through German fighters and flak, however, both of which would be extremely heavy and deadly. We flew in support of the Bulge operations below, and our anxiety grew when we learned our fighter escort would not be with us on today's mission.

We began our initial point of the bomb run very close to Denmark. We did not want to violate their airspace and made a hard right-hand turn against a 150-mile-per-hour wind. We were now in a severe crosswind to the target and tried to maintain our positions while crabbing into the wind. We looked like a scattered flock of geese as we approached the target. The excessive turn made by the lead squadron caused big problems for the high and low squadrons. The high squadron could not hold its position and had to make S turns out and back above the group. A gap was created that diminished our bomber-box effectiveness—an easy and tempting target for German fighters. The low squadron was ordered to move in and fill the void, as the high squadron would now be the last ones over the target.

Crabbing thirty-plus degrees toward the target, it was the slowest and most torturous bomb run I had ever been on. The flak gunners had us zeroed in as "black death" exploded all around and through us. Our B-17 took hits all over the place as we took our turn in the shredder. Flak took out all the number-two engine oil lines, the copilot's intercom, the bombardier's interphone, and the waist oxygen system. I had a piece of flak come through the glass by my left ear, hit the bulletproof glass on the gun sight, and ricochet out the other side by my right ear! We were the lucky ones.

Our left wingman was hit by flak, nosed over, and collided with another B-17 that was just below the lead element. The lead squadron also lost a third B-17 to flak while on the bomb run. The high squadron fared no better, losing four B-17s during this long-drawn-out bomb run. Gaps began to form as the remainder of the group reached the release point.

Two B-17s from the low squadron, low element, were hit and shot up badly; one entered a tight spin and crashed below. The two remaining B-17s in the low element, Lt. Glen Rojohn in *Little Skipper* and Lt. William G. MacNab in *Nine Lives*, closed in on one another for protection.

With bombs away, the lead squadron dropped down one thousand feet to confuse the flak batteries and turned into the 150-mile-an-hour headwind, beginning its slow-motion crawl back home. The low squadron was now following the lead squadron at the same altitude. The instant the flak stopped, the German fighters poured in. Fw 190s, Bf 109s, and Me 262s tore into us from all directions as trails of wretched black smoke and flame could be seen pouring out of the engines on many of the B-17s. Cannon and tracer rounds filled the sky as aircraft on both sides hammered away at one another.

I told Major Martin what was happening behind us, and, through his commands, the formation closed tightly as the three squadrons slowly became one group. With our left wing exposed, two B-17s attempted to fill the slot: Rojohn in *Little Skipper* from above and MacNab in *Nine Lives* from below. Both were trying to find protection and fill the void on our left wing. The only thing they found was each other.

It was surreal as they came together, not with a resounding crash but rather a melding of two planes. I stared in disbelief at the "piggyback" B-17s in front of me. Eight engines turning in unison, two B-17s stuck together, each with a death grip on the other. They were almost perfectly matched, wingtip to wingtip, with *Little Skipper* above just to the left of *Nine Lives*' tail. I could only imagine what was going on inside those two helpless B-17s as we flew back above the North Sea.

View from the top turret gunner's position showing B-17s pulling contrails as they make their way to the target. The Luftwaffe fighters loved these white-scribed lines because they were easy to spot.

Later, Sgt. Paul Zak, flying in the high squadron, said that he, too, saw the two B-17s collide: "I was the ball-turret gunner on Harold Bucklew's B-17, named *Silver Dollar*. We had just left the target area as I began to search for German fighters. The target in Hamburg was burning behind us as we headed home. I looked right behind me and below, and I saw two B-17s latch on to one another with all eight engines still running! It was the most unbelievable thing I had ever seen! The two B-17s made a graceful circle to the left, and I called our navigator and gave him the tail numbers on both B-17s as they passed below me. I began to count the chutes as they came out of the bombers and I watched the helpless pair of B-17s fall behind and descend until they disappeared from my view."

As I talked to Rojohn in the museum, he described how he and his copilot, Lt. William Leek, fought to save their ship and crew. Gunning the engines and attempting to pull their B-17 off of MacNab's proved to be impossible. To make matters worse, *Little Skipper*'s ball turret was embedded into *Nine Lives*. There was nowhere to go but down as the two B-17s made a gentle turn to the left.

Rojohn said that finding that his elevators and ailerons still functioned properly, he and Leek turned the hybrid B-17s slowly and reentered German airspace. With one of MacNab's engines now on fire, Rojohn gave the engine shutdown command to Leek, and they feathered the props and cut all four of their engines. Lieutenant Rojohn rang the bailout bell for the remainder of his crew, who frantically tried to free Cpl. Joseph Russo from his ball turret, which was slammed right through the top of MacNab's fuselage.

Rojohn told me that he thought that both MacNab and his copilot, 2nd Lt. Nelson B. Vaughn, in *Nine Lives* below him were either killed or severely injured by fighters moments before the two B-17s became one. Head-on firing passes by German fighters were the probable cause of their injuries. For the rest of MacNab's crew, it was time to "get while the getting was good." From my position, I saw four members of MacNab's crew successfully bail out and begin their long descent to earth.

I later heard that as the conjoined B-17s neared the German coast, flak batteries began to take aim at the approaching targets, thinking it was some new kind of American bomber or a secret eight-engine wonder weapon. According to the stories, however, the German antiaircraft officer in charge refused to give the order to fire. He realized it was only a matter of time before these poor souls would crash.

Passing quickly through ten thousand feet, Rojohn said his crew reluctantly gave up on trying to free Corporal Russo from his ball-turret tomb. He said they were flying with both sets of feet on the instrument panel and the yokes buried in their stomachs, as they fought to keep the two B-17s level. Corporal Russo recited Hail Marys over the intercom, and the other members of *Little Skipper* began to bail out of their stricken ship.

"Leek saved my life," Rojohn said. "I ordered him to bail out with the others, but he sternly refused my command. Without Lieutenant Leek helping me hold the yoke back, there was no way I could control the two planes."

In Lieutenant Rojohn's mind, Lieutenant Leek was the true hero, willing to sacrifice himself so others could live. Lieutenant Rojohn made the same choice, but he refused any credit or praise.

According to Rojohn, where the two B-17s would land or crash was anyone's guess. The fire below, deep inside *Nine Lives,* intensified, and .50-caliber ammunition began to cook off and explode as the B17s descended toward northern Germany. One hundred thousand pounds of Boeing aircraft were about to make their mark on German soil. Falling fast and gliding like a rock, the two airplanes, with *Nine Lives* on the bottom, hit hard and pancaked into the frozen ground near Wilhelmshaven. Acting as a cushion for the top B-17, *Nine Lives* disintegrated like an eggshell. The force of the impact lifted *Little Skipper* and sent the B-17 on its last mission. I personally think it's rather ironic that in its last dying act as a US Army Air Corps bomber, B-17 *Little Skipper* destroyed its final target, smashing into a German HQ building and leveling it.

When the smoke and dust settled, Rojohn and Leek found themselves both very much alive! Sitting in their seats still attached to the nose and cockpit section, they simply undid their straps, stood up, and climbed out from their twisted wreckage with only minor injuries. A scattering of broken and bent metal lay behind them. Unfortunately for Corporal Russo, still trapped in his ball turret, Lady Luck was not with him on this flight; it is believed he was killed on impact.

Rojohn said he pulled a cigarette from his pack and put it to his lips, but a young-looking, very nervous German soldier snatched the cigarette before it could be lit. Pointing to the ground with his rifle, both Rojohn and Leek saw the cause for his alarm: fuel had spilled everywhere, including the wing they were standing on.

After convincing their German captors that they were not flying a secret weapon, Lieutenants Rojohn and Leek, along with eight other survivors, became guests of the Luftwaffe and spent the rest of the war in a POW camp. Of the eighteen men total that made up both crews, eight were killed in action; five men from MacNab's B-17 and three men from Rojohn's gave the ultimate sacrifice for their country. Had it not been for the heroic actions of both Lieutenant Rojohn and Lieutenant Leek at a time when their worlds collided, the killed-in-action count would have been much higher.

After this chance meeting at the museum, Glen Rojohn and I became fast friends and continued our relationship for many, many years. Reminiscing about the "piggy-back" answered long-overdue questions. My hat goes off to Glen and his copilot; this is the stuff heroes are made of!

A stateside B-17 crew poses while in training. All of the men had to work as a team while inside the Flying Fortress.

1945

THE END IN SIGHT

The harsh winter weather that descended upon the scattered Allied lines that were stretched thin across the Ardennes Forest in mid-December 1944 was a bittersweet triumph for Adolph Hitler. Although his ground troops used the horrible weather conditions to their advantage, concealing buildups for their eventual forward thrust into the overwhelmed GIs, his once-vaulted blitzkrieging Luftwaffe sat helpless on the fog-covered frozen ground as the Battle of the Bulge commenced.

The original plan, code-named Wacht am Rhein (Watch on the Rhine), called for coordinated ground and air attacks forecasted to cripple the Allied air power that had decimated the Luftwaffe in recent months. If this plan could be accomplished, the Allied ground push to Germany would be halted in its tracks, and without protective air cover, the

The Fw 190 was one of the Luftwaffe's all-around best fighters—it could bomb, strafe, and dogfight with whatever the Allies threw at it. With a mixed bag of cannons and machine guns, it was scourge of bomber streams.

Allies would be thrown back into the channel. It was all wishful thinking on the Führer's part, however. Hitler lived by the sword, and now he was about to die by it.

The Führer had to wait for something he had no control over: clearing weather conditions. By the time the fog and low clouds had lifted, the Germans were advancing to the rear with the Allied army hot on their heels. As the new year approached, Hitler used his final trump card and unleashed over eight hundred of his Luftwaffe fighters in a frantic act to save himself and his homeland.

Operation Boden Platte (Ground Plate) was a desperate attempt by a desperate man to turn around the course of the war. Convinced of overwhelming success, Luftwaffe planners and pilots prepared for what was hoped to be Germany's victorious start to the new year: the surprise attack by German fighters on western Allied airfields in Europe.

UNINVITED GUEST

FELDWEBEL (FLYING SERGEANT) OSCAR BOESCH, STURMSTAFFEL FOCKE-WULF FW 190

I had just flown my last mission of the year, a support sweep for our ground troops fighting in the Bulge area. My Fw 190 had earned its keep once again, evidenced by my blackened gunports like those on the other 190s as the rest of the Staffel pilots taxied in and shut down next to me. Thoughts of celebrating on this New Year's Eve were short lived as we entered the operations building.

> By order of the *Geschuaderestab* [commander] the pilots of *Geschwader*
> IV JG3 "Udet" are restricted to base with no alcohol, no party and to be
> in bed by 10 pm. Do not talk to anyone as a very important mission is in
> the planning for early next morning. Happy New Year German Fighter
> pilots! Dismissed!

On January 1, 1945, our wakeup call came at 5:30 a.m. A top-secret mission, Operation Boden Platte, was laid out for us at the morning briefing. We pilots studied detailed maps of our route and target area — Eindhoven Air Base, Holland — and listened to last-minute instructions before making the short walk to our Fw 190s.

I was surprised how calm my nerves were and felt somewhat refreshed knowing that it was now our turn to attack Allied aircraft that were hopefully still on the ground. Finally, I thought, some payback and our day for revenge against the bothersome Allied escort fighters. They called us targets of opportunity, but they left their bombers and dropped down to go looking for us. We were always outnumbered when we took our daily beatings. Every day we had to endure attacks by Mustangs, Spitfires, Lightnings, Thunderbolts, and Typhoons. They shot up everything they saw; even a man on a bicycle was not safe on the streets! As I strapped myself into the 190, I believed this important mission would bring some much-needed reprieve from Allied superiority on the western front. I also knew, however, that if this mission failed, it would spell disaster for all of us and the tactical end of the Luftwaffe.

Shortly after 8:20 a.m., our Staffel — squadron — of nineteen Fw 190s quickly lifted off from the snow-covered field at Gütersloh and disappeared into the western sky. We quickly rendezvoused with the rest of the Geschwader "Udet" near Lippstadt and formed up with other 190s, becoming a strike force of sixty Fw 190s. To prevent detection by enemy radar, our flight level was on the deck. We flew between chimneys and around church steeples to avoid detection.

This Fw 190 is painted in the markings of Oscar Boesch. As a young Luftwaffe pilot, Boesch was tasked with attacking the bomber streams that flew over his homeland on a daily basis.

Leading us to Eindhoven was our "Mother Goose," a Ju 88 that did all of the navigating and communicating; radio silence was mandatory until we reached the target. With good visibility and flat terrain, we flew over the front lines undetected by antiaircraft guns. Fifty kilometers behind Allied lines, we dropped our belly tanks and charged our guns, and I tightened up my straps as Eindhoven Air Base came into view.

In front of us was a huge parking lot full of Spitfires and Typhoons. Hundreds and hundreds of Allied aircraft were right before my eyes, and this time they were all on the ground! I saw four Spitfires being fueled at a gas booth, and I aimed for the center one. My cannon rounds tore into them, and huge explosions ripped the Spitfires apart; they all began to burn. All around me were black-and-red fireballs where Allied aircraft once sat.

Streaks of cannon shells zipped through the snow and mud into burning aircraft as Eindhoven Air Base was chewed to bits by our Fw 190s. I made pass after pass on the fully engulfed field and saw Typhoons and Spitfires trying to taxi through the chaos. Other Fw 190s sealed their fate as cannon shells found their mark and ignited the Allied fighters before they could get airborne. Heavy antiaircraft fire began to arc in my direction as the British defensive gunners tried to retaliate. It was like flying in a damn hornet's nest, with tracer rounds swirling everywhere!

On my fourth and last pass over Eindhoven, I ran out of machine-gun ammo and my cannons jammed on me. I was just above the treetops when the fires from the burning aircraft threw thick black clouds of oily smoke into the air, completely obscuring visibility. Suddenly, out of the smoke and haze came a fellow Fw 190 right in front of my nose!

A fraction of a second sooner and we would have collided. That's when I thought, *Oh boy, it's dangerous—time to get the hell out of here!*

With my cannon still jammed and my machine guns out of ammo, it was a wakeup call for me to leave. On the deck at full throttle, I turned east for home. As it was so often after a battle, I was all alone. About five minutes' flying time from Eindhoven, I saw a low-flying aircraft ahead of me and thought it was a fellow Fw 190. As I got closer to my newfound wingman, however, a chill ran up my spine. This was no 190—this was a hostile Typhoon!

I was right behind him, one hundred feet away and, luckily for me, right in his blind spot. The Typhoon was one of the Luftwaffe's most hated and feared Allied aircraft. It had done so much damage to our ground units, particularly our armor. It was fast, and, when heavily loaded with rockets, it turned our tanks into Swiss cheese. I recharged my jammed cannon and got a green light!

The Typhoon made a thirty-degree turn to the left, and I stayed with him out of sight. I had him bull's-eyed in my gun sight, and at such close range, how could I miss? I pulled the trigger on the thirty-millimeter cannon and hoped he would fall with the rounds I had left. I squeezed the trigger again and again . . . nothing! The only thing that worked was that damn green light!

I was fifty kilometers behind enemy lines on the backside of a ferocious tiger. He had superior speed and firepower, and probably lots of ammunition. Had I been over Germany, I may have rammed him or chewed off his tail, but on his side of the line, I had no chance to survive a tangle with him. The Typhoon went into another turn and I followed him through it, still unnoticed. I had a ten-second window of opportunity to leave before I became a Typhoon victim.

I carefully maneuvered myself out of harm's way and the golden opportunity for the Typhoon pilot to get an easy kill. I wished I knew his name to let him know how he and I got away—then we could both celebrate!

There was no celebrating when I returned to Gütersloh, however. Bad news was in the making as the Luftwaffe losses were colossal. Two hundred and eleven pilots and over three hundred aircraft had been lost; the damage we inflicted seemed minimal in comparison. This would be the Luftwaffe's final large-scale operation on the western front as we held out for as long as we could. The month of May was only four months away, and it came very quickly.

SAINT VALENTINE'S DAY MASSACRE

LIEUTENANT CHARLES E. "CHUCK" MINAHAN
AND SERGEANT NOBLE HOLLAND, USAAC
MARTIN B-26 MARAUDER

For centuries, February 14, Saint Valentine's Day, has been associated with the exchange of love notes between adoring couples. Traditionally, this was a day set aside for giving gifts from the heart, but on February 14, 1945, there was not much love for mankind as World War II and the devastation that followed staggered through another year. There was still a lot of giving, though, as Allied planes pounded Axis Germany in round-the-clock bombing raids.

The "giving" had begun one day earlier, as British Lancaster and Mosquito bombers began the firebombing of Dresden. American heavy bombers continued the daylight action as the fires of hell engulfed the ravaged German city. Elsewhere in Europe, the German army reversed course and was in retreat, falling back across the Rhine River into the heart of the fatherland. Hitler's dream of the one-thousand-year reign of terror would fall well short.

As the strategic heavy bombers from the Eighth Air Force concentrated on Germany's industrial targets, the tactical Ninth Air Force committed over six hundred A-20 Havocs, B-26 Marauders, and A-26 Invaders to the fleeing German army. Their targets were marshaling yards, troop concentrations, railway stations, barge traffic, and bridges. Included in this mission were men and aircraft from the 344th Bomb Group, 495th Bomb Squadron, flying B-26s from their base at A-59, Cormeilles-en-Vexin, France. Of the hundreds of men who gathered for the morning briefing, two of them had flown almost twenty missions together inside the belly of a B-26. Each one had a different view of the sky and chaos to follow because they sat at opposite ends of the aircraft. This is their story.

The airplane commander, Lieutenant Chuck Minahan, had been flying B-26s in combat since August 1944. During that time, he had been responsible for the lives of five other men: copilot Ben Huffman, bombardier/navigator Leo Armstrong, flight engineer Ben Longstreth, radio operator John Regan, and the back seat of eyes and protection, Sgt. Noble Holland—tail gunner/armament. As the men gathered for their early-morning briefing, they learned that one of their number, John, could not fly with them because of an illness that had sidelined him to sick bay. His replacement was Vick Ellis, and, unfortunately for him, today would be his last mission.

LIEUTENANT MINAHAN RECALLS THE FEBRUARY 14 MISSION BRIEFING

Our target was a railroad bridge over the Rhine River near Koblenz. We were told that the Germans were retreating but had stalled out on the other side of the Rhine. The thing that caught everyone's attention, though, was the flak patterns around the target. Generally speaking, they were red circles that were enclosed at the outer periphery of the target. Within those red areas, it reminded me of a large bunch of grapes, except each grape represented multiple eighty-eight-millimeter flak guns. There had to be over a thousand guns in an area of twenty square miles, with overlapping fire from each of the guns. This was by far the worst flak concentration we would ever fly over.

Having flown more than twenty missions, we had been briefed in the past about heavy gun emplacements and, thankfully, encountered none. In other situations, though, we had flown over the undercast and had not been shot at. I always looked for the good and bad signs before a mission, like weather reports, target type, and so on. Today we were told that we would have clear skies all the way to and over the target—a bad sign in my book. Things only got worse from there on out.

Our engine start time was supposed to be at 8:00 a.m. We had finished the preflight and loading of our B-26, which included the four thousand pounds of bombs we carried, and strapped ourselves into our respective positions to wait for the signal of the green flare to crank our engines. The only thing we saw was the morning sun growing higher in the sky and the "red reds" repeating the never-ending delays. This was a maximum-effort mission, with each of the three squadrons putting up eighteen B-26s and each plane carrying a full bomb load and a crew of six men.

Inside the Marauder's cramped quarters, we passed the time with the thoughts of the mission at hand, which only intensified our anxiety. As a cure for that, I thought about home and my wife and the name I gave to one of the B-26s I normally flew. Most of my missions were flown in a Marauder I dubbed *Lak-a-Nookie*, which was named for a promise I made to my wife back in Texas on what I wouldn't do overseas. I kept my promise to her, but it was damn difficult, especially around all those French girls! Today's mission found me in the left seat of another Marauder. The hands on my watch were creeping into the noon hour when a green flare finally arced across the blue sky. The sound of fifty-four Marauders roared to life as we taxied into position.

Our squadron, the 459th, was the lead group on the February 14 mission, and the entire group was led by Maj. Lucius Clay. We flew in a six-ship formation box, with Major Clay out in front and a B-26 on either side of him. I flew the number four-slot with the nose of my B-26 just below and behind Major Clay's tail. I, too, had a B-26 on either side of me as we formed up over France and made our way to Germany. Little did I know at the time that I would never see most of these men again.

With our formation zigzagging back and forth across Germany, our crewmen searched for the Luftwaffe fighters, which, thankfully, never showed up. But they didn't have to, as flak opened up ahead and all around us. We settled down into the bombing run and had just started to level our wings as we completed our turn to the IP. We were less than fifteen minutes out from the target when all hell broke loose and the sky faded to gray.

A B-26 ground crewmember paints on black-and-white invasion stripes in prepartion for the invasion of Normandy. *LIFE photo*

The Germans didn't shoot at single B-26s; they just filled a box in the sky and darkened it with black death. Those eighty-eights were well coordinated, and they had us pegged to our exact position and height. With the flak bursting all around us, it sounded like handfuls of gravel being thrown against a tin shed as tiny strips of metal tore into our B-26. We were the lucky ones.

We were hit aggressively for fifteen minutes on our bomb run, and in that time I saw two bright flashes of light above my left and right wings. I could feel the transmission of heat come through the Plexiglas as the number-two and number-three B-26s vaporized before my eyes. This was not something I could easily ignore, and I was scared silly, but I concentrated on maintaining my position in the formation, or what was left of it. Things were not much better behind us.

SERGEANT NOBLE HOLLAND RECALLS WHAT HAPPENED NEXT

In less than a minute's time, the clear, blue, sunny sky behind me turned black with powder and shrapnel everywhere. I saw orange bursts above me, below me, and level with me. Those sons of bitching high ones were the ones I didn't like because they had to get upstairs to detonate, and if they went through us we were goners for sure.

B-26 Marauders unload their bombs on German targets below.

I saw a B-26 behind me in another flight explode after taking a direct hit—a million tiny pieces of aluminum went every which way. I looked out my window to one side and saw the right wing of a B-26 with only the engine and propeller still attached— it looked like someone had jerked it off the plane and turned it loose. It was an eerie thing to see the propeller turning at full bore as the wing fell back to earth. The whole scene was totally chaotic, and the sky was full of turmoil. Then the chaos entered our Marauder.

LIEUTENANT MINAHAN RELATES WHAT HAPPENED UP FRONT

My eyes were glued to Major Clay's B-26, which drifted above my nose eight feet away. This was by no means a casual, loose formation; my right hands jockeyed the throttles on and off, on and off. I felt like a whiskey runner in Texas as I jammed my throttles back and forth. Just before the intercom was knocked out, I heard a call that the waist gunner had been hit by flak and needed help, but there wasn't much I could do for him as Major Clay's bomb-bay doors opened and his bomb load tumbled downward. I could sense our own bombs coming out, and the lightening of our load forced the Marauder upward. I gave the wounded waist gunner a quick thought and hoped someone could help him as I concentrated on keeping the B-26 upright.

SERGEANT HOLLAND, TOO, REMEMBERS THE CALL FROM THE WAIST GUNNER

Vick Ellis called me and said he was shot through the shoulder. I asked him if he was bleeding badly, and he said, "No, not bad at all." I told him that I would wait until some of this flak calmed down before I crawled forward to help him. I had a lot of armor plating around my ass, and I didn't want to venture too far away from it! Back up front in the cockpit, things began to unravel for Lieutenant Minahan.

Major Clay started a mild left turn with a flight of B-26s above us to our right and a flight below us to our left. They, too, were a shadow of their former box as Major Clay and I represented what was left of the lead box of B-26s. As I turned left with them, my forward speed increased and I began to overtake Major Clay. I pulled the power back and found that my left engine linkage had been severed at the control column, with the left engine roaring at full throttle. My left engine began to overpower the drag of the right and I realized I had a runaway. It was difficult to take my eyes off the B-26 above me and yet try to deal with an overspeeding engine, but my attention shifted to inside the cockpit as my B-26 began to roll right.

As the Marauder went beyond the vertical, the formation rose above my belly and the ground below filled my windscreen as I fought to control the roll. I found out quickly that I had no aileron control, either, because the cable on my control wheel had been completely blown away. My copilot, Ben Huffman, wondered out loud, "What the hell are you doing?!" He thought I was deliberately maneuvering away from Major Clay, and it wasn't until I yelled "Help me!" that he realized that something was wrong. Lieutenant Huffman's aileron cable was still intact, and he wrestled with his control wheel while I pushed full right rudder in as fast and as far as I could. Our B-26 completed its sloppy roll, losing four thousand feet of altitude in the process. I wanted to keep it flying long enough so the guys in the back could jump, but I had no idea what was going on back there. Things in the back were not much better.

I could see black smoke coming from the left engine, as I crawled forward to aid Vick Ellis. I saw that Vick was bleeding from the top of his shoulder, so I gave him a shot of morphine and dumped the whole bag of sulfur powder on his wound. As I was bandaging his shoulder, I looked up and saw the bombardier, Leo Armstrong, motioning for me to bail out. The wind was howling through the back area, and it was impossible to speak or hear over the noise, but I could see his lips moving telling me to jump. Hydraulic fluid was flying around, spraying me in the face, stinging my eyes as I helped Vick Ellis with his parachute—God, I hated the smell of that crap!

I motioned to Vick and pointed to his parachute. He nodded yes, but I could see there would be no way for him to pull his ripcord with that bad arm. I attached a twenty-foot strap to his chute and anchored it to the inside of the Marauder in hopes that once he fell, it would jerk the parachute open. As we got ready to jump, Vick changed his mind and shook his head no, pointing to his injured shoulder. I wasn't about to leave him and neither was the rest of the crew, so we settled in for the ride of our lives. I put a pair of earphones on to listen to what was going on up front, and I heard Major Clay yell "Regroup, regroup!" trying to pull the other B-26s back together. Then the intercom went dead.

Rare in-flight photo of Chuck Minihan's B-26 *Lak-a-Nookie* before taking flak damage.

LIEUTENANT MINAHAN

I could see Major Clay pulling up and away from us, but my main concern was getting that left engine shut down. I pulled mixture control and then pulled the prop control back, worrying that the Curtiss Electric prop motors had crystallized and would shear off my propeller blades. Thankfully, it didn't happen as I feathered the props, knowing full well we were going to be here for a while. Ben and I got it half-assed trimmed up and slowly advanced power on the right engine, easing it into a reasonably mild, descending,

single-engine flight and pegged the airspeed at 140 knots. I knew that once we reached three thousand to four thousand feet, the B-26 would hold altitude. The question was, for how long?

I called bomber command on the UHF frequency and told them to find me an airfield or we were going to leave this sucker. After what seemed like a lifetime and a half, they came back and said there was an airfield up ahead near Reims, France. What they forgot to tell me was that it was still under construction!

It was starting to get late when we reentered French airspace, the bottom of the sun beginning to touch the horizon. I could see the airfield up ahead and shouted to the crew in the back to hang on, not knowing whether they could hear me or not. I threw the gear handle down, and of course the never-ending bad luck held out—the hydraulics were gone, and the gear remained upright. I got the attention of the flight engineer, Ben Longstreth, and motioned for him to hand crank the gear down. I knew we only had one shot at this, and I wondered how much longer the Marauder would hold together.

SERGEANT HOLLAND

I couldn't see into the cockpit, so I didn't know what was going on up there. I knew something was wrong when the flight engineer motioned for me to come up to the bomb bay. We found the landing gear practically frozen shut as we stood in the bomb bay to hand crank it down. It took a long time for the main gear legs to lock, but we did it. The nose gear, on the other hand, was a bigger problem because we couldn't even get it to unlatch. We tried and tried, but it wouldn't budge. I crawled back to the waist area, made sure Vick Ellis was secure, and sat next to him, waiting for the crash-landing to follow.

The last B-26 still flying today is owned by Kermit Weeks. This B-26 is painted in early US Army Air Corps colors. *EAA/Jim Koepnick*

LIEUTENANT MINAHAN

I took some power off, and at the same time I adjusted the rudder trim. I could see the field was still under construction because concrete mixers were working on parts of the runway. I came in hot, without flaps, and touched down on the mains as I held the nose off. I was literally tearing apart the runway because it was made of wire mesh and not the pierced steel planking I had been used to. I missed one of the concrete mixers by a few feet as I went roaring by, tearing up the mesh like a peeled orange.

I got the plane slowed down to seventy knots, but I knew if I didn't do something quick, we were going to run out of runway. I reached up and pulled the red handle above my head that activated an air bottle, which in turn locked the brakes. The nose pitched down and went skitching and skidding across the wire mesh. My heels began to get hot as the nose of the Marauder ground off, destroying the Norden bombsight before I finally got her stopped. I popped the double overhead hatch as people scrambled over my head to get out. I shut off all the switches I could find, and it was hell trying to climb down that nose. It was a lot worse for the guys in the back, though, like Noble Holland and Vick Ellis, because they had to jump out of the waist window that now stood more than ten feet off the ground.

I counted noses and found everyone to be OK, standing far away since we expected that sucker to blow at any minute. It never did, though, and a group of 82nd Airborne soldiers that were housed nearby gathered around us and threw us into the back of a six-by-six truck.

SERGEANT HOLLAND

We sat in the back of that truck, just staring at one another. Some GI came running up from behind us and tossed in a bottle of cognac—it went around the six of us inside the truck and tossed out the back empty! That mission made me start believing in God. On all the missions I flew afterwards, I had no fear. I had a calmness come over me. I believed that when it was my time to go, there was nothing I could do about it, so why worry about it?

LIEUTENANT MINAHAN

We were housed in a champagne factory that night, and we helped ourselves to the liquid bubbly. It helped calm my nerves, but it also gave me one helluva headache the next day! It took us two days to get back to base, where I found out Major Clay was the only one to make it back from our flight. After our debrief, I further found out that my crew had put me in for the Distinguished Flying Cross, which I received at a later date. One of the lines of the citation read, "Saving his aircraft and landing it safely when it should have been abandoned." That jarred the hell out of me, because I knew each of these guys would have done the same for me.

> Chuck Minahan completed thirty-three missions in Martin B-26 Marauders and retired from the US Air Force with the rank of colonel. Noble Holland completed his tour as Chuck Minahan's tail gunner and lived peacefully in Iowa until his death in 2009.

WORLD AT WAR: In order for the Allies in the Pacific theater of operations to deliver a death blow to Japan, they needed to obtain some Axis-occupied island real estate from which they could launch their new long-range bomber called the B-29 Superfortress. The Japanese, however, were prepared to stand and fight to the death. These battles were some of the bloodiest of the war, and they called for Allied aircraft big and small to help secure a victory.

DEVIL'S DARLING
PACIFIC ISLAND HOPPING
WITH A WARBUG

LIEUTENANT THOMAS ROZGA, USMC (RET.)
STINSON OY-1 SENTINEL

Thomas Rozga was born in 1923 and followed in his older brother's footsteps by earning his wings of gold in the US Marine Corps.

You can't always get what you want.

I entered the service in late December 1941 for two reasons: First, my brother Tony had earned his wings in 1940 and I wanted to be just like him. Second, and more importantly, the Japanese had bombed Pearl Harbor and I wanted to return the favor. When I earned my wings, I was commissioned as a second lieutenant in the Marine Corps and assigned to fly Corsairs. Unfortunately, I had a little mishap with one during a landing, so they decided I would be better suited to flying the PBY Catalina. The PBY was old and slow, but it was also reliable and could do just about anything . . . at half the speed of a scooter! I have to admit the scenery was quite nice flying around the Caribbean in 1943 looking for German U-boats, but I still wanted to get into some action. In early 1944, I got more than I bargained for when I received orders to report to Quantico, Virginia, to join a VMO—a Marine Observation Squadron.

VMO: EYES AND EARS OF THE MARINE CORPS

The VMOs were the eyes and ears of the commanding officers of the various marine divisions. Able to communicate via two-way radio, we could tell the troops on the ground what was happening on the front lines, scout out targets of opportunity, and then direct artillery fire onto enemy positions. Unfortunately, all of this was performed in an unarmed, tandem two-place, fabric-covered "warbug" called the Stinson OY-1. Otherwise known as the L-5, the Stinson was constructed using chromoly steel tubing and fabric covering with a wraparound Plexiglas greenhouse, giving the pilot and observer an unobstructed view. It was powered by a six-cylinder, 190-horsepower Lycoming O-435 engine, giving it ample power to get in and out of most short-field situations. Some models carried an observer in the back seat, and others carried a stretcher behind the observer so we could fly our wounded away from the battlefield.

I have to admit that the first time I saw this airplane, I scratched my head and wondered out loud, "We're flying these in combat?" Compared to the PBY, the OY-1 looked like a toy model. I was disappointed, to say the least, until I actually flew it. After a familiarization cockpit checkout, I quickly learned why the OY-1 was the obvious choice for battlefield missions. You could stall it, spin it, loop it, and land it in a few hundred feet.

It wasn't going to set any speed records, but boy oh boy, was that little Stinson maneuverable. After months of training, we headed west to San Diego, loaded our airplanes and ourselves aboard a "baby flattop" called the USS *Whiteplains*, and headed for Hawaii. Eventually, five of us joined the 4th Marine Division and VMO-4. I entered combat for the first time at a place called Saipan.

A DAY AT THE BEACH

Saipan was over thirteen miles long, almost six miles wide, and a perfect place from which to launch B-29 Superfortresses to strike Tokyo. The only problem was it just happened to

Lieutenant Tom Rozga poses in front of his bazooka-equipped Stinson OY-1 named *Lady Satan*.

be the headquarters for the Japanese Pacific Fleet and housed almost thirty thousand Japanese troops.

On June 17, 1944, two of us took off from our carrier in our OY-1s, and I became the first American airplane to land on Saipan on D + 2. I ended up landing on a thick, sandy road about a half mile from the front lines. It's a good thing I was in a full stall configuration because it was like landing in peanut butter, which stopped my OY-1 in a hurry.

I shopped around for a better site and found a chunk of concrete runway that hadn't been bombed at Charan-Kanoa airstrip. There was no time for rest, both of our OY-1s were pressed into service; we carried no observers on that first mission as we called in artillery fire to the targets below. I tried to stay at around five hundred feet, constantly adjusting my altitude to confuse the Japanese gunners below who tried to knock us down. No matter what battlefield we were over, the Japanese gunners always tried for the cockpit area or the engine. After a while, I lost count how many holes I had in my airplane. Thankfully, most of them whizzed through the fabric covering and kept right on going!

But that wasn't the only thing we had to fear. Soon, our own artillery and shells from the ships at sea came roaring over our heads—we could feel vibrations from them passing close by. It was unsettling both around the airplane and inside as well.

I saw firsthand that day how serious this business of war truly was when my wingman got hit by Japanese ground fire. Wounded, he tried to make it back to base but couldn't pull up quickly enough and ended up crashing into an ammo dump. Sadly, he had just been informed by the Red Cross that morning that he was the proud father of a baby boy. It was a tragic loss of a good friend, and unfortunately there would be many more to follow.

A few days later, the rest of the squadron arrived at the airstrip. We were located near a small town where some Japanese civilians lived—part of the over twenty thousand who

OY-1s belonging to VMO-2 on Isley Field, Saipan, in June 1944. *Jack Cook collection*

called Saipan home. Due in part to the emperor's indoctrination of how the Americans were nothing but murderous soldiers, they ran from us when we arrived; hundreds of them hid in caves on the north side of the island and tragically began to jump to their deaths. We were able to capture some of the civilians and convince them to fly with us in our OY-1s.

Rigged with a large speaker and microphone, we flew overhead with our back seater pleading for them to surrender. The ones who wanted to were convinced by armed Japanese soldiers to jump or be shot in the caves. The others, some holding small children in their arms, believed what the emperor had told them and willingly threw themselves off the cliffs.

Eventually, after we secured Saipan, we moved over to Tinian to do it all over again. By mid-August of 1944, we were withdrawn and sent back to Hawaii to rest, regroup, and retrain for an even bloodier campaign.

IWO JIMA

By January of 1945, I was the new commanding officer of VMO-4, and we were on our way back to the front, headed for Guam to pick up a couple of new OY-1s to go with the others we had aboard the USS *Wake Island*. With our aircraft secured on deck, we set sail for Iwo Jima. As the skipper, it was my duty to go ashore with the mud marines and pick out a suitable landing spot for the rest of the squadron. After jumping into the Pacific and wading ashore with the rest of the soldiers, I spent the rest of the day and night hugging a sand dune with Mount Suribachi off to my left and the Japanese firing down our throats.

On day two, it was time for some payback, and I ordered the first two airplanes to come in and land on a five-hundred-foot section of runway that we had captured. Unfortunately,

the Japanese were concealed at the other end of the runway and pounded us with mortar rounds and machine-gun fire as the Stinsons landed. They quickly learned, however, that an OY-1 overhead meant that death and destruction were on their way in the form of artillery rounds. By day five, all of the OY-1s from VMO-4 were on the island and ready to hunt. The Japanese were smart, though, and concealed themselves in the foliage, keeping quiet with just some sporadic rifle shots. Then, as the sun set and night fell over the island, they unleashed their own hell on us. Their artillery was quite accurate; they had zeroed in on every blade of grass on the island before our arrival. Eventually, one of our generals had enough of the sleepless nights and came up with an idea to stop them.

NIGHT STALKER

General Clifton Cates asked me to find a volunteer to take off at 11:00 p.m. and try to pinpoint where the Japanese artillery was hidden. He was quite upset that his men were being prevented from getting a restful night's sleep! I informed the general that whoever accepted this mission would have to fly at a certain level to avoid being hit by our own artillery. The general smiled and said, "Oh yes, Lieutenant, I understand, and incidentally, I have invited the navy in on this as well."

I told him that the navy shoots low and the marines shoot high, and the guy flying would only have about a four-hundred-foot box to fly within as incoming shells zipped by below and above. I asked the general whether he was sure he wanted to do this tonight. He said he was, and I told him then I was his volunteer—if I couldn't do it, I didn't want to risk any of my pilots.

At 11:00 p.m., I had six guys lined up with flashlights staggered down the runway to show the width of the strip. I lifted the OY-1 off OK, but once I got airborne, I had no

A Stinson OY-1 assigned to VMO-2 takes off from Saipan to go out on another spotting mission. *Jack Cook collection*

horizon in the pitch-black darkness. It wasn't until I had a few hundred feet under my wings that I could make out small fires from exploding shells, which helped me to determine where the front lines were. I had one eyed glued to my altimeter because I needed to stay above four hundred feet and below seven hundred feet for fear of running into one of our incoming artillery shells.

The first time the Japanese guns opened up, I radioed the marines and navy guns their position and waited for the fireworks show. I could feel the black air I was flying in begin to churn like a swollen river. The OY-1 was getting tossed around—my wings rocked and the big tail shook. Those shells were too damn close!

With the shells raining down, darkness became daylight as everything inside that circle of death was quickly annihilated. The Japanese never came out again that night. After two hours of flying solo, all was quiet below and I returned to land. The next day, General Cates came up to me and thanked me for allowing his boys to get a good night's sleep. Then he added, "No more night flights, Lieutenant. With that many shells coming in, a guy could get killed up there." I saluted and replied, "You're not kidding, general!"

BAZOOKA MUD MOVER

The fact of the matter was that as a marine observation pilot—droning around above a battlefield, talking on the radio, calling in artillery—most of us were frustrated fighter pilots. We wanted in on the action, and with only .45-caliber pistols slung on our hips, we knew we had to come up with something bigger to do any damage. One of the pilots in our squadron had the mindset of an ordnance man, and he came up to me one day and asked, "Skipper, how's about we mount some bazookas on the airplanes?" I laughed and replied, "Do you really think it can be done?" He nodded his head up and down like an excited little boy and said, "I know it can be done!"

My concern was that the fabric-covered tail section or elevator on the OY-1 would be burned completely off from the flame that exited the rear tube of the bazooka. The smile from the pilot's face departed when I mentioned this, and he became more serious, thinking about the question I posed. "I guess it's possible, Skipper, but we won't know unless we try it out. Want me to mount one on each side?"

I thought about it for a second and said, "Hell if we're going to do this right, then let's put three bazookas on each side. Now go find some bazookas!"

Finding bazookas on Iwo Jima was like a kid finding candy on Halloween, and we mounted three tubes to the wing struts of each wing on an OY-1 that was adorned with the nose art of *Lady Satan*. We then installed six toggle switches on the instrument panel, one to fire each of the bazookas. By that afternoon, it was ready to try out. Our engineering officer, Lieutenant Kelly, asked if he could be the first. Before I could say anything, he was already airborne.

He fired one bazooka, looked back, and saw that his tail wasn't on fire, so he cranked off another round. Satisfied, he fired the remaining four rounds and came back in to give his report: "The handling was beautiful. No adverse effects whatsoever, and no fire exiting the rear tube. As a matter of fact, once the projectiles have left the bazooka, it becomes a hollow tube with no resistance and excellent airflow. It's time for some marine observation payback!"

From then on, the biggest problem I had was breaking up the fights between the pilots, because they all wanted to fly *Lady Satan*. Thankfully, rank has its privileges, and even I got into the action with our lone bazooka-equipped OY-1.

An actual OY-1 combat survivor is owned by Chris and Jerri Bergan, who painted it to look like Tom's *Lady Satan*.

The procedure was to get up to altitude—never really that high—select a target below, and then push the nose over into a shallow dive. Most of the time, I fired all of them at once, and they zoomed toward their target below. The Japanese learned to keep their heads down as the marines on the ground waved and cheered us on. Honestly, they weren't that accurate, but they made a hell of an explosion when they hit, and it sure made us feel like fighter-bomber pilots for a while! I found out later that the brass in the Pentagon had spent an ungodly sum of money trying to figure out how to properly mount a bazooka on an airplane. We wrote them a letter, and it read, "From VMO-4. Reference to our bazooka mounted OY-1s. It didn't cost us anything—just some USMC ingenuity!"

We flew missions from dawn to dusk; sometimes three OY-1s would be up at one time. VMO-4 ended up with hundreds of missions flown over Iwo Jima before we were withdrawn in April of 1945. And for me, I will never forget my time in the OY-1, which I often referred to as old faithful.

In February 2010, Tom Rozga was reunited with an old friend—a fully restored Stinson L-5 that he flew in the service in 1945.

WORLD AT WAR: While the soldiers on the ground during World War I had endured the horrors of trench warfare—poison gas, bayonet charges, machine-gun nests, and flame throwers—the pilots from both sides who flew observation airplanes overhead were much more civil to one another. Shortly before fixed weaponry was bolted to these fabric-covered aircraft, the observation airplane was the only game in town. These early warriors of the sky were more like modern-day traffic reporters as they flew over battle-fields and enemy front lines documenting troop movements, buildups, and potential weaknesses. When two opposing observation airplanes encountered one another over the skies of Europe, these "great men of honor" smiled and exchanged pleasantries to one another as they flew by. Chivalry, at least in the air, was far from dead; that was until someone threw a brick at their opponent.

Soon, new, more aerodynamic weapons such as grenades, rocks, and pieces of rope with grappling hooks were brought aloft and hurled at one another in an attempt to bring down a passing foe. But the one true facet that forever changed how the airplane would be used in combat was the first time an observation pilot brought a pistol to a rock fight. As the first shots of aerial combat rang out high above the trenches, the killing machine of the air was born.

Now, fast forward to more than thirty years later, during one of the last air battles of World War II, and fly along with two observation airplanes—one American and the other German—as they battle one another in flimsy, fabric-covered aircraft, just like their early forefathers did.

APRIL 1945

DUEL OF THE LIGHTWEIGHTS

CUB VS. STORCH

LIEUTENANTS MERRITT DUANE FRANCIES AND WILLIAM S. MARTIN, US ARMY (RET.) PIPER L-4 CUB VS. FI 156 STORCH

MERRITT FRANCIES

To me, the Piper J-3 Cub was just about the nicest airplane I had ever flown. When I joined the army on December 10, 1941, I had already earned my private pilot's license flying Cubs through the CPTP in my hometown of Wenatchee, Washington, in February of that year. Because of my prior flight experience, I was slotted to become an army liaison/artillery-spotting pilot. I was even more delighted to learn that the airplane I would fly in combat was the military version of the J-3, called the L-4. Although the L-4 was still powered by the same reliable sixty-five-horsepower Continental engine that the yellow-and-black, lightning-bolt-bearing J-3 carried, it seemed much more powerful in its army olive-drab color, with a white star on the fuselage and wing.

To the victors go the spoils! Here, Lieutenants Martin and Francies examine their air-to-air victory and the treasures found inside the fallen Luftwaffe "fighter."

Although most Storchs carried a small machine gun that was fired through the rear window, these slow-moving airplanes were no match for prowling Allied fighters.

The L-4 had also picked up a nickname, "Grasshopper," because of the way it hopped and skipped across the uneven roads, dry streambeds, and cow pastures we used as takeoff and landing fields.

Aside from its paint job, another wonderful improvement the military model had was the "greenhouse" canopy that afforded the pilot in front and the observer in back much greater visibility. Although the empty weight of the L-4 was around 740 pounds, our maximum takeoff weight was almost double that. We carried radios to communicate with our artillery units on the ground along with message pouches to drop maps, correspondence, and notes to our front-line field commanders. But some of the other L-4 pilots in other units must have been frustrated dive-bomber pilots, because they affixed bazookas to the struts of their planes and went on the offensive looking to tangle with German armor. The only weapon I ever carried was my .45-caliber pistol—and it would come in quite handy late in the war.

By February of 1944, I was stationed with the 5th Armored Division in Liverpool, England, while we prepared for the invasion of France. By late July of 1944, I was winging my way across the English Channel at the controls of my L-4 as the rest of the 71st landed at Utah Beach. My primary mission was artillery spotting in support of our advancing troops. Depending on how broad the front lines were that particular day, we would launch anywhere from one to four L-4s to spot artillery. I have been told that the Germans were more afraid of a single unarmed L-4 flying overhead than they were of a whole squadron of Thunderbolts or Mustangs. They knew that if they had been spotted by us, they could rest assured that in a few minutes a God-awful artillery barrage would rain down on their position. But that's not to say they didn't try to shoot us down when they could.

I flew at altitudes that I thought would provide the most safety for me—usually just below the cloud cover. If I began to take ground fire, I would simply duck into a cloud bank until I passed the threat. The problem with that, though, was sometimes the clouds were a lot thicker than I thought they were, which made for some very interesting recoveries in a non-instrument-condition-equipped airplane! And the pot shots from the ground were not the only thing I had to worry about; we were easy targets for the Luftwaffe fighters.

While on a mission over Luxemburg, I was jumped by a group of Bf 109s who made a bunch of running passes on me. All I could do was turn and dive as their machine-gun rounds tore into my engine and wings. At six hundred feet, my engine stopped dead, and I looked for a place to land. I dead-sticked the L-4 into a small pasture and ran as fast as I could to one of our Sherman tanks that came roaring up to rescue me. Later on, our mechanics patched up the holes in the fabric and replaced the engine; the L-4 was as good as new. I remember thinking the versatility of the Grasshopper was unbelievable as I flew it out of that field.

By early 1945, we were hopscotching our way across occupied Europe into Germany. Most of the days were the same: fly around, look for something to shoot at, and, when we burned off half of the twelve gallons of fuel we carried, turn around to land and refuel. On one particular mission, stuffed in my back seat was Lt. William S. Martin, who had flown quite a number of missions with me. Bill was a former tank commander and a heck of an artillery spotter. We had destroyed a lot together, including an L-4!

WILLIAM MARTIN

I had been with Lieutenant Francies on an earlier mission when he landed his L-4 in a very small field to pick me up. Getting into the field was bad enough, with just the weight of the pilot in the front seat, but getting out, with the addition of me in the back seat, was going to be impossible. We took off anyway because we had a mission to fly, and as we rolled forward with the tail slowly coming up, the wheels remained firmly on the ground. Lieutenant Francies tried to steer through an open gate on the fencerow, but it wasn't wide enough as one of the L-4's wing struts caught a fence post. The L-4 reared up and then flopped on the other side of the fence. I thought Lieutenant Francies was hurt because it took him more than a minute to turn around and speak to me. When he finally did, he just smiled and said, "I bet I get a new L-4 now!"

APRIL 11, 1945: VESBECK, GERMANY
LIEUTENANT FRANCIES

I had named my new L-4 *Miss Me!?* for two reasons. One was that I wanted the Germans to miss me when they shot at me, and the other is I that hoped someone was missing me back home. On today's mission, Lieutenant Martin was again spotting from the back seat as we flew out ahead of the advancing column looking for targets. We were flying at between six hundred and eight hundred feet when we spotted a German motorcycle with sidecar that came racing out of a tree line below. This guy was parallel to the front lines, and we assumed he was a messenger. Our plan was to see where he was going, then fly alongside of him and pop a couple of rounds off at him from our .45s. We were all set to do just that when all of a sudden, a German Fieseler Fi 156 Storch flew right below us at treetop level.

The Storch was the German observation equivalent of the L-4, but it was a lot bigger, weighed twice as much, flew faster, and was sometimes lightly armed with a machine gun. But, at the time, I didn't give any of that much thought because we had the altitude advantage—and besides, he hadn't seen us yet. This guy was in a big hurry, skimming the treetops, and he must have thought his camouflage would blend in with the terrain below. He thought wrong; those German crosses were as clear as day as he headed east above the trees. I lifted the side-door window of the L-4 up and pushed the door down to give Lieutenant Martin and me more room to shoot at him. I pushed the stick forward and the nose of the L-4 pitched down, diving onto the Storch.

LIEUTENANT MARTIN

We came up from the Storch's blind side as Lieutenant Francies tried to cut in front of him. While Lieutenant Francies was diving down on him, he yelled to me through the swirling wind in the cockpit, saying that he was going to try to chase this guy toward our tank column so they could get a shot at him. The Storch wouldn't go along with the chase idea, however, and instead the German pilot cranked that big wing over and started going around and around in a great big circle. We circled above him trying to figure out what we were going to do next; that's when I saw Lieutenant Francies unholster his .45 and push the L-4 closer to the Storch.

LIEUTENANT FRANCIES

The Storch tried his best to outmaneuver us, but it is darn near impossible to outmaneuver a Cub! I flew at him head-on, and neither one of us was changing course or altitude. At the last minute, I jinxed back on the stick and we flew over him, missing him by a few feet. I remember thinking there were a lot of glass windows over the Storch's cockpit, and I realized that both the German pilot in the front and the guy in the back had seen us—their eyes were as big as saucers. Lieutenant Martin and I started to fire at him with our .45s as we passed overhead. The Storch was thirty miles per hour faster than we were, but instead of running, he tried to circle upward for altitude. I could turn tighter than he could, however, so it didn't take us long to get back into a firing position and let loose again with our handguns; this time I unloaded my entire magazine.

LIEUTENANT MARTIN

Our tank column was only a half mile away, and I had been talking with them the entire time while we danced around with the Storch. I remember yelling through the microphone, "We got him! We got him!" The trouble was, the battalion commander on the ground thought I said, "We got hit!" The only thing that got hit was the Storch—our rounds began to find their mark.

LIEUTENANT FRANCIES

I had to hold the L-4's stick with my knees as I dropped my empty magazine out of the airplane; there was no way I wanted that to lodge under my rudder pedal. I continued to fly with my knees as I put a fresh magazine into the .45 and began to fire at the Storch again. I was getting close to him at that time, still above him and I leading him just a little bit. When I thought I had the right lead, I began to crank off rounds as fast as I could. I saw a small flash near his engine cowling and on his fuselage, so I knew I was hitting him, especially when I saw fuel streaming from one of the fuel tanks. The Storch began to turn left and climb, and then suddenly it made a hard right and dived into a corkscrew turn. I was still above him when I emptied my last magazine into him.

With its unique flaperon system, not only was the Fieseler Storch able to operate at very slow speeds, it could literally land on a postage stamp! *EAA/Jim Koepnick*

I had him pretty well boxed in from above as he tried to turn away from me. We were finally able to drive him into the ground as the Storch tried one last turn. Because his wings were much longer than mine, he misjudged his height, and his right wing dug into the ground. It was more of a controlled crash than it was a landing as the Storch plowed into a beet field, wiping out his gear and right wing. One thing was certain—that German pilot didn't want any part of us! A couple of minutes later, I set the Cub down as close as I could to the Storch and Martin and I made our way over to the wreckage. I went for the guy who was still in the back seat while Lieutenant Martin went looking for the pilot, who had taken off running.

LIEUTENANT MARTIN

We saw that the guy in the back had been hit in the foot, so Lieutenant Francies tended to him. I retrieved the carbine rifle that was stuffed in the back of the L-4 and went after the pilot, who had run north and was hiding behind a pile of beets. I yelled in German to him, "Hands up!" He stood up, and for a minute he thought I was going to shoot him.

Eventually, all of the troops in the area who had been watching our "dogfight" came racing up to our position. I turned over my prisoner, the pilot, to some MPs. One of my friends in a half-track jumped down and cut the tail number and swastika off the tail of the Storch and handed it to me as a souvenir. I then found Lieutenant Francies playing doctor as he tended to his patient.

LIEUTENANT FRANCIES

When I found the observer in the rear seat of the Storch, he was shaking and trembling—he thought I was going to kill him. I could see some blood oozing out of his boot, and I helped him get out of the Storch. I had retrieved my medical kit from the back of the L-4 while Lieutenant Martin stood guard over the German observer. I pulled his boot off to bandage his foot up, and when I turned the boot over, I saw a .45-caliber slug fall to the ground. As soon as I patched him up, he was turned over to the MPs as Lieutenant Martin and I looked over the Storch. We saw a few bullet holes in the cowling, one in the windshield, one in the fuel tank, and a couple in the fuselage. We also found a lot of paperwork and learned that this plane had been based at a temporary field with a bunch of other Storches. Unfortunately for its pilot, he was the tail-end Charlie guy, and all his help was fleeing eastbound away from the advancing Allied troops.

I also found the German flag that flew over their airfield stuffed inside the Storch, and I grabbed that for a souvenir. The entire duel had lasted no more than ten minutes, but it sure felt like an hour to me. Lieutenant Martin and I hopped back into the L-4 and completed our observation of the front lines. We had been told to cover a certain area, and that's exactly what we did—we went back to spotting artillery fire as if shooting down the Storch was all in a day's work.

The front office of the Piper L-4 Cub was spartan at best. But with its unique clamshell doors, which folded both up and down, it offered both the pilot and observer an unobstructed view of the world below.

SEVENTY-FIRST ARMORED FIELD ARTILLERY BATTALION COMMENDATION

It is a pleasure to forward to you the attached certificate crediting you with the destruction in aerial combat of a German Fieseler Storch aircraft. The certificate makes official and a matter of record your participation in this very unusual event which brought the following comment from the Ninth United States Army:

"Reminiscent of World War I action was a claim recently awarded for a Fieseler Storch reconnaissance plane. An L-4 from the 71 Armored FA Bn, piloted by 1st Lt. Merritt D. Francies with 1st Lt. William S. Martin as observer, was flying over a column when they saw a Fi 156 flying at treetop level below them. Circling down on the German plane they cut loose with their pistols and hit the gasoline tank. Lt. Francies then dove on the Storch, forcing it to the ground where it hit a fence and was demolished. The L-4 landed nearby and captured the two occupants, one of whom had been wounded by the firing."

I.B. Washburn
Lt. Col., F.A. Commanding

WORLD AT WAR: The concepts of naval warfare prior to World War II were largely that of surface ships firing main batteries on enemy targets. With the advent of the floatplane being catapulted from their decks, however, the "eyes" of the navy grew larger and more far-reaching.

The primary purpose of these planes was to search for enemy ships and shore targets, and to direct naval gunfire onto them. Radar had limited use during shore bombardment in support of amphibious operations. Therefore, fire control by surface ships relied heavily on these overflying observation/scout planes. As war clouds began to build, so, too, did the navy's inventory of aircraft. In the late summer of 1940, a brand-new observation/scout plane was delivered—a radical departure from the typical biplane aircraft the navy was accustomed to.

The Vought OS2U Kingfisher could be operated from water or land, or it could be catapulted from a ship. Powered by a 450-horsepower Pratt & Whitney R-985 Wasp engine, the dual-controlled Kingfisher contained a crew of two. The pilot in front was responsible for all flying and navigation, while the rear seat was manned by a gunner/radio man, for whom twin .30-caliber machine guns were mounted around a ringed "bathtub." Using a single main float with attached wingtip floats, it ruled the seas. From the dark early days of Pearl Harbor to the culmination of the Japanese surrender aboard USS *Missouri*, the Kingfisher was there in the forefront.

Not as glamorous as the battle-tested navy gunfighters Wild Cat, Hellcat, and Corsair, the Kingfisher nevertheless had one little lifesaving trick up its sleeve. Many downed Allied pilots thanked their lucky stars at the sight of a lumbering Kingfisher splashing down and taxiing toward them in shark-infested waters. And for one young OS2U pilot, a "day at the beach" was anything but pleasant!

A FISHER OF MEN

COMMANDER ALMON P. OLIVER, USN (RET.)
VOUGHT OS2U KINGFISHER

Almon Oliver was born in 1924 and entered combat in the Pacific when he was still twenty-two days shy of his twentieth birthday, making him one of the youngest naval aviators of World War II. He earned his wings in 1943.

In early 1944, I was placed into the OS2U program. I first learned to "fly floats" with a navy N3N, but after earning my water wings, I moved right into Kingfishers. I was very impressed by the size of them and wondered how they could stay afloat. I soon learned what kind of beating the Kingfisher could take and still bring a "bunch of wet guys" home.

Probably the thing that impressed me the most was the catapult launch. With the plane resting on a sixty-foot steel track atop the ship's deck, I sat and waited for the bang. Built into the catapult rail was a system of pistons, pulleys, and cables, and an eight-inch shell filled with black powder was fired into a chamber. In essence, this amounted to being fired from a cannon! Acceleration from zero to sixty knots took only a few feet of travel.

Situated behind your head was a support unit. A handle for your throttle hand was built in so you didn't lose throttle control at this very critical moment—it's one helluva bang, and you have to get a grip on yourself! I've lost everything at various times: feet off the rudders and my hand chasing the stick. Better than any damn thrill ride!

Normally, we would be launched into the wind. However, as it seemed to be the case for most of my launches, we could also be "banged" cross deck. This meant that after the first Kingfisher was launched, the second catapult was trained across the fantail and its Kingfisher shot off. For the pilot, it was a little unnerving.

The first thing you see rocketing down the track is the hand rail you just missed by less than three feet. The plane is shuddering something fierce, and you're on the verge of a stall. The burble from the superstructure causes you

A Vought Kingfisher taxis quickly to catch the wire to be loaded back aboard a destroyer.

A Vought OS2U Kingfisher on patrol in the Pacific. A welcome sight to downed allied airmen, the Kingfishers were catapulted from a rail system atop destroyer decks and, when they returned to the ship, had to be hoisted back aboard. *US Navy*

to wobble less than fifteen feet above the water. As rpms build and catch up with your beating heart, you regain control and begin your mission.

Returning to land had its own set of problems. The ocean has several motions that affect not only the ship but a landing Kingfisher as well. Swells are a rhythmic action of the water and could be judged by the pilot, posing no big problem unless they were extremely high. Choppy water, however, was a problem.

This could be dealt with by the ship creating a "slick": as it turned from the stern, it would cause the surface to be smoothed by knocking down the chop. Landing in the slick area, the pilot immediately taxied to a sled, a heavy rope tied into a series of one-foot squares, which was towed from a boom. Measuring ten feet wide by twenty feet long, a spring-loaded hook attached to the bottom of the main Kingfisher float would engage the sled, and the plane would be towed. A sling from the front cockpit was attached to the aircraft crane. The Kingfisher was then hoisted aboard and placed in a cradle atop the catapult track. Communication between the ship and the aircraft during these recovery times was by blinker, code, or signal flags, so it was essential that pilots became proficient in all aspects of naval communications. I did and so, too, I became a Kingfisher pilot.

In April 1944, I was posted at Fort Island, Hawaii. After going through operational training, I was placed into a pilot pool with about thirty other guys, and we simply waited for our orders to come in. Little did I realize it at the time, but a series of heroic events were taking place off a Japanese-held island called Truk. I was about to fill some mighty big shoes.

On April 30, two Kingfishers launched from the battleship *North Carolina*, one of them flown by Lt. John Burns. Originally sent out to pick up one downed pilot, Lieutenant Burns multiplied his rescue tenfold, rescuing not only the downed airman but also the other Kingfisher crew. After delivering his three airmen to the submarine USS *Tang*, Lieutenant Burns and his rear seater then answered another call of a downed navy flier.

Picking up his fourth rider Burns saw two TBMs, carrying three men each, ditch nearby, and he was able to rescue these six fliers. With nine people now aboard, he was a little overweight! The Kingfisher looked like a floating frat house as he slowly taxied to the USS *Tang*. With his Kingfisher taking on water, he, along with the rest of his passengers, safely boarded the sub.

All men were now safe and secure, thanks to the durability of the Kingfisher. Unfortunately, it had become damaged in the multiple rescues. In a cruel twist of fate, this life raft of an airplane was purposely sunk to keep it out of Japanese hands. The *North Carolina* was now without any Kingfishers or pilots and steamed for Hawaii. My destiny was now sealed.

On May 10, I boarded the *North Carolina* along with other replacements, including two brand-new Kingfishers, and we soon set sail for the war-torn Pacific. We were put to work immediately at places such as Saipan, Guam, Iwo Jima, and Okinawa. Wherever the war went, so too did the Kingfisher. Spotting gunfire was our major function in this deadly arena.

Probably the worst hit I ever took was at Iwo Jima. Here was this little island sur-rounded by hundreds of Allied ships—the amount of incoming firepower being thrown

The US Navy Kingfisher was an angel of mercy, saving the lives of many downed airmen.

at that strip of land was astronomical. I got a call on D+2 from some marines asking for help because they were being overrun near the airfield. From my position circling overhead at about one thousand feet, the situation looked serious.

In order for me to help the ground pounders, I had to put the fire right on top of them. Dialing up Combat Information Center, I explained the situation to them. I began to direct a series of five-inch shells into the area and walk the rounds toward the Japanese. Once the range and target area were found, the ships put it on automatic and fired a series of ten five-inchers as fast as you could spit. It may have been close to the marines, but it was right in the guts of the Japanese.

Later, I was then called to fly over and investigate some Japanese vehicles hidden in a little canyon. I dived the Kingfisher to the deck and leveled out at two hundred feet above the canyon floor. Simultaneously, and unbeknownst to me, there was a whole flight of TBM bombers heading southbound. As I began my trip through the woods, the ground beneath me erupted in smoke and flame—the TBMs had unloaded their bombs right

into my flight path. And just for good measure, the Japanese on the ground began to fire at me as well. When all was said and done, I miraculously came out of that valley of death. I had holes in each wing that straddled the cockpit, and it was anyone's guess whether they had been caused by the Japanese or our own bombs going off underneath me! I was pretty shaken up, but that tough old bird of an airplane flew on as if it were no worse for wear.

During a fighter strike on a Japanese naval air base near Ominato Bay on August 9, an F4U Corsair flown by Lt. j.g. Vernon T. Coumbre was hit by enemy ground fire. Lieutenant Coumbre was able to fly five miles off shore of the Japanese home island of

A Royal Navy Kingfisher is hoisted aboard a destroyer to be placed on a catapult rail.

Honshu. Dead-sticking his Corsair into the sea below, he clambered aboard his life raft to await his rescue. If Lieutenant Coumbre didn't have bad luck, he would have had no luck at all! The wind whipped his raft and drove him into shore: the Japanese mainland!

At about 4:00 p.m., we got a call aboard the USS *North Carolina* that a pilot had ditched in the bay near Ominato. Although we had the duty on this day, we figured that with the sun setting and the distance we needed to travel, there was no way we

Al Oliver proudly displays the medal he was awarded for saving the lives of his fellow downed pilots off of Japan proper in August 1945.

would make it back to the ship before dark. It was decided to wait until daylight and pass the mission on to a cruiser, which had the duty the following day. Forgetting about the downed pilot, I went to bed.

Meanwhile, Lieutenant Coumbre settled in for the night, hiding in a clump of bamboo thicket and hoping and praying no one would forget about him. He also prayed that the Japanese who were beating the bush nearby wouldn't find him. The Japanese continued their search throughout the night looking for the intruder who dared step foot on their sacred soil.

The next morning, an orderly shook me awake. "Get out of bed. Get your flight suit on. You're going to Ominato.

"Ominato what?" I answered. "I'm not supposed to fly today!"

Once fully dressed, I dragged myself up to the deck. Not getting any breakfast was bad enough, but when I stepped outside, it was horrible. Drizzle, low overcast, and patchy fog greeted me as I walked to the Kingfisher. I guess we had the duty today!

The mission was simple: fly 150 miles to northern Japan, land, and pick up an American pilot who was camping on a beach that belonged to the enemy. It sounded so simple that maybe the Japanese would have some sake waiting for us, too! In all seriousness, though, I hoped the poor guy on the beach was doing OK.

At 8:30 a.m., two Kingfishers were launched from the *North Carolina*, the rescue mission headed by Lt. Ralph Jacobs. I was launched seconds after Lieutenant Jacobs, and our planes joined up. We left our radiomen behind to conserve fuel and weight. If we planned it right and didn't loiter too long looking for this guy, we should have enough fuel to make it home. We knew, however, that nothing ever worked as planned!

Inbound to Ominato Bay, we picked up our escort. Four F6F Hellcats and four F4U Corsairs would be our top cover and bodyguards, just in case any Zeros thought a slow-flying Kingfisher was an easy target. The area we were headed to was a hornet's nest of Japanese military facilities. To the south was an army base and to the north was a combination airfield and naval base. And when we arrived, we knew they would have a welcoming party waiting for us. Sure enough, the whole coastline erupted in antiaircraft fire and shore batteries. It was very surreal as hot lead and shells burst all around our flight. And yet, there, standing on the beach, was the reason we had all come here: Lieutenant Coumbre, waving at us! Lieutenant Jacobs radioed me and said he was going in to pick him up.

The winds and waves were really rough that day, but the Kingfisher was accustomed to such conditions, and Lieutenant Jacobs settled the main float onto the boiling sea. As five-inch shells continued going off all around him, he began to taxi toward the beach

A US Navy Vought Kingfisher on patrol.

and Lieutenant Coumbre. Watching from above at 1,500 feet, I began to get nervous, wondering what was taking so long. I never noticed the flak bursts around me as my eyes were glued to the Kingfisher below.

The surface winds were over thirty knots, blowing directly into the beach and causing a high and treacherous surf. As Lieutenant Coumbre tried to fight his way through the twisting sea, Lieutenant Jacobs must have realized he would never make it to the Kingfisher. Lieutenant Jacobs stood in the cockpit, leaving one foot inside and one foot on the sea-slicked wing to try to throw a lifeline attached to an inflatable donut to the floundering Lieutenant Coumbre.

Suddenly, two five-inchers straddled the Kingfisher and blew geysers of water into the air. With shells going off around him and waves slamming into the Kingfisher, Lieutenant Jacobs was knocked overboard. As he fell backward into the water, his foot caught the throttle and jammed it forward; the pilotless Kingfisher was off to the races!

All I saw of this , however, was the plane in motion. *Finally*, I thought, glancing down. *He's got him. Let's get the hell out of here!* Lieutenant Jacobs was making a fine run, but I wondered why was he taking so long to get airborne. The Kingfisher began to do a lot of crazy things on the water below. I knew the sea was rough, but it wasn't that big of a problem. I pushed my Kingfisher over and went down for a look. I flew alongside her and looked in: empty!

Now we had a big problem. I flew back to where I had last seen the attempted rescue. Not one but two pilots were now waving at me from the beach! The shore batteries continued to fire at me as I splashed down. The only way to get these guys out of there

This navy Kingfisher is about to make a big splash as it comes in for a landing.

was for me to come to them. I backed the Kingfisher onto the beach—by using full flaps and "blipping" the engine on and off, I was able to let the wind do the rest and push me to shore like a sailboat. As my main float hit the sand, Jacobs and Coumbre scrambled aboard. I leaned back and yelled to Jacobs, "You help that guy into the seat! I'll get him out of here and have someone come and get you." Jacobs looked at me, then at the shells bursting all around us, gritted his teeth, and said, "Hell no!" The next thing I knew, I had two great big soaking wet guys in my back seat.

Heavy fire from the beach caused plumes of water to explode nearby as I made my takeoff run. The Kingfisher lifted off effortlessly, not even noticing the extra weight I carried in the back. As we flew out of Ominato Bay, I witnessed an unbelievable sight: there before me were navy fighters strafing the runaway Kingfisher going full bore across the waves. Lieutenant Jacobs' abandoned plane began to burn as we headed for home. I crossed my fingers as I stared at the fuel gauge.

After almost seven hours to the minute of constant flying, I began to set up for landing behind the *North Carolina*. Visibility was reduced to less than a half mile, my fuel gauge was reading empty, and I had two wet guys in the back; why did this have to be the time I got a bad slick?! I had been in combat over fifteen months, and never ever had I gotten a wave-off from landing. I went around again to give it another try. This time, *North Carolina* gave me the slick I needed, and I splashed down. After we were hoisted aboard and the Kingfisher secured, the plane captain told me I had less than a cup of gas left.

One of the doctors came up to me and said, "You look like you could use a drink." One full bottle of brandy and two days of sleep later, I awoke and was told I had flown my last mission: the only pilot to rescue a person—or persons—from Japan proper.

After the war, Almon Oliver continued to fly for the US Navy and progressed up to jets. After twenty-five years of continuous service, he retired as a commander, with fond memories of flying the Kingfisher.

PANDORA'S BOCKSCAR

CAPTAIN CHARLES DON ALBURY, USAAC (RET.)
BOEING B-29 SUPERFORTRESS

Charles Albury was born in Miami in 1920 and began test-flying B-29 Superfortresses in 1943.

In Greek mythology, the god Zeus gave Pandora a gift in the form of a simple box. Along with this box came specific instructions that she never open it. Giving in to temptation and curiosity, Pandora ignored the warnings and opened the box, and misery, evil, misfortune, and calamity spilled from it, afflicting mankind until the end of time. On August 9, 1945, the same afflictions ravaged a US Army Air Corps B-29 bomber as it made ready for the second atomic flight over Japan. Here is the story from the copilot of that flight as he flew right seat in a B-29 called Bockscar.

As far as I was concerned, the air corps couldn't build a big enough airplane for me—the bigger the better! I was grinning from ear to ear when they sent me to Kansas to fly the new state-of-the-art, war-ending bomber called the B-29 Superfortress. God, she was awesome!

The B-29 was just less than one hundred feet long and had a 141-foot wing span. Bolted to her wings were four 2,200-horsepower Wright engines turning four-bladed Hamilton Standard full-feathering propellers, all of which rested on tricycle landing gear. We flew in pressurized comfort surrounded by glass, aluminum, and every new bell and whistle that had been invented. This wasn't like the B-17s I trained in, but the B-29 did have some teething problems.

Most of those problems were with the engines, which had a tendency to overheat and start on fire. The initial B-29s that I flew were considered unsafe, with an engine life of only ten hours before meltdown. We didn't get to fly them that much, and to conserve the ten-hour time between overhauls TBO, we were towed to the end of the runway where we did our startups. After takeoff, we had to stay at three hundred feet to keep the engines cool until

Charles "Don" Albury at the controls of a Boeing B-29 Superfortress.

the needles settled back into the green.

Boeing worked out most of the bugs, and B-29s began to pour off the assembly lines. After scrounging as much stick time as I could, I was sent to Eglin Field and became part of a cadre of men who tested and modified the central fire-control system on the plane. My boss was Col. Paul Tibbets, who was a great commander and a superb leader. I had a lot of respect for him; I would have gone to hell and back with him and almost did near the end of the war.

As B-29 production increased, so did the need for pilots to fly them. A small problem soon devel-

The last atomic bomb is dropped on Nagasaki, Japan, by B-29 *Bockscar.*

oped, however: the air corps found that they were almost out of instructors. I was sent back to Pratt, Kansas, where I rejoined Paul Tibbets, along with my future squadron commander and copilot, Maj. Chuck Sweeny. I took my turn in the ring and helped train new pilots. It was good living, even with the moments of sheer terror as I wrestled the controls back from excited student pilots.

One morning, I was called up to see Tibbets in operations, and he asked me if I wanted to join him at a place called Wendover, Utah. I had never heard of that place before, but if Tibbets was going, then I would go, too! We soon boarded a brand-new B-29 for the long flight. In the air, Tibbets told me he was getting an outfit together to go overseas and wondered if I wanted to go along. My beaming smile and the nod of my head was acknowledgment enough. Tibbets then said, "I can't tell you where we are going or why we are going, but we have a new weapon that has the capability to destroy a whole city. I am also hopeful it will save countless lives and end the war." I sat in stunned silence as I wracked my brain, wondering what he was talking about. I found out soon enough.

When we touched down at Wendover, I knew I wasn't in Kansas anymore. The place was desolate. A couple of runways ran smack dab into the side of a mountain—not a good place for a fully loaded B-29. But this place also had a never-ending runway, otherwise known as the salt flats. I, along with the rest of the 509th Composite Group, would call this forsaken, inhospitable desert home.

The B-29 *Bockscar* crew of the last atomic mission. Don is standing, center.

I was part of the 393rd Bomb Group and was pilot in command of a B-29 called *The Great Artiste*. She was named after our bombardier, Kermit Beahan, who at the time was dating a nurse and wasn't quite forthright with her about some of his past conquests. The story is that before going overseas, we had been sent to Cuba on a training mission—we were to drop twenty two-hundred-pound practice bombs on a target in the Atlantic Ocean. We approached the target and Beahan dropped ten of the bombs on one side and the other ten on the other side of the target. All of us in the cockpit roared and shouted over the intercom, using his girlfriend's nickname for him, "Hey Honey Bee, that was a great drop!" Beahan answered back, "That's the Great Artiste!" We named our aircraft to honor him. He was a great and likable man, and a helluva bombardier, too!

Kermit, along with the rest of us, got plenty of practice over the desert dropping large, rotund bombs we called pumpkins. These pumpkin flights tested the bomb casings and tail-finned configurations that the scientists from New Mexico developed. Eventually, the right combination was found. They named the longer, thinner one "Little Boy" and the large, round one "Fat Man." They also called them atom bombs, but we didn't hear that term until we arrived in the Pacific.

We left Wendover AAF base in mid-1945, flying seventeen brand-new, identical Superfortresses that were stripped of all defensive guns except the twin .50s in the tail. We had highly modified equipment, including reconfigured bomb bays with new doors installed, allowing for the larger-than-normal bomb we would carry. We also had fuel-injected engines that turned full-reversing propellers—a feature that would later save my bacon on Okinawa.

Early on in our training, we had been briefed by Colonel Tibbets and high-ranking intelligence people that "What you hear here stays here—understood?!" I never asked questions about what we were doing, and I never talked to anybody else about what they were doing. So when I got my briefing on Tinian about the new atomic bomb project, the intelligence guy didn't believe me when I told him I had no idea what he was talking about. He kept badgering me, demanding, "Then how come Fred Bock knew what was going on?!"

Fred was the aircraft commander on a B-29 named *Bockscar*. He liked to read the funny papers and especially loved the Flash Gordon stuff. Flash always talked about atomic ray

Currently, the only airworthy B-29 flying is operated by the Commemorative Air Force and is named *FIFI*. *Jim Koepnick*

guns and atomic weapons, so I guess that's how he knew about their little secret. On August 6, 1945, I saw firsthand what "atomic bomb" meant and why it was so secretive.

Although I was aircraft commander on *The Great Artiste*, I moved over and gave up my left seat every time our squadron commander, Chuck Sweeny, flew. Major Sweeny always picked our B-29 when he wanted to fly, and it was no exception when we were selected to follow Colonel Tibbets into the air to make our way to a target city on Japan called Hiroshima. Tibbets carried the Little Boy bomb in his B-29 *Enola Gay*, while we carried the blast-measuring equipment in our belly.

Everything on that first mission went off as planned. We rendezvoused on time and together. The bomb run over the target was precise and clear as we fell in behind *Enola Gay* while her bomb bay doors swung open. Sweeny and I wore welder's goggles for protection, but it was hard to see the instruments, especially with another B-29 right in front of us, so we took them off. After Colonel Tibbets released Little Boy, he peeled off one way and we peeled off the other as shock waves raced up to greet us. It felt like the whole damn airplane had been punched with a huge fist. The first atomic mission was orchestrated with precision and accomplishment. It was everything the second mission wasn't.

The decision to drop another atomic bomb had already been made the day before. Originally it was planned for August 11, but because of a typhoon in the area, they moved it up to August 9, with Kokura, Japan, designated as the recipient of Fat Man. Colonel Tibbets selected Major Sweeny to command the second mission, so naturally we thought *The Great Artiste* would carry the bomb. There was just one little problem: *The Great Artiste* was still fitted with the blast-measuring equipment from the first drop, and removing it and replacing it on another B-29 would take days. Colonel Tibbets ordered a swap of airplanes, and we soon found ourselves scheduled to fly Fred Bock's B-29 *Bockscar*, while he and his crew took ours. They were all identical anyway, so it was really no big deal, except for a small fuel problem in *Bockscar*.

Most of our B-29s carried a reserve fuel tank of six hundred gallons located in the aft bomb bay. The gas tank was mainly used for ballast, and I don't recall ever having to tap into it on earlier missions. The problem we found was that the fuel transfer pumps were not working and the 3,600 pounds of fuel in the back became dead weight. After a lengthy discussion, Major Sweeny and I agreed, "We never used it before, so let's go ahead and go!" At 3:49 a.m. on August 9, we lifted off of Tinian Island in an overloaded B-29 and headed to our rendezvous point carrying a fully armed atomic bomb strapped inside our bomb bay. Things only got worse from there on out.

Normally, we flew with a crew of eleven men, but on this mission, we had some extra riders. One of them, US Navy Cmdr. Frederick C. Ashworth, was the weaponeer for Fat Man. At 4:15 a.m., Commander Ashworth climbed into the bomb bay, replaced the green plugs with red, and announced that the bomb was armed. He also told us to maintain an altitude above five thousand feet because the bomb could pre-detonate below that altitude. Thoughts of past engine failures crept into my mind as we climbed higher for added insurance. Even if we wanted to turn back, we couldn't. It was all or nothing, and nothing was not an option!

We were already an hour behind schedule because of the fuel pump problem. Our two advanced weather B-29s, *Up and Atom* and *Laggin Dragon*, headed for our primary target at Kokura and our secondary target at Nagasaki, respectively. They would orbit the area and report back weather conditions as we approached the target. Weather was already a problem well before we reached Japan.

Initially we were to hook up with *The Great Artiste* and *Big Stink*, our photo plane, over Iwo Jima, but because of a fast-moving typhoon, we had to fly farther west at a higher altitude to a new rendezvous point. Both of these changes in plans made for higher fuel consumption, none of which we could spare. The thought of that useless six hundred gallons sloshing around in the back began to peck at my brain.

Before we had left Tinian, we had been given two very important directives by Colonel Tibbets: drop Fat Man visually, not by radar, and wait no longer than fifteen minutes at the rendezvous point before heading to Japan. We not only broke the second order, we smashed it!

We found *The Great Artiste* right away as we circled, looking and waiting for *Big Stink* to show up. We were at thirty thousand feet making small circles, and unbeknownst to us, he was at forty-one thousand feet making big, wide circles. We never saw each other, and

A rear view of the massive four-engine B-29 bomber. Note how large the tail is compared to a B-17 Flying Fortress. *Jim Koepnick*

after forty minutes of boring circles in the sky, burning precious fuel, *Bockscar* and *The Great Artiste* jumped on the Hirohito Highway and headed for Japan.

As darkness faded to light, I had a certain sense of security as we flew over the Pacific. Down below us were cruisers and destroyers, and in the air were PBYs and B-29 "Super Dumbos," all gathered in case one of us had to ditch on the way home. What was once a possibility was fast becoming reality as our fuel tanks filled with air.

At 10:20 a.m., we arrived over Kokura late and found our target obscured by smoke. The day before, our B-29s had firebombed a small city thirty to forty miles away, and the thick smoke from the fires covered our primary target. We made a series of three separate runs over Kokura, and each time we got to the IP, Beahan, said, "I don't see the aiming point—target covered by smoke!" We had been at it for over forty-five minutes and were really eating up a lot of fuel. A veil of smoke had saved Kokura—we turned for Nagasaki.

On our way to our secondary target, Major Sweeny and I had a discussion about the possibility of a radar drop and the large developing cloud cover that we were now flying

in and out of while cruising at over thirty thousand feet. Commander Ashworth insisted that we have a visual on the target before we drop Fat Man. As we neared Nagasaki, our discussion became a little heated.

"Look, Navy," said Major Sweeny, "we're either gonna drop it by radar or we're gonna have to punch it off out over the ocean 'cause we sure as hell can't take it back with us!" No one said a word as we began our radar run on Nagasaki. Finally, Commander Ashworth said, "If you have to drop it by radar, then go ahead and do it." Thirty seconds later, Kermit shouted over the intercom, "I think I see it!" as he peered through his bombsight.

At 11:58 a.m., Beahan was now piloting *Bockscar* as he made his adjustments and released the ten-thousand-pound bomb. Major Sweeny and I cranked *Bockscar* into a 155-degree dive to the left as *The Great Artiste* mirrored us to the right. At 12:02 p.m., Fat Man exploded at an altitude of around 1,800 feet. The gates of hell opened up and erupted over Nagasaki.

A tremendous amount of dust and smoke began to billow up from below. Three separate shock waves raced upwards and around the ascending mushroom cloud. The horrific sight of the force of over twenty-two thousand pounds of TNT going off created

B-29 *Strange Cargo* was part of the B-29 squadron that carried out the atomic missions.

some of the most beautiful colors I had ever seen. Pinks, reds, greens, and every known color in the world swirled though that towering cloud; it looked like Lucifer's rainbow.

As we turned south for home, so did our fuel gauges. The nagging thought of our untouchable fuel made us instinctively tap our fuel gauges as if they would somehow show full tanks. We raced the devil back home, knowing full well we would never make it, even at reduced power. Our conversation soon turned to the best way to belly-flop a B-29 in the ocean. We looked for all the ships we had seen on the way over and found none. No rescue aircraft, either, not even a damn Japanese fishing boat!

What had happened was during the mission, someone in another B-29 broke radio silence and said, "Hey Chuck [Major Sweeny], where are you? Have you aborted?" We didn't respond, and they heard the transmission back home, thinking we had scrubbed the mission. That's when they recalled our rescue team.

We made up our minds to fly toward Okinawa as long as we could, hoping to come across a small island and ditch nearby—no amount of praying was going to get those fuel needles to rise. Somehow, we were granted a small miracle, and Okinawa came into view. As our heart rates dropped from high rev to normal cruise, however, the tower on the ground wouldn't answer our radio calls!

They had some alert going on down there, and after three attempts to raise them on the air, we shot off the flares of the day. They wouldn't answer those, either. Finally, Major Sweeny gave the order, "Shoot all the damned flares off!" We had the makings of a huge Roman candle as multicolored flares arched over the island.

We could see what runway they were using as we set ourselves up to land. Turning toward the runway, we cut behind a B-29 just about to touch down and another B-29 turning final. We carried a few extra knots and maintained 150 instead of the normal 120, just in case something else would go wrong—and it did! That's when we lost the first engine.

At five hundred feet above the ground, our number-three engine began sucking air, and the effect was immediate. Major Sweeny and I were too busy to even curse as we fought to control *Bockscar*'s descent. As we touched down, the number-two engine gasped and coughed for the last time as it, too, was starved of fuel. Sweeny and I slammed on the brakes and threw the two running engines into full reverse. We stopped five hundred feet from the end of the runway. Our clock showed it was 1:00 p.m.; it had been the longest nine hours of my life!

All kinds of people and rescue vehicles gathered around our plane as we came to a stop. We were under strict orders not to tell anybody where we had been. As Major Sweeny and Commander Ashworth went on ahead to send a message back to Tinian, the rest of us got off the plane to get some chow. Some GI came up to me and said, "Hey, did you hear they just dropped another atomic bomb on Japan?!"

I bit my lip and asked sheepishly, "They did?"

He replied, "Yeah, and it was dropped by a P-47 Thunderbolt!"

"Wow!" I said. "Those Jugs sure can carry one heck of a load. I wonder how much fuel he used."

When we checked our gas tanks, we found thirty-three gallons of usable fuel on board, with another six hundred gallons safe and sound in the back! At 1:20 p.m., *The Great Artiste* and *Big Stink* landed on Okinawa. Somehow *Big Stink* made it to Nagasaki and took photographs as Pandora's Box was thrown wide open. The world would never be the same again.

After the war, Don Albury continued to fly "large airplanes" and became an airline captain with Eastern Airlines. He passed away on May 23, 2009.

INDEX